THE ANCIENT GUIDE TO MODERN LIFE

THE ANCIENT GUIDE TO MODERN LIFE

Natalie Haynes

P

PROFILE BOOKS

First published in Great Britain in 2010 by
Profile Books Ltd
3A Exmouth House
Pine Street
London ECIR OJH
www.profilebooks.com

1 3 5 7 9 10 8 6 4 2

Typeset in Garamond by MacGuru Ltd
info@macguru.org.uk
Printed and bound in Great Britain by
Clays, Bungay, Suffolk

A CIP catalogue record for this book is available from the British Library.

ISBN 978 1 84668 323 7
eISBN 978 1 84765 293 5

The paper this book is printed on is certified by the © 1996 Forest Stewardship Council A.C. (FSC). It is ancient-forest friendly. The printer holds FSC chain of custody SGS-COC-2061

FSC
Mixed Sources
Product group from well-managed
forests and other controlled sources
Cert no. SGS-COC-2061
www.fsc.org
© 1996 Forest Stewardship Council

For Dan
tecum vivere amem, tecum obeam lubens
Horace, *Odes* 3.9

Contents

Introduction

I have been obsessed with the ancient world since I was eleven years old, when I began learning about Roman Life at school. We read about Julius Caesar, looked at pictures of Hadrian's Wall, and made scale models of temples from cardboard boxes (complete with a cotton-wool sacrificial sheep bleeding red nail varnish over one corner of the box). When I turned twelve, Roman Life became Latin, and the Cambridge Latin Course took over. These brightly coloured books introduced a new generation of classical scholars to Caecilius and his wife Metella, who lived in Pompeii and so had a death sentence hanging over them from Book One. 'Caecilius est in horto,' we would chant, before grimly observing that he wouldn't survive the impending eruption from the garden, no matter how nice his triclinium was. I also remember some twins called Loquax and Antiloquax, about whom I can recall nothing else, although a residual suspicion of identical twins remains somewhere in my brain.

When we chose our GCSE subjects, it never occurred to me that I wouldn't take Latin, and if I was going to do Latin, I might as well take Greek, too. Luckily, my parents didn't see a need for any other living languages. French was enough. And this way, after all, there was no risk of a sullen German exchange student pitching up and moaning about everything in our house (which had happened with my brother's the year before. I think my brother then made up for it by going to Germany and eschewing wurst). If I'd thought the whole thing through, of course, I would have borrowed the Italian girl from the year above me at school, taken her home, dressed her in a sheet and pretended she was my Roman exchange, but I had less imagination in those days, and got the giggles too easily to carry off that kind of thing well.

My future in Classics was probably determined by the set texts I was given to learn for GCSE. Book Two of Virgil's *Aeneid* was the Latin verse – it's about the fall of Troy, the story of which we all thought we knew from those books on Greek myth we'd read as children. Book Two explains the bit with the Trojan horse that previously had never made any sense: seriously, you had the Greeks camped outside your city for ten years, and then they go away, leaving a big, Greek-army-sized wooden horse outside; and you take it into the city, and are then surprised when it turns out to be full of soldiers with death on their minds. No wonder the Trojans had lost the war. They were idiots. 'Beware of Greeks bearing gifts' didn't really cover it. 'Beware of Trojans, they're too stupid to live' was closer to the mark. How had they survived ten years of war without accidentally stabbing themselves through the eye with their own spears?

It turns out, when you actually read Book Two of *The Aeneid*, that the Trojans were not idiots. They did question the Greeks. Their priest, Laocoön, busted the horse right from the start. He's the one who says the line about beware the Greeks bearing gifts. He says the horse is full of Greek soldiers, or if it isn't, it's some kind of infernal siege engine, designed to trash their city in some way. He even guesses who had the idea for the horse – Ulysses (or Odysseus, to give him his Greek name). Laocoön throws his spear into the horse's flank and it vibrates there. You can only imagine the Greeks inside, holding their breath, thinking they were discovered. But then comes the Greeks' master-stroke: Sinon. Sinon is a Greek, left behind by his countrymen when they sailed away. He's dishevelled and unassuming, and he plays the Trojans like a cheap violin. He presents himself as a victim of Ulysses' machinations – Ulysses has hated his family for years. And then he refuses to say any more. Why don't the Trojans simply kill him, he asks. That would please the Greek leaders – Menelaus, Agamemnon, Ulysses. The Trojans are hooked. Why would killing him please the Greeks? What has happened? Aeneas, who narrates this story, reminds his audience that the Trojans just weren't used to the Greeks and their lies. So, of course, they fell for it. Sinon, apparently unwillingly, continues with his tale of woe. The Greeks had sacrificed Agamemnon's daughter, Iphigenia, to appease the gods when they first set out for Troy. The offering had ensured safe passage across the seas. Now they were giving up and going home, they needed to kill someone else for a safe return journey. Their priest, Calchas, would decide whom Apollo wanted as his victim. Eventually, bullied into it by Ulysses, he chose Sinon. No one argued: rather Sinon than them. Sinon was dressed up as a sacrificial victim: all the trappings that would normally adorn an animal were placed upon him. The scene he describes is horrifying. So he did a runner, and hid. Even as he tells the story, he begins to cry.

The kindly Trojans cannot bear his unhappiness. King Priam orders him to be freed from his bonds. Forget about the Greeks, he says. You're one of us now. By the way, what's this big wooden horse they left behind? Sinon appeals to the gods. He must keep Troy safe, now they have shown him such kindness. The horse is a religious arte-fact, made by the Greeks to appease the goddess Pallas Athene. The reason it's so big is so that the Trojans can't get it into their city. If they do, the offering will benefit them, rather than the Greeks. But if they damage the horse in some way, destruction will rain down upon Priam and the Trojans instead.

Sinon gives an award-winning performance. Even so, the Trojans aren't completely sure. Maybe they should believe Sinon, maybe they shouldn't. But then the gods intervene. Two huge sea-snakes appear near the shore. They head straight for Laocoön, and snatch his two small sons. Laocoön tries to rescue them, but the snakes seize him too. He stabs at them with his sword, and is soon covered in venom and blood. The snakes escape and hide in Athene's temple: it's surely a sign that she has sent them. The Trojans make their decision. The snakes had attacked Laocoön because he had violated the wooden horse, hurling a spear at it. They should take care of the horse, and wheel it into their city to keep it safe; offer prayers to the goddess to make up for the spear-chucking incident. The Trojans aren't stupid, they're out-flanked: the twin persuasions of sneaky human being and supernatural monsters are simply too much for them.

The Greeks were incredibly lucky and incredibly smart – they had a much better plan than just leaving the horse behind and hoping for the best. Sinon could have come straight from the pages of John Le Carré, saying just enough to sound plausible. Before the end of Book Two of *The Aeneid*, there is fighting, slaughter, sacrilege, raging fire and two ghosts. I was as hooked as the poor Trojans.

At the same time, over in Greek lessons, we were reading about Odysseus as hero, rather than villain. Our set text included his escape from the cave of Polyphemus, the Cyclops. Odysseus claims his name is No One, blinds Polyphemus – the original poke in the eye with a sharp stick – and then ties himself beneath a small team of sheep, sneaking past the Cyclops as they scamper outdoors. When the blinded Cyclops shouts out for help, he bellows that No One has hurt him. The other Cyclops assume he is deranged. Why cry out for help when no one's hurting you?

It is no exaggeration to say that these books changed my life. I could have taken science A-levels and become a vet, like I had planned to, aged eight. Instead, I took Latin, Greek and Ancient History A-levels, then a Classics degree, just so I could keep reading stuff like this. I realise this isn't something many people get the opportunity to do now – very few schools teach Latin and Greek, and tuition fees have made it difficult to choose a degree subject because you like it, rather than because you think it will be useful. So, all I can say is this: the Classics are worth whatever time you give them. Whether you study Latin verb-endings every day for a year, or simply wander into the cinema to watch the latest sword-and-sandal spectacular, you're in for a treat (unless the film is *Troy*. Then you're in for a snooze). Classics have informed so much of our lives – our politics, our laws, our history, our culture, our language. We live in a world where a defiant refusal to acknowledge anything but the present is commonplace: the past is considered too boring and the future too scary. But the past is full of people just like us, people who lived ordinary lives in extraordinary times. Spend some time with them, and we might learn more about ourselves. So that's what this book is – a collection of some of the best stories from the ancient world, stories which are interesting, funny, sad or peculiar, and especially stories which seem impossibly contemporary even though they're a couple of millennia old, like the one about Vedius Pollio, surely the world's first Bond villain. Myths are debunked – Julius Caesar's last words weren't 'Et tu, Brute?', gladiators didn't salute the emperor when they were about to die, and the

Romans weren't chucking Christians to the lions every mealtime. This book is about how the ancient world has shaped the present one, and how our present is illuminated by the past. Ancient history doesn't just belong in dusty classrooms and dog-eared textbooks, it belongs in our lives now. As Thucydides, the Athenian historian, once wrote, 'It will be enough for me if these words are judged useful by those who want to understand clearly the events which happened in the past and which (human nature being what it is) will, at some time or other and in much the same ways, be repeated in the future. My work is not a piece of writing designed to meet the taste of an immediate public, but was done to last for ever.'

1

Old World Order

It's tempting to believe that we no longer need to think about politics. After all, voter apathy is high in countries all over the world, and voter cynicism about our elected officials is even higher. Does it matter who's in office when they all use it as a chance to feather their own nests and take advantage of their positions? Can politicians really make a positive difference to our lives, or is it just so much empty rhetoric? And what can we possibly learn about politics from the ancient world, where citizens (no women, no foreigners) were the only ones allowed to vote, let alone stand for office?

Well, yes, of course politics matters. Although we shrug in the UK when reminded that we're technically subjects of a monarch rather than citizens of a democracy, we live like citizens. We vote, and by voting, we have some control over our own and our country's destiny. If choosing between the major political parties sometimes feels a little like deciding whether to be drowned in salt water or fresh, it still beats the alternatives. Like it or not, wherever we are in the world, most of us are governed by someone. An elected chamber, a prime minister, a president, a queen: someone has the right to tell us what to do. We can either retire to the mountains, stockpile tinned food and arm ourselves to the teeth, or we can accept it. And if we're going to accept governance, that means we also need to question and challenge it.

Trevor J. Saunders, late Professor of Greek at Newcastle University, put things most succinctly in his introduction to Aristotle's *Politics*: 'The society that loses its grip on the past is in danger, for it produces men who know nothing but the present, and who are not aware that life has been, and could be, different from what it is. Such men bear tyranny easily; for they have nothing with which to compare it.'

Ancient writers give us everything we need to ask ourselves and our leaders difficult questions. Greek and Roman philosophers, historians, playwrights and comedians were all keen to assess the political situation in which they lived, wanted to live or believed people could live. They wrote extensively about politics, both domestic and foreign. Whether it was the direct democracy of fifth-century BCE Athens, or the civil wars that ravaged first-century BCE Rome, the ancients were keenly aware of how profound, and instant, an effect politics could have on an individual life.

Aristotle summed up our relationship with politics in a bon mot that survives to this day: Man is, by nature, a *politikon zōon* – a political animal. In other words, we are designed to live in a city-state, a polis. That's how we thrive, being the sociable creatures we are. Our nature intends for us to live among others, which presumably explains why so many of us pile into overcrowded cities to live and work in them. We can't help ourselves. And if we're going to live alongside other people, we need to have some system for doing so. Anarchy, after all, has never really caught on. It just seems like so much trouble. The suffix *-archy*, by the way, comes from the Greek verb *archein*, meaning 'to rule'. So, anarchy: an absence of rule; monarchy: one ruler; oligarchy: a small group of rulers; patriarchy: the rule of a father; matriarchy: the rule of a mother. Over time, various Greek states managed to test out virtually every system of government: kings, tyrants, oligarchs. The Spartans even managed a diarchy, where two kings from separate royal families ruled jointly. But it is Athens that has always inspired us the most, with its extraordinary, seemingly impossible democracy.

Athenian democracy wasn't representative, as democracies almost everywhere are now. In America, in the UK, in virtually every country that uses a democratic system of government, we vote for someone to represent our interests: a constituency MP or a congressman, for example. They go to vote on matters of state, while we go to our place of work, safe in the knowledge that they will vote as we would vote. That is, at least, the theory. And it sometimes works, too – how many times have you seen an MP acknowledging that power stations need to be built, or airports extended, or affordable housing created, just not in their constituency?

But the Athenians did things differently. Their democracy was direct. In other words, they didn't vote for someone else to turn out and make decisions for them. On days when the Ekklesia – or Assembly – was held, the citizens of Athens walked to the Pnyx, a hill near the Acropolis (and a Scrabble-player's delight, now that proper nouns are allowed), listened to arguments for and against, say, a military expedition to Syracuse, and then they voted for or against the proposal themselves, by show of hands. The whole process was administered by ordinary men like them, who were appointed by lot. A council of 500, called the Boulē, drew up the agenda for Assembly meetings. The council comprised of fifty men from each of the ten Athenian tribes, and each tribe ruled the council for a tenth of the year, the order again decided by lot. The ruling tribe was called the prytany, and it had a chairman who decided what business they should undertake. He, too, was chosen by sortition – lot – and would be in charge for one day and one night. Aristotle, in his *Athenian Constitution*, tells us that no one was ever allowed to serve for longer than a day, or a second time. So any nefarious scheme hatched to acquire undue influence over the chairman of the prytany would be almost impossible to administer, and even if it succeeded, would be mayfly-brief.

Anyone who worries about an elected representative's salary or expenses may be interested to know that the Athenians serving on the council, or in the prytany, would receive a sum of a few obols (a low-skilled worker's wage) for each day they served. And they got free communal dinners during their time in the prytany. These small benefits were essentially to make up for any earnings lost while men did their democratic duty, rather than payment for their service to the state.

It was, obviously, an egalitarian system. Office wasn't limited to those who could afford to hold it, because the stipend made it possible for all. In the words of the Athenian historian Thucydides, 'When it is a question of putting one person before another in positions of public responsibility, what counts is not membership of a particular class, but the actual ability which the man possesses. No one, so long as he has it in him to be of service to the state, is kept in political obscurity because of poverty.'

It's hard to imagine Marx himself dreaming of a more even distribution of authority – farmers, smiths, merchants and gentry all served the people in turn. And during the time they formed the prytany, they lived and ate together, too. But the question arises: did you get the best man for the job? What if the lot fell upon a person of chronic stupidity? The cheering truth is that someone could only hold a position of real authority, the chairmanship of the prytany, for twenty-four hours. And though one hesitates to test the talents of modern politicians, how much damage can really be wrought by one official in twenty-four hours? The rest of the time that man would be one of fifty men in the prytany, or 500 in the Boulē, or several thousand in the Assembly. One assumes that the wisdom of crowds must have more than compensated for the stupidity of individuals. But then, didn't the Athenians also face the contrary problem? What happened if you found the perfect candidate – efficient, and self-effacing – and you lost him twenty-four hours later?

Perhaps the Athenians thought in those terms, but if so, we have no record of a city pining for a civil servant they had loved and lost. It seems rather to have been the case that they simply assumed everyone would be reasonably competent. There were other jobs one could be elected to hold, mostly notably the ten *stratēgoi* – generals – who were in charge of Athens' military campaigns. But even those key posts were voted for annually. And a vote of confidence in the generals was held during each prytany, too. If a vote of no-confidence was carried, the general would be tried in court for his failures. When politicians today make their glib statements about 'the court of public opinion', they really have no idea how lucky they are. Trial by media may be unfair, but it's probably less traumatic than a monthly assessment of your competence by a random selection of your peers. For all their occasional impetuousness, we must assume that the Athenian people were actually far more tolerant of mistakes than we are now. If we instituted monthly competence checks nowadays, starting on 1 January, it's difficult to imagine most politicians or military leaders staying in office past February.

And the consequences of being tried and convicted of military incompetence were severe, as the historian Thucydides experienced himself directly. Thucydides wrote a history of the Peloponnesian War that tells us much of what we know about the latter half of fifth-century

BCE Greece. The Peloponnesian War was a disastrous conflict between the Athenians and their one-time allies against Persian invaders, the Spartans. For thirty years they conducted campaigns against each other – each summer the Spartans would travel to Athens for battle, and the Athenians would withdraw inside the walls of their city. The Spartans were the greatest warriors that the Mediterranean had ever seen. Conversely, the Athenians had the greatest naval force that the ancient world had known. They were perfectly matched.

The town of Amphipolis was an Athenian colony on the coast of Thrace, north of Athens; much of Greece had been divided into supporters of Sparta or Athens, whether they liked it or not. It was a tough time in history to try to be neutral, as we'll see with the Melians later on. In the winter of 424–423 BCE, Brasidas, a Spartan general, offered the Amphipolitans good terms if they would surrender to him. Thucydides, who was an Athenian general that year, arrived too late to save the city, and the Athenians decided he was to blame for their considerable strategic loss. They recalled him from battle, and exiled him for twenty years, some of which he spent in Sparta. It's perhaps a sign that his heart was in history rather than military leadership that he manages to find a lugubrious bright side, even to this indignity: 'I saw what was being done on both sides, particularly on the Peloponnesian side, because of my exile, and this leisure gave me rather exceptional facilities for looking into things.'

Amphipolis' loss is perhaps history's gain: Thucydides certainly believed his exile gave him a unique viewpoint on the Peloponnesian War, so why should we doubt him? But one presumes most generals wouldn't be so sanguine about a twenty-year exile. Yet we never read of the slightest suggestion that men weren't prepared to put themselves forward for this potentially risky job. Something else to bear in mind, perhaps, when we're repeatedly told that politicians need a pay-rise or we won't attract the best people into politics. It seems that the opportunity to wield power, exert influence and make oneself known is a powerful lure, even in the face of poor remuneration and possible exile. An ungenerous person might suggest that history teaches us we could offer our politicians a hefty pay cut and still get plenty of perfectly competent candidates ready to take on the job.

It's very tempting, when considering Athenian democracy, to become rather giddy at how accessible and instant everything was. People turned up and voted about matters that had direct, personal consequences for themselves. Take the example of the war. The Athenians would vote, in the Assembly, for or against certain military campaigns. Should they assemble a force to resist the Persians, make an expedition against Sicily or destroy the rebellious city of Mytilene (the capital city of the island of Lesbos)? They weren't voting, as politicians do now, for other people to gather up weapons and head off to war. Athenian voters were the same men as those who rowed Athenian triremes – ships with three banks of oars. They were the infantry or the cavalry, depending on their wealth: you could only be a cavalryman if you could afford to provide yourself with a horse. So one can criticise the Athenian Assembly for its occasional mistakes, its impetuousness or its folly, but one can't suggest that the men involved in the decision-making process were ever divorced from the consequences of their actions. Even those too old to fight would be voting their sons or brothers into the battle lines. One contrasts that with the scene in the 2004 movie *Fahrenheit 9/11* in which the polemicist director Michael Moore tries to persuade Members of Congress to sign their own kids up to fight in a war for which they have voted. Only one congressman was the father of a soldier serving in Iraq.

Certainly, we can and should take lessons from ancient Athens with regard to our political attitudes. The notion of political apathy is very modern: only once you have rights can you afford to become bored with them. And the widespread modern feeling that the political classes are quite separate from the rest of us is an ugly one, and not one which the Athenians would have understood. Because they all took an active role in administering their democracy, the ruling class wasn't separate from the voting class. The notion that it doesn't matter who or what you vote for because they're all the same would not have struck a chord in Athens.

Can we rediscover this sense of civic pride and duty now, when voter turnout is low and often getting lower with each new generation? The example of President Obama suggests we can: his election campaign was funded by many small donors rather than a few big hitters. In other words, he had popular support from the masses, rather than oligarchic support from a small number of businesses or individuals. Whether you like his politics or not isn't really important; what matters is that he has reminded people, en masse, that they should care enough about themselves and their country to participate in electing their leaders. The enemy of political progress is the belief that nothing will ever really change. And indeed, if we believe that, we render it true. It's the civic equivalent of saying that you don't believe in fairies, and then watching one fall dead at your feet, its little fairy wings broken by your cynicism. The Athenians had plenty of failings, but one thing they really got right was the understanding that participation was the way to effect change. Why stand outside something with a placard when you could be changing it from within? The Athenians should inspire us to become school governors, patient representatives, local councillors and Members of Parliament. They should persuade us to stop shrugging and sighing when we could instead be improving our lot. We could stop huffing at the hospital closures or airport expansions we oppose and stand against them at the next election instead.

We need reminding that people power isn't just for trivia. We love voting – look at the success of reality television, which depends on it. If we didn't want our opinions heard, there would be no *Big Brother*, no *X Factor* or *American Idol*, no *Dancing with the Stars*. And while I'm prepared to concede that many people might prefer things that way, that is hardly the point. The point is that we vote when we care about the outcome, and we can see that our vote will have an effect, even a tiny one. Almost 100 million people voted in the 2009 *American Idol* final: if voters, especially young voters, are as apathetic as we're led to believe, why would they bother to be one small voice among millions? The answer, surely, is that they see there's a real choice to be made, even if it may seem a rather trivial one.

The real causes of political apathy are being ignored because it's so much easier simply to blame the young. But if people aren't voting in elections, maybe the problem isn't the voters but the elections themselves. Look at the turnout in Ireland for European Parliament elections, for example, which buck the Europe-wide trend for decreasing turnout. Across Europe, voter turnout has dropped at every European Parliament election since the first one, in 1979. But in Ireland, although that trend was followed last century, it was reversed dramatically when voter turnout shot up from 50.2 per cent in the 1999 elections to 58.5 per cent in 2004. According to the *Irish Times*, this was because a referendum on citizenship was held on the same day. Whatever the incentives, over 57 per cent of Irish people voted in the 2009 elections, which, Europe-wide, attracted a turnout average of about 43 per cent.

People vote when they're persuaded that the consequences of voting, or not voting, are important. Is it time to acknowledge that some voters don't vote for MEPs because they simply don't want them? And if they don't want them, then why have them? What would be different, for example, if Slovakia, where only 19 per cent of voters cast a ballot in the 2009 European Parliament elections, went unrepresented in the European Parliament? Would anything really change in the countries that didn't vote? And if things would change, for the worse, then how hard can it be to explain that to the electorate, to show them what they get in exchange for turning out and voting?

Nowadays, we are insulated from the consequences of political inaction. If I don't vote for the London mayor, London doesn't end up without a mayor. It just gets the one other people voted for – which, let us be honest, is what might well happen even if I did vote. The received wisdom is that people don't bother voting when they know that their vote can't really change the outcome. But the *American Idol* voters disprove that completely: it just isn't the case that we only vote when we think an election will be a tight race. We vote when we care, and our politicians need to remind us how much we really do care. The Athenian example should inspire us to try to reduce the distance between political cause and effect. We need to see what we're getting when we put our cross in the box, just as they did when they raised their hands on the Pnyx.

But for all their glittering ideals, the Athenians' definition of democracy was decidedly limited; and when we admire, as we should, their directness, involvement and participation, we have to bear in mind what was missing. The Athenians lived in a world where every citizen had the right to vote. But, as previously noted, their definition of who counted as a citizen was profoundly limited. For a start, citizens had to be male adults. Women, as so often in the ancient world, and indeed in many parts of the modern one, didn't count. Although some philosophers – Plato, for example – could see that there was something decidedly screwy in allowing half the available talent pool in any society to go untapped, the Athenians were not mould-breakers in the world of gender equality. They were also fiercely xenophobic when it came to civic rights. To be an Athenian citizen, it wasn't enough to live in Athens. You needed to have been born there, with two Athenian parents. A woman may not have had the right to vote, but she could still ruin your right to citizenship if she hailed from another part of Greece.

You couldn't move from Thebes to Athens and acquire voting rights there, the way you can move from Chicago to New York and find yourself voting for the New York mayor thirty days later. Citizenship – the right to own property as well as the right to vote – was a closely guarded privilege. Athens had a vast population of metics, or resident aliens, as it is usually translated (if that sounds neither too Sting nor too *X-Files*). The idea which permeates the extremes of modern political discourse – that those who were born somewhere have greater rights to it than those who arrive there later – was prevalent in the ancient world. If you wanted to live somewhere as glamorous as Athens when you'd been born on a Mediterranean backwater island, no one would stop you. But you would never be allowed to think of yourself as Athenian, the way those of us who now pitch up in a country's capital can call ourselves Parisians or Londoners. And you wouldn't be able to vote on matters that affected you in your city of residence.

Perhaps still more disquieting to modern eyes even than the thousands of disenfranchised women and resident foreigners is the fact that Athens could not have had its democratic systems if it hadn't also had slavery. If an Athenian citizen was going to turn up and vote in person at some or all Assembly meetings; if he was going serve on the council, and be part of one of its presiding tribes for thirty-six days in a row; if he was going to participate in his direct democracy at all, in other words, he couldn't also work on those days. And if he was a farmer, or a blacksmith, or pretty much anything else, he would need someone to cover for him; the harvest wouldn't wait until he'd gone into town and voted. That someone was most probably going to be a slave. So is Athens really a place we should look up to at all? Or is admiring their political system on a par with admiring the management theory of plantation owners?

Well, both of those things are partly true. The Athenians were so extraordinary, so modern, in so many ways that it is rather difficult to forgive them when their value system clashes with ours so entirely. But, in their defence, they lived in a world where slavery went unquestioned by everyone. Every ancient society had slaves, one way or another. That's how they got so many huge building projects realised without running years late and billions over budget. Time, as the hymn goes, makes ancient good uncouth, and what seemed normal and reasonable to the Greeks seems considerably less so to us. While no one in their right mind would defend the institution of slavery, it is a pointless exercise to demand that every society throughout history value the same things that we do.

The real weakness of Athenian democracy, according to ancient writers, wasn't the people it left out, but the people it let in. The writers whose work survives – Plato, Aristotle, Thucydides, Aristophanes – were far less exercised by the lack of universal civic rights than they were about the calibre of voters. To these critical right-wingers, democracy was only a whisper away from ochlocracy – mob rule. The word 'democracy' has a very different resonance for us now, so often seen as something to aspire to, for societies which lack the freedoms that many of us take for granted. When George W. Bush talked repeatedly about trying to foster democracy in the Middle East, people may have scoffed at his cultural insensitivity, but they largely agreed with the premise: to most of us, it seems that democracy might be flawed but it is still, in the words of Winston Churchill, 'the worst form of government, except all the others that have been tried'.

That was certainly not the opinion of ancient authors, who were usually oligarchic in their views. They considered the best form of government to be the rule of an elite (which is what, originally, the word 'aristocracy' meant – 'the rule of the best' – before it came to attract rather more negative, inbred connotations). The *dēmos*, or people, could be a terrifying prospect to the upper classes. They were a noisy, brutish mass: impetuous, emotional, easily led into stupid decisions. Thucydides tells us rather censoriously, for example, of their changeable mood during the Mytilene Debate. In 428 BCE, near the beginning of the Peloponnesian War, Mytilene, the capital city of Lesbos, revolted from Athens. The traditional punishment for this kind of rebellion was the mass execution of all adult men, and the enslavement of all women and children. It was, in essence, genocide. And once the Athenians found out that Mytilene had rebelled, they voted to accept a proposal for this severest of retributions, made by Cleon, a demagogue (literally meaning 'people-leader', but always used pejoratively). And a trireme was dispatched to carry the orders to Mytilene.

Cleon received a terrible press from Thucydides, who called him 'remarkable among the Athenians for the violence of his character'. Cleon's family were probably tanners, and he was therefore very much a representative of the *dēmos*. Cleon was ruthlessly parodied in several of Aristophanes' comedies, especially *The Knights*, where he was portrayed as a thuggish, vicious-minded steward who flogged the slaves and misled his master, Dēmos. And the real Cleon's proposal for the gravest punishment for Mytilene must have helped to create his reputation for thuggishness: the day after they had voted for mass execution, the Athenians reconsidered. When they questioned their harsh decision of the previous day, Cleon did his utmost to persuade them that they had chosen wisely. But the Athenians decided to be more merciful, and a second trireme was immediately sent out, to try to catch up with its predecessor. The second boat arrived just in time to prevent the death sentences being carried out.

Thucydides tells this story with a sort of weary resignation, as though this is the kind of thing you have to accept with a democracy: idiot crowds making idiot decisions at the behest of idiot speakers, then promptly regretting them. But in defence of the Athenian masses, they very rarely made such a volte-face. They made mistakes, certainly. They committed to the wrong military campaigns, and they could be blood-thirsty and unforgiving. But not often. Just as we wring our hands when extremist right-wing parties thrive in local elections, high-minded political theorists like Plato and Aristotle sometimes despaired of the lowbrow men who decided crucial affairs with their emotions rather than their brains. But actually, the Athenians should fill us with hope: they made a lot of excellent decisions, and when they made bad ones, they could be men enough to admit it and perform a speedy U-turn. If only our politicians, and perhaps our media, could be so open about their errors, then we might yet live in a more sensible world.

But as the fifth century drew to a close, so too did Athenian hegemony of the ancient world. They had done untold damage to themselves by deciding on a foolish and unnecessary conflict with Sicily between 415 and 413 BCE, which cost them the best part of a generation of young men. And their long war with Sparta was finally lost in 404 BCE. Sparta, however, couldn't press home their advantage for long: they were drastically weakened by the revolts of the Helots, a serf people whom the Spartans treated rather as one might a race of alarming and unloved wild dogs. The legendary Spartan land force, so lethal against the Athenians, was crushed by Theban soldiers in 371 BCE, in Leuctra, a village near Thebes. But the Thebans, similarly, were unable to shine for long. Soon a new power arrived: Philip II of Macedon, followed by his son, Alexander the Great, tutored by Aristotle in politics and philosophy, and quickly demanding new worlds to conquer.

After Alexander's early death, in 323 BCE, the Hellenistic (another word for Greek) period followed. Macedon tried to retain its control of the Greek world, and rivals emerged from as far afield as Carthage, in modern-day Tunisia. But it soon became clear, despite the best efforts of Hannibal, his elephants and his rock-breaking tactical brilliance, that there was room for only one superpower, and that wasn't in Greece or North Africa. It was the biggest, brashest ancient society of all: Rome.

In other words, the rise of Rome didn't just follow on automatically from the Athenian Empire. It was hard-won over a long period. And Rome's biggest rivals were the Carthaginians. The Punic Wars – the conflicts between Rome and Carthage – spanned from 264 to 146 BCE. Punic, by the way, comes from the Latin word *punicus*, meaning Carthaginian. Easily the best known today is the Second Punic War, during which the Romans (under the command of Publius Cornelius Scipio then later his son, Scipio Africanus) fought Hannibal Barca in a series of battles recorded by the historian Livy. Livy was born in 59 BCE and died in CE 17; he lived and worked through the collapse of the Roman Republic and the beginning of its empire, and wrote an immense history of Rome, *Ab Urbe Condita* – 'From the Founding of the City'. The traditional date of Rome's foundation was 753 BCE, so Livy's ambitious history covered more than seven centuries over 142 books. Only thirty-five of these books survive today, and of those, ten are devoted to the seventeen-year war with Hannibal.

The mere mention of Livy may provoke weary sighs from all

those who tortured themselves with his difficult, complicated battle descriptions at school. I myself, aged perhaps seventeen, was almost daily reduced to tears by Hannibal's endless encounters with shaggy, shabby mountain men as he crossed the Alps. But that just goes to prove that teenagers are better designed for inappropriate relationships and binge-drinking than reading military history, something which I suspect in our hearts we already knew. Pliny the Younger, after all, was so engrossed with a book of Livian history that he didn't bother going to see the eruption of Vesuvius in CE 79. That may make him, by any standards, a joyless swot, but it certainly kept him in better health than his uncle, Pliny the Elder, who died in his attempts to rescue those trapped by the volcano. Lest one be in any doubt, here is evidence that history saves lives. Or at least one life.

Hannibal, the Carthaginian general, was the ultimate bogeyman for the Romans. The image of Hannibal standing outside the gates of Rome was one that still terrorised them in literature centuries after it occurred. He seemed capable of impossible feats of daring. Who else would have realised that his best chance of success against the Romans lay in taking them by surprise, after going the long way round – over the mountains rather than across the sea – from Carthage to Rome? Who else would have brought a herd of elephants across the Alps? If this makes him sound more like a circus ringmaster than a military tactician, go to your nearest zoo and look at the size of an elephant. Then imagine several of them. Then imagine them outside the cage and angry. Then imagine you have a short sword and not much else to repel them, and you begin to see why elephants formed such a huge psychological threat in ancient battles. Of course, elephants are considerably harder to control than, say, horses, so Hannibal's elephants were often as much of a hazard to his own men as his enemies. But that is hardly the point – if you want to win a war, you need your enemy to believe that you will stop at nothing. And herding elephants across one of the highest mountain ranges in Europe, or on to rafts to get them across large bodies of water, certainly shows that you mean business.

Hannibal even cracked his way through solid rock in his attempts to reach Rome. As Livy explains, it was the only possible route:

> When they needed to cut through the rock, they felled and lopped the huge trees nearby, and made a great pile of logs. As soon as the wind blew hard enough to catch a spark, they set the wood on fire, and they poured vinegary wine on to the burning rock to soften it. Once they'd heated the rock, they cracked it open with their tools. They made gentle zigzags in the cliff, so that not only the pack animals, but even the elephants could be led down it.

Hannibal was eventually beaten by the younger Scipio at Zama, in North Africa, in 202 BCE. The victory was so crucial that the Roman general was given a new cognomen – thereafter known as Scipio Africanus – as a mark of his success. But Zama was a close-run thing. Hannibal was very nearly victorious himself, but betrayal by a former ally, Masinissa, left him fatally weakened, and he was routed by Scipio's men. The Carthaginian senate, who had never really trusted Hannibal anyway, were quick to make terms. If wars are usually won by generals and lost by politicians, then Hannibal was an early casualty. And Carthage had left the future clear for the inexorable rise of Rome.

Athens may stand in our minds as the political ideal, but Rome is the ultimate pragmatist. The Romans had their ideal political system – the Republic – but they lost it in messy civil war. A system that worked well for hundreds of years, the Roman Republic was much loved and lamented by many surviving writers. Nobly born men competed to hold office and follow an electoral hierarchy: the *cursus honorum*. A man wishing to achieve the heights of political honour needed to serve for ten years in the Roman army. At the age of thirty, he could stand for election as quaestor, an administrative position. A few years later he could try to be elected aedile, a position of superior administrative responsibility. At the age of thirty-nine, he could try to be considered for the position of praetor, a judicial role. Then, and only then, aged forty or more, and theoretically older and wiser for it, a man could try to be elected as one of the two consuls, the major political posts in Rome. A consul could command armies, chair the Senate and even give his name to the year. At every stage there were fewer jobs available than at the previous stage – twenty quaestors, six or eight praetors and two consuls.

The flaw in this otherwise excellent system, as you have doubtless noticed, is that it encouraged a far larger number of men to believe they had a future in politics than there was ever really space for at the top. The American phenomenon of 'going postal' has been linked to precisely the same problem: if you tell every child that they can grow up to become president, you aren't necessarily doing them a favour. For while the self-belief you might foster can only be a good thing, the moment when reality crashes in and makes it clear that only the very talented or the very rich have a hope of a successful political career is a painful one. Once someone realises that, far from becoming president, he or she will instead be working in the post room of a minor corporation until death, it's no wonder the occasional person picks up a shotgun and demands a recount.

This problem was exacerbated in Rome. Once a man had entered the political arena, he might well not want to go home early. Certainly, there were men who succeeded, like Cicero, forever patting himself on the back for making it to the consulship in 63 BCE, in spite of being a *novus homo* – literally a 'new man', meaning that none of his ancestors had served as consul. But there were many more who felt they had been unjustly passed over, or who wanted more power than a year or two at the top would provide. It could only end one way.

The Roman Republic collapsed into civil war in the first century BCE. It reached its nadir in one of the best-known scenes of all ancient history. Julius Caesar, who had tried to make himself dictator (quite a step up from consul, and certainly not part of the *cursus honorum*), was assassinated on the steps of a theatre. No wonder Shakespeare couldn't resist the story: all that dramatic tension, and a theatrical backdrop to boot. Caesar's final words, though, were not 'Et tu, Brute?', in spite of what Shakespeare would have you believe. He actually spoke his last words in Greek: 'Kai su, teknon?' – 'Even you, my son?'

Brutus' mother had been having an affair with Caesar for so long that there were rumours he might even be Brutus' father. Timings make that unlikely, but either way, as he lay dying, Caesar called Brutus his son. Isn't that death scene a lot more tragic with the Oedipal over-tones of a father killed by his own child? If Margaret Thatcher had hit John Major with a line like that (albeit that Clytemnestra would have been a more appropriate Freudian figurehead for her than Oedipus), his career might have been as short-lived as that of Brutus, who committed suicide two years after Caesar's murder, in 42 BCE.

Civil war raged through the Roman world until the Battle of Actium in 31 BCE, where Octavian finally triumphed over Mark Antony. The Republic, however much nostalgic Roman writers would wish otherwise, was over for good. The Romans began an imperial system, which was sufficiently stable for them to conquer a vast empire and rule it in relative peace for centuries. It was the ultimate triumph of spin over reality – Octavian, now renamed Augustus, had seen the fate of Julius Caesar (his adoptive father), when he appeared to his contemporaries to be a dictator, almost a king. Augustus had no intention of being stabbed on the steps of any entertainment venue, so he cloaked his power with egalitarian names. He wasn't a dictator; he didn't have ideas above his station. He was simply *princeps senatus* – the chief man of the senate. He was *primus inter pares* – the first among equals; it would be almost 2,000 years before George Orwell's pigs recognised the powerful truth behind this idea: some animals really were more equal than others. Augustus wasn't trying to be king; he had no more power than any elected official might have. He just had the power of all the elected officials rolled into one: he became the first Roman emperor.

Imperial Rome is surely the time most of us think of when we think of ancient Rome. Whether it is from *I Claudius*, *Gladiator* or *Quo Vadis*, our vision of Rome usually has an emperor in its midst. The emperors were the celebrities of the ancient world: faces on coins, and names on buildings. And their characters have survived the ages intact: Augustus, the elder statesman, Claudius and his stammer, Nero fiddling while Rome burned (as much the victim of a myth as Marie Antoinette and her mistranslated brioche). Few political institutions can have inspired so many, from poets and novelists like Robert Graves, to dictators like Mussolini. And that's before one remembers Gaius Caligula, the mad emperor, who both provided an unassailable definition of madness (he threatened to make Incitatus, his favourite horse, a consul), and gave his name to *Penthouse*'s highest-selling porn film of all time, still shifting 3,000 copies a month, thirty years after it was released.

The emperors still define the way we think of modern leaders today, so often do they seem to foreshadow men who came to power thousands of years later. JFK was Titus, loved by the people, but destined to die young. Tony Blair was Augustus, the master of spin. Berlusconi is Domitian, running his state amid secrecy and lies. Kim Jong-Il is Claudius, disguising physical weakness, after his rumoured stroke, with a streak of war-mongering machismo. Our penchant for celebrity politics, with one figure defining a country at home and abroad, makes it almost too easy to match modern leaders with their imperial counterparts.

But there is plenty more we can learn from the ancients, particularly when it comes to foreign policy. Western relations with the Middle East, for example, didn't just become difficult with the clash of Christianity and Islam. It has always been a flashpoint. The emperor Vespasian and his son Titus fought immensely aggressive wars in Judaea in the first century CE. Josephus, the Jewish historian, tells us that more than a million people died in the siege and subsequent destruction of Jerusalem in CE 70. Anachronistic critics have accused almost every Roman emperor of anti-Semitism, Titus understandably more than most. Yet for this to stick, they have to overlook his long, illicit love affair with Berenice, a Jewish queen.

He was, of course, carrying on a noble Roman tradition of falling for an unsuitable and reviled Eastern queen. A century earlier, Mark Antony had given Rome its own version of Osama Bin Laden: Cleopatra. An Eastern figure, commanding considerable local support, she achieved an almost totemic status as Rome's enemy and represented everything Rome most feared. Whether because of her beauty, her politics or her charm, she was enough to persuade a good Roman like Mark Antony to turn on his country. But for all their overt hostility towards the East, the Romans were conflicted. They themselves were mythically descended from an Eastern kingdom: the founder of Rome was Aeneas, once a prince of Troy, who travelled away from his burning city and eventually became an Italian king. Just as we wish to have a productive relationship with the oil-bearing Middle East, while fearing we may be fostering enemies for the future, so the Romans were both drawn to, and repelled by, the East.

One point to consider: the USA, with regard to its foreign policy, is often compared to Rome. As they are the only superpowers in their respective worlds, it's tempting to link them closely. Certainly, the popular image of Americans, speaking no language abroad but their own, is one that should ring a bell. The word 'barbarian' comes from the inability of the Romans – and before them the Greeks – to understand what foreigners were saying. To them, all foreign speech sounded like 'Bar bar bar'. And so the word 'barbarian' came to mean an uncultured, uncivilised person, a non-Roman, in a world where Rome was everything (even though, ironically, the Romans took the word from the Greeks). But the Romans, like the Americans, get a lot of criticism for their bigotry, or racism, or religious intolerance. And not all of it is deserved. The Romans didn't hate the races they conquered. They simply viewed themselves as superior in every possible regard, and demolished anyone who got in their way. It took a British chieftain, named Calgacus, to summarise their foreign policy succinctly, when he said, 'Ubi solitudinem faciunt, pacem appellant': 'The Romans create a desert, and call it peace.' Even America's harshest critics might stop short of quite such a devastating remark.

So, if the world seems off-balance when only one superpower is in the mix, what happens when there are two? Is some sort of war, hot or cold, inevitable? Well, since Rome brooked no rivals, to answer that we have to go back to ancient Greece. The Athenian Empire arose from an earlier alliance of Greek city-states called the Delian League, named after the Mediterranean island of Delos, where their meetings originally took place. The League came together in 478 BCE in order to repel the threat of future invasions from Persia, modern-day Iran

– another indication that Middle-East/West relations have always been fraught.

The first Persian War had been fought in the 490s BCE when Darius, the king of Persia, sent his men to invade Greece. But the Persian warriors eventually received their comeuppance at the hands of the Athenian soldiers, in the legendary Battle of Marathon in 490. Although better remembered now for the myth of a soldier sprinting twenty-six miles to Athens to report the victory and inspiring a thousand fun runs, Marathon was far more important than that. It was the moment the Greeks realised that, even with a smaller fighting force, they could still beat the Persians and retain their freedom. Darius never forgave the Athenians, and plotted one day to return. But he died a few years later, before he had the chance. His son, Xerxes, became king, and decided to avenge his father's honour, with a second invasion in 480 BCE. One could perhaps argue that sons of fathers who have been defeated are all the more bellicose because of it. Certainly, Xerxes was prepared to throw everything he had at this war: he hoped to conquer all of Greece. This time, the Greeks were more ready than ever. The Athenians took the fight to sea, against the Persian fleet at Artemisium. Although they were forced to withdraw after a few days, they sailed to Salamis, and crushed the Persian fleet there.

Sadly for the Athenians, few people now remember their role in this war, as they were so wholly upstaged by the 300 Spartans who fought a suicidal battle at Thermopylae. Leonidas, a Spartan king, held the pass of Thermopylae ('hot gates' is the literal translation) for a week against a vastly superior Persian force. And he might have lasted even longer had not the Spartans and their allies (probably no more than 1,500 men altogether) not been betrayed by Ephialtes, a traitor who showed the Persians a secret path that would bring them out behind Greek lines. If you haven't watched Zack Snyder's film *300* about this conflict, then do give it a go. It may be full of giants and supernatural hybrid rhinoceroses, but it is well worth a watch, and has some excellent pieces from Herodotus – the Father of History (if you're a fan) or the Father of Lies (if you aren't) – lurking within it. This includes a scene that illustrates the Spartans' lack of enthusiasm for diplomacy. Ambassadors were treated with the utmost respect in the ancient world; they were sacrosanct. But when the Persian ambassador had arrived in Sparta demanding that a symbolic tribute of earth and water be paid to Xerxes, his king, the Spartans gave his words only the briefest consideration. Then they pushed the ambassador down a well and pointed out that he could find plenty of earth and water down there. Luckily they were good enough in battle to defend their shocking manners, or Sparta might have died out pretty quickly.

So after the successful defence against this second Persian invasion, the Greeks formed the Delian League, under the leadership of the Athenians. It took more than twenty years for the League to morph into the Athenian Empire. Instead of the city-states contributing ships to the war effort, they were gradually compelled to pay money instead, allowing Athens to equip her mighty fleet. One doesn't need to be a military historian to see that if city-states contributed ships to a collective navy, those ships could also be used to defend the city-state that had contributed them. But once they started giving money instead, they were simply paying for Athens to become more and more powerful at their expense. Just as after the Second World War, two powerful allies became two implacable enemies. Athens and Sparta had combined to make an unbeatable force against the common enemy of Persia. But without that common enemy, they simply couldn't live with each other.

So what can we conclude about the modern political world from what we know about the ancient one? It seems hard to avoid the deterministic interpretation that if the Middle East was a focus of factional war two and a half millennia ago, things will never change. Well, adopt a defeatist attitude if you must, but knowledge should be a help rather than an excuse. Just because East and West have a long history of disagreement doesn't mean that they can't ever agree, after all. Perhaps the sense of perspective we acquire from looking at the ancient world is the very thing needed to make everyone more reasonable in their dealings with one another. Don't we want to stand on the shoulders of the Greeks and the Romans, instead of biting at their knees? Our lives are considerably nicer, less brutish and longer than the lives of our ancient predecessors. And we have all the resources of time, money and historical perspective at our disposal. So perhaps we should stop viewing political issues of any kind – foreign or domestic – as intractable problems. The ancients didn't always do things in the kindest, or the most effective, way, but they always tried something, and sometimes it worked. Our inventiveness, coupled with the keen political will we could borrow from them, might be just what the modern world requires.

2

How Many Angry Men?

Any society, ancient or modern, needs laws. We have an innate sense of justice, or more properly, of injustice. That's why we have all, at some point or another, wailed the phrase, 'It's not fair.' When a child sees that her sister has been given a larger biscuit than hers, she doesn't need to have come to terms with Socrates' assertion that we are all born with an ideal form of equality in our minds. She just looks at the biscuits, and she knows she is being short-changed. No wonder weeping ensues. We have a schizophrenic (literally a 'split mind') attitude to the law: we call it an ass and make cheap jokes about lawyers (What's the difference between a lawyer and a vulture? Frequent flyer miles). But at the same time, we believe in it fervently. We are shocked if someone suggests a trial without jury for crimes that carry a prison sentence. We're appalled when the UK government proposes reforms to the legal aid system, even though it's creaking at the edges. We look to the law to protect us, the little guy.

For their many failings, the Romans spent the best part of a thousand years refining their laws. The Twelve Tables, their earliest laws, regulated property, marriage, inheritance and plenty more, and they dated back to the fifth century BCE, when Rome was still a backwater, and Athens ruled supreme. Even as a backwater, the Romans wanted a legal system they could understand, use and be proud of. And as Rome grew in power and size, senators and, later, emperors began to enact new and improved laws. In the mid sixth century CE, the emperor Justinian finally codified the statutes of previous emperors into the Corpus Iuris Civilis, the Body of Civil Law. It formed the basis for most legal systems right up to the present day. When someone asks what the Romans have done for us, the law isn't a bad place to start.

Laws defined people in the ancient world. They were a means to distinguish humans from beasts, on the one hand, which knew no laws, and the gods, on the other hand, who abided by none. Laws might be human in origin, like those of Thurii, an Athenian colony, whose whole constitution was devised by the philosopher Protagoras. They might equally be divine, like the 613 commandments given to Moses in the Old Testament, which range from 'Thou shalt not kill' to 'Don't get a tattoo.'

In Athens they had a lawgiver so legendarily severe that he is still an adjective to this day. The word 'draconian' isn't derived from *draco*, the Latin name for a dragon – although *draco* does give us *dracul* (the Romanian word for 'dragon', hence Vlad Dracul, Count Dracula and other unsavoury dinner guests). Rather, draconian laws are named after Draco, the seventh-century BCE lawgiver. According to his first-century CE biographer, Plutarch, almost every type of crime was liable for the death penalty, and even those convicted of idleness were executed. Those who stole fruit or vegetables received the same punishment as those who committed sacrilege or murder. A fourth-century demagogue named Demades apparently quipped that Draco's code was written 'not in ink but in blood'.

Many of Draco's laws were repealed in the sixth century BCE by the more lenient Solon, Athens' next great lawgiver, 'because of their severity and the excessive harshness of their penalties'. Perhaps even Draco's contemporaries felt the death penalty for idling was a bit much: 'Draco himself, they say, when he was asked why he had made death the penalty for most crimes, answered that he thought the minor ones deserved it, and for greater ones there was no heavier punishment left.'

Although it might be tempting, therefore, to think of ancient Greece as a place where one had less freedom than Winston Smith in *1984*, and as much hope of penal clemency as Jean Valjean in *Les Misérables*, things weren't quite that bad. Solon repealed the death penalty for everything but homicide, and Athenians viewed their legal system with considerable pride. As the great fifth-century Athenian statesman Pericles says, 'When it comes to settling private disagreements, everyone is equal before the law.' And Aristotle, in the fourth century BCE, went a step further: 'For as man is the best of all animals when he has reached his full development, so he is worst of all when divorced from law and justice.' In other words, living without a fair and just legal system would make human beings less than human, less than other living creatures. It's a view that surely any human rights organisation would agree with today, even if that organisation might phrase things rather differently.

Ancient legal systems were just as idiosyncratic as ours are. The laws in Sparta, for example, the militaristic city-state in southern Greece, were far more stern than those in Athens, post-Draco. Sparta also had a celebrated lawgiver, named Lycurgus, who conducted a several-pronged attack on wealth, seeing it as an evil that made Spartans soft, and prone to crime. He eliminated gold and silver coinage, and made iron the only valid currency, assigning a low value to it, so that Spartans needed a vast amount to buy anything. And as Plutarch observes, 'Once this was made legal tender, many types of crime disappeared from Sparta. For who would set out to steal, or accept as a bribe, or rob, or plunder something which could not be hidden, excited no envy when possessed, and could not even profitably be chopped up?' Lycurgus also ensured that the men of Sparta all ate together in mess-halls. No matter how wealthy a man might be, he wouldn't be able to sit at home all day on a chaise longue, eating the Spartan equivalent of violet creams. He was compelled to dine with his fellow Spartans, so that they all ate the same meat and grain, and no-one developed a taste for luxury. No wonder the word 'spartan' retains its meaning today.

But perhaps the most pragmatic of ancient lawgivers was the little-known Pittacus, ruler of Mytilene between 589 and 579 BCE. Aristotle tells us of his extremely sensible attitude to binge-drinking excesses: 'a particular law of his is that if drunks commit any offence they should pay a larger fine than sober men would. Since more drunken men than sober insult and mistreat people ... he ignored the question of pardoning them and focused on expediency.' It's hard not to have a little fellow feeling with Pittacus here: there really is no point in becoming exasperated with the over-exuberant drunk when one can simply fleece him instead. Given the plague of drunken tourists that descends upon the Greek islands every summer, Lesbos might do worse than to consider reintroducing Pittacus' law.

Perhaps the most marked difference between modern and ancient legal systems is the presence, or absence, of law enforcement. The ancients didn't have police officers, in any sense that we do now. If you broke a law in Athens, no one would turn up on the doorstep with an identifying badge and demand that you accompany them to the station. If you stole something from a neighbour, that neighbour wouldn't contact an arresting officer and demand that he interrogate you. There was no equivalent of the Crown Prosecution Service or the district attorney to decide whether to bring charges against you. Things were, as so often in the ancient world, rather more direct than that. If you stole a statue from the garden next door, the person most likely to deal with you was its owner, who wouldn't need a policeman, because he could go straight to the courts and sue you himself. If the case went to court, you and he might be rich enough to hire advocates, such as Lysias or Antiphon, to speak on your behalf. Or you might simply represent yourselves in court, argue your case and hope for the best. Demosthenes, the legendary fourth-century BCE Greek orator, discovered in his teens that his inheritance had been snaffled by his guardians, and spent his childhood studying the great orators, so that he could argue his own case against the malefactors. He eventually won damages against his embezzling guardians, and began a lifetime career in the law.

In Rome, things worked on a rather grander scale. The Romans didn't have a police force either, but they had several alternatives. The closest thing to a modern police force were the vigiles, who were both the firemen and nightwatchmen of ancient Rome. Their name, like our word 'vigilant', comes from the Latin verb *vigilo*, meaning 'to keep awake' and thus 'to keep watch'. They would keep an eye out for runaway slaves, muggers and burglars, and helped to keep the city safe at night. But their real job was firefighting; the crime-busting was a decidedly secondary affair. Rome maintained civil order, for the most part, without assistance. The city was badly scarred by the first century BCE, with its endless warring factions, assassinations and civil war. Augustus' reign, beginning in 27 BCE, heralded a calmer time for the city. And it returned to chaos only briefly, in 69 CE, the year of four emperors. The suicide of the emperor Nero in 68, after an increasingly lunatic reign, left the city open once again to rival bids for power – four rival bids, to be precise: Galba, Otho and Vitellius, who ascended the throne in quick succession, then finally Vespasian, who ruled peacefully for the next decade.

Rome, in other words, had lost her taste for internal conflict. She did, however, still have the urban cohorts, a military wing stationed in the city. They wouldn't have dealt with vandalism, insurance fraud or burglary, but they were formidable riot police. Indeed, riot police today still use Roman military techniques: when they cover themselves with riot shields, interlocking them around themselves and above, they are employing the testudo formation. This tactic – named after a tortoise, for obvious reasons – wasn't invented by the Romans, but they used it to devastating effect, as the historian Cassius Dio explains:

> One day, when they fell into an ambush and were being struck by dense showers of arrows, they suddenly formed the testudo by joining their shields, and rested their left knees on the ground. The barbarians, who had never seen anything of the kind before, thought that they had fallen from their wounds and needed only one finishing blow; so they threw aside their bows, leaped from their horses, and drawing their daggers, came up close to put an end to them. At this the Romans sprang to their feet, extended their battle-line at the word of command, and confronting the foe face to face, fell upon them, each one upon the man nearest him, and cut down great numbers.

So, Rome was well-equipped with soldiers who could maintain order. The *cohortes urbanae* were also a check on the power of the emperor, who had the Praetorian Guard as his personal bodyguard, serving much the same function as Saddam Hussein's Republican Guard once did – although it was a foolish emperor who would completely trust them: both Tiberius and Gaius Caligula were killed with the aid of their Praetorian prefects. Macro, Tiberius' assailant, was said to have smothered him with a pillow. And Gaius Caligula incurred the wrath of Cassius Chaerea, his Praetorian prefect, with unkind teasing about Chaerea's effeminate manner: 'When Chaerea asked for the watchword, Gaius gave him "Priapus" or "Venus"; and if he came to give thanks, Gaius always stuck out his hand in an obscene gesture.' One hesitates to imagine. Chaerea eventually stabbed Gaius Caligula in the neck, and split his jaw. Perhaps the moral of this story is not to tease a policeman, as even the effeminate ones are armed, and some of them may bear a grudge.

The Romans may not have had policemen, but they did have a rather more alarming force policing the higher social orders: informers. Or, as the historian Tacitus preferred to describe them, 'an evil which for many years ate away at public life'. Informers flourished under the reign of Tiberius; it was the McCarthyism of its time. Tiberius liked to give his enemies enough rope, and Tacitus' account of his reign is pure, sinister HUAC: 'He could have stopped all Libo's words and deeds. He preferred to make note of them.'

Marcus Scribonius Libo Drusus, whose case Tacitus relates in detail, was charged with necromancy, and faced a barrage of accusers. He eventually killed himself, by stabbing himself twice in the stomach. Tacitus leaves us in no doubt why someone might choose to accuse a man in court, irrespective of whether or not he had committed a crime: 'Libo's property was divided among his accusers, and extra praetorships were given to those of senatorial rank.' Money and political promotion? No wonder informers were clamouring for more lives to ruin. We even see examples of Roman citizens facing trumped-up charges purely because they had especially nice houses that their accusers hoped to acquire in the post-conviction division of spoils.

Entrapment was also par for the course in these informer-led cases. Libo, whom Tacitus damns with a customary thumbnail character sketch as 'easy prey for the fortune-tellers', was encouraged by a friend, Catus, to pursue interests in astrological predictions, magical rites and reading of dreams. His necromancy, in other words, was mere vanity of ambition (he came from a line of powerful ancestors, which can often lead a man to imagine himself in a position of power, or occasionally even to acquire one) combined with silliness. Tacitus calls the documents used against Libo in court 'vaecordes' – 'insane' – and it's hard not to agree. One of them stated that Libo had asked a fortune-teller if he might one day be rich enough to pave the Appian Way with money as far as Brundisium. The childish nature of this request, so ludicrous that it must have been true, makes one almost weep for Libo and his foolishness.

Catus encouraged him in his nonsense until he had entangled him in evidence. 'Once he had enough witnesses – including slaves who knew the facts – he asked to see the emperor.' Other prosecutors were soon involved, and Libo was accused, among other charges, of making secret and terrible markings next to the names of the emperor and various senators. He denied the handwriting was his. His slaves claimed it was. Roman practice was to interrogate slaves under torture if they were witnesses in legal cases, as only then could one be sure they were telling the truth – or at least be sure they were saying whatever they thought was most likely to stop the torturer. But an ancient senatorial decree forbade torturing slaves in capital cases against their masters. Even the Romans, who lacked finesse and kindness in matters such as these, realised that someone might not get a fair trial if his or her life depended on a tortured slave telling the truth, the whole truth and nothing but.

Legal niceties, however, stood no chance against Tiberius at his most grimly efficient. He ordered Libo's slaves to be sold to an agent of the Treasury. Since they were no longer Libo's slaves, they could now be tortured with impunity, and testify against their former master on a capital charge, with the senatorial decree remaining intact. It was not the only case of maintaining the letter of the law over its spirit during Tiberius' principate. The imperial biographer Suetonius was a man who loved scurrilous gossip above all things. He was born out of time: anyone who took such undisguised delight in reporting the sexual peccadilloes and violent tendencies of every one of his subjects missed his calling as a tabloid journalist. Nonetheless, even he seems shocked when he writes about some of those executed during Tiberius' reign. Their bodies were dragged to the Tiber with hooks – 'inter eos feminae et pueri', 'among them women and children'. He goes on to explain that tradition dictated that virgins couldn't be strangled. But Tiberius' men weren't going to let a little thing like that stop them: 'Immaturae puellae ... uitiatae prius a carnifice, dein strangulatae.' Young girls were raped first by the executioner, then strangled. Sometimes the Romans can be very hard to love.

There is, of course, no point in criticising the Romans, the Greeks or any other ancient society for having different, indeed unarguably worse, values from our own. Even in a country like contemporary Afghanistan, where laws are in place allowing men to starve their wives for refusing them sex, people would probably blanch at raping a child so they could then strangle her with legal impunity. But we do need to remember the failings of ancient societies: the temptation to see them as places where tunic-clad men wandered round declaiming Ciceronian witticisms from scrolls is a powerful one for those interested in the classical world. And an understandable one, too. Most of us would rather study a culture we like. Classicists have often romanticised the past: they have made the ancient world seem so close to ours that we can find ourselves viewing a society which has been defunct for a couple of millennia as though it weren't defunct at all, but simply far away and impossible to reach. Indeed, popular culture has such a passion for the ancient world that it often contributes to this mental glitch: how many times does one see ancient Rome, for example, presented as a toga party to which our invitation went astray? *A Funny Thing Happened on the Way to the Forum, Carry On Cleo, Up Pompeii, Caligula* are but a few examples. Even the makers of *Star Trek* threw in the odd planet that resembled ancient Rome. So perhaps in some part of our minds we tend to view Rome as though it were topographically, rather than temporally, separate from our world. And because of that glitch, we have to make a mental choice: either we face up to their realities and are shocked and horrified by what we see, as though Rome were a rogue state in the modern world; or we shroud ourselves in ignorance and concentrate on the beautiful poetry, or admire the astonishing architecture, refusing to imagine how many men must have died to build an aqueduct, a temple or a column. Why dwell on the bad stuff?

But if we really want to understand the ancient world, and use it to help us to understand the modern one, we must try to correct this glitch, and remember that time, or at least history, really is a one-way street. While it is perfectly reasonable, if rather culturally imperialist, to expect contemporary societies to match up to our standards of what is right and wrong, there is absolutely no point bringing this sensibility to a study of the ancients. When we deplore the attitude to women's rights in, say, Saudi Arabia, or the behaviour of the governing parties of Sudan, or Burma, we do so because the people who live in these countries live in the same world as us. It requires only a small leap of imagination to see our loved ones or ourselves in the position of a woman flogged for wearing trousers, or a man imprisoned for using the Internet. But the past is more than just another country where they do things differently. And if we hold it up to modern standards, it can only disappoint: why should the Victorians be regarded as such great engineers when they didn't even invent computers? How can the Spartans be considered good at fighting if they didn't have guns or nukes? The famous 300 at Thermopylae would have been wiped from the face of the earth in one short air-strike. Ability is relative: it's about what you achieve with what is available to you. And ethics are relative, too: expecting the Romans to shudder at the same things that revolt us is a waste of time and thought. This is not the place for a liberal wail about their use of torture.

This is, however, precisely the place to point out that even the Romans, with their routine lack of humanity when it came to those they had enslaved, knew that torture was essentially useless. Yet the rationale behind Roman thinking on evidence from slaves was pretty logical. If person A is owned by person B, person B has the power of life and death over person A. So if Antoninus is the slave of Brutus, he cannot be expected to give honest evidence about Brutus' actions in court, because the very fact that Brutus could injure him, brand him or even kill him is too powerful an influence. Most of us wouldn't promise to tell the truth – no matter what – with a gun to our heads. Or, rather, we probably would promise, but then lie, which obviously serves justice far less well than a refusal to speak at all. The Romans astutely realised that they wouldn't get honest answers from slaves unless they proposed an alternative both more frightening and more immediate than their masters' potential retribution. So if a slave's evidence was to be used in court, the slave had to be tortured. Torture wasn't being used as a punishment, or a threat, although the Romans had no hesitation in using it for those purposes too. But the systematic torture of slaves giving evidence was used as a strategy to counterbalance the enormous power a master exerted over his slave.

It's hard to assess the quality of evidence elicited from these slaves. With the twin evils of a torturer on the one hand and a furious master on the other, it may well have been largely a matter of chance whether the truth was ever uncovered. And what is interesting about Libo's case is that it reveals the Romans knew that too. They tortured slaves to get to the truth. But when a man's life was on the line, his slaves couldn't be tortured, presumably because their evidence was known to be unreliable. After all, if you were a cruel master, then a slave might cheerily sing like the proverbial canary, just to be rid of you. Even if you were a kind master, slaves still might say whatever came to mind, just to make the pain of the torture stop. A man could not face a capital charge on those terms, even in a society that had no problem with death sentences or imposed suicides. Roman justice might look shaky to us, but one only has to read the letters of the ever-boastful Cicero to see how proud they were of it. And Tacitus, in spite of his legendary promise to write 'sine ira et studio' – 'without anger or bias' – is clearly appalled by Libo's case. The persecution of innocents and the subversion of legal protocol are tangibly shocking to him.

So perhaps the question that should arise in our minds from the trial of Libo is this: if the Romans knew, 2,000 years ago, that those being tortured will say whatever is necessary for the torture to stop, why does the argument about torture continue to this day? Why are we still presented with the exhausted 'ticking bomb' scenario, in which a captured terrorist knows where a nuclear bomb is planted in the middle of, say, Melbourne. Do the police torture him to reveal its whereabouts, thus saving hundreds of thousands of lives at the cost of simply injuring one man? Who could argue against such a simple premise? Well, perhaps those Roman senators (whose decree preventing the torture of slaves in capital cases prompted Tiberius' weaselly subterfuge), who knew that torturing people produces more lies than truth. So when we consider the infamous ticking bomb scenario, which thankfully belongs more amid the ticking time of the TV show, *24*, rather than the world in which the rest of us live, we are considering a fallacy. We don't need to worry about what happens in one ticking bomb scenario, because bomb scenarios rarely happen just once. We need to worry about what happens in five or ten ticking bomb scenarios.

Say the first time you capture the terrorist, you torture him and find out the bomb's whereabouts. A result for the forces of freedom and Jack Bauer. But what happens the next time a bomb is ticking, and you capture the terrorist and torture him to find out where the bomb is planted? His fellow conspirators (since we can assume that most nuclear-bomb-planting lunatics require some division of labour), not merely believing but knowing that he will be tortured, and that the human body can only take so much, detonate the bomb immediately, to prevent him from giving them away. While previously they might have negotiated for a hefty sum in a Cayman Islands bank account and a helicopter to reach it, they now refuse to do anything of the kind.

And then the third time you capture the terrorist, he has seen the earlier torture revelations on the news, and has been trained to withstand torture at any price. He will die before he gives up the bomb. Rather than brandishing that fact, after the fashion of Daniel Craig in *Casino Royale*, he convincingly persuades his interrogators of a false location. While the men on the ground waste time trying to reach a place where the bomb isn't, the bomb goes off. The fourth time you capture your terrorist and torture him, he talks. But because of your previous cases, it becomes clear that you have literally no idea if you are being told the truth or not. You are in precisely the same situation, knowledge-wise, as you would have been had you never begun this torturing lark. Only now you are brutalised by your experience of causing unimaginable pain to another human being, and you go home and kill your wife and kids before turning the gun on yourself. Not a good day at the office.

So, once a lawsuit was finally brought before a court, do Greek or Roman justice systems start to look more like ours? As so often with the ancient world, the answer is yes and no. Athenian courts, on paper, might look a great deal like ours: they had a jury, a speech from the prosecution and one from the defence, witnesses and evidence. But the differences shouldn't be glossed over. Firstly, the jury was, for want of a better word, massive. Juries of 501 or 1,000 men were commonplace. Even Henry Fonda might have needed more than a day to change that many minds. The jurors were allotted their cases through an incredibly complex system of random allocations, using tokens, staves, acorns and blocks. If you wished to bribe a jury in Athens, you would need extremely deep pockets. It's impossible to know how many potential jurors turned up each day, or how many cases might run concurrently, but common sense would suggest that you would need to bribe literally hundreds of men to have a fighting chance of getting enough of them in your courtroom to make a difference to the verdict.

It would also be impossible to know if your juror had taken the bung and voted against your wishes. Aristotle explains the workings of the law courts in minute detail, so we know that jurors would be given two ballots, which looked the same. The only difference was one of weight: one was solid, the other hollow. Jurors would drop their ballots into jars at the end of a trial. So, two ballots, one representing the prosecution, and one the defence. Two jars, one made of bronze, into which you dropped the ballot matching whichever speaker you thought had proved his case; and one made of wood, into which you dropped your other ballot. Even someone staring hard to see if they'd spent their bribe money wisely would be unable to tell for whom each juror was voting.

And it wouldn't be any easier to bribe those counting the ballots. Once all the jurors had voted, the ballots were counted in public, in the courtroom, and a herald proclaimed the result straightaway. Interestingly, if the votes were exactly equal (unlikely with a jury of 501, but certainly possible with a jury of 1,000), the defence won. In Athens, you really were innocent until proven guilty.

If you're wondering how Athens managed to find so many hundreds of willing jurors when we live in a time where weaselling out of jury service is commonplace, the answer is very simple: they paid them. Jurors were paid a small stipend, like those doing civic duty in the council. It was only a couple of obols, which was roughly the same wage a man would get for doing a day's unskilled labour. It wouldn't make up for the loss of work if you were a highly skilled craftsman, for example. But then, a craftsman wouldn't have to volunteer for jury service. The majority of jurors would be, if Aristophanes can be trusted, old men.

In his play *The Wasps* the chorus is a gang of old men who serve on the jury courts as often as they can. They are too old to do manual work, and enjoy getting out of the house and socialising at the courts. They also enjoy the power it gives them: they like to sting those pleading their cases in court, that is why they are dressed as wasps. Aristophanes, it must be remembered, was a comedian, and one who often created humour with hyperbole. But that is no reason to presume there isn't a grain of truth in what he says: quite the reverse, in fact. Exaggeration isn't funny unless there's some truth at its centre. If there isn't, it's simply fantasy. So when, in the play, a son locks his father in the house to prevent him from doing jury service because it's made him so litigious that no one can bear it, we can assume that this isn't a documentary. Certainly, when the old man presides over a court at home instead, and hears the case of a dog, prosecuted for stealing a cheese, we can assume (even before the dog offers his verbal defence) that we are in the realms of comic invention. But the joke wouldn't be funny if his audience couldn't see the starting point as realistic – the jury courts probably were populated by the elderly, while the young were busy fighting in the war, or working.

And although Aristophanes painted the old men as aggressive jurors, likely to find a man guilty because they enjoyed exercising their power, it's hard not to think that the Athenians were on to something. Modern societies often can't work out what to do with the elderly. We boot them out of their jobs at sixty-five, and then complain that their pensions cost us money. We seem to believe that old people should just shuffle off and die, unless we are personally related to them (and sometimes even then: one hesitates to judge). We have, in other words, lost centuries of respect for acquired wisdom. Why should they know best, just because they're older?

At the same time, we roll our eyes in irritation whenever a trial is abandoned because it has gone on for too long, or become too complex for a jury to understand: this is especially true in complicated fraud cases. We're determined to have a trial by our peers, but plenty of us try to get out of doing jury service. So would it be so bad if our juries were, on average, a little older than some of us? There must be plenty of pensioners who would cheerfully subsidise their pensions with a little paid jury service, and whose considerable skills and wisdom are currently ignored by society at large. Who would you rather have hearing a fraud case: a retired economics teacher, or a self-employed woman whose eye is on the clock, knowing she's losing money every minute she's in the courtroom? We might not wish to create a class of professional jurors, but some semi-professional ones would be no bad thing. The law isn't the Olympics; jurors don't need to be amateurs to keep the whole thing fair. And the current crop of retired people were teenagers during the summer of love, so let's not imagine that anyone over the age of sixty will suddenly start behaving like a dyspeptic colonel in an Agatha Christie novel.

The size and grandeur of law courts surely emphasises how important they are to our society. It is impossible not to be impressed by the Old Bailey in London, even if one sometimes disagrees with the judgements made within. And the Justitiepaleis in Brussels would make the most hardened criminal quake: according to UNESCO, it was the largest building constructed during the nineteenth century. Ancient Athens had two major courts: the Heliaia, which judged the trials of Pericles and Socrates, among others; and the Areopagus (literally 'Hill of Ares', after the god of war was tried there for murdering Poseidon's son. Well, in myth, anyway).

The Greeks were used to seeing the courts immortalised in their culture, too. Aeschylus' *Oresteia* is a trilogy of plays that follow the tragedy of the House of Atreus. Atreus had two sons, Agamemnon and Menelaus. Menelaus married Helen and lived in Sparta. His household was thrown into disarray when Paris turned up and ran off with Helen to Troy, whereupon she became the face that launched a thousand ships. If you think Paris sounds like a cheap adulterer, try to remember his back-story: one day, the goddess Eris (whose name means 'strife') chucked a golden apple down among three other goddesses: Athene, Hera and Aphrodite. On the apple was inscribed the phrase *tē kallistē*, which means 'for the most beautiful'. All three goddesses wanted to claim the apple as her own, and they began to quarrel. They asked Zeus to judge who was the most beautiful, but he knew better than to get involved in an epic session of girl-war. He appointed Paris to decide instead. The goddesses, naturally, tried to bribe Paris, each according to her own speciality. Athene offered him wisdom and skills: success in war. Hera offered him power: dominion over Europe and Asia. And Aphrodite offered him Helen: the most beautiful woman the world had ever seen. Paris chose Aphrodite and claimed Helen as his own. The problem with these celestial spats is that no one considered the feelings of the wronged husband. So Menelaus had to sail to Troy to try to regain his wife. The other leaders of the Greeks accompanied him, including his brother, King Agamemnon of Argos, or Mycenae (in southern Greece). The role of the gods is crucial in the Trojan War: they intervene all over the place, depending on the vicissitudes of their favourites. The version of Mount Olympus we see in the film *Jason and the Argonauts* gives us a pretty good representation of how the gods behave in Homer. Humans are their playthings, and they intervene like petulant children when the mood takes them.

The gods gave Agamemnon a difficult decision at the very beginning of his campaign. The Greek armies were massed and ready to sail to Troy. Somehow, Agamemnon offended Artemis, the goddess of hunting, perhaps by killing an animal sacred to her. She took revenge by preventing the fleet from sailing – suddenly, there was no wind and without it, they were stuck. The prophet Calchas declared that Artemis could only be appeased if Agamemnon sacrificed his own daughter, Iphigenia. Comparative religion enthusiasts will see a parallel with the Old Testament patriarch Abraham, and the deity's demand for him to sacrifice his son, Isaac.

Isaac, of course, was saved by an angel at the crucial moment. Iphigenia wasn't so lucky. But Artemis was propitiated, and the fleet sailed to Troy. Ten years later the Greeks finally sacked Troy and sailed home. When Agamemnon arrived back in Greece, he was slaughtered by his wife, Clytemnestra, and her lover, Aegisthus. She had not forgiven the sacrifice of her daughter, and she exacted retribution, a life for a life. Yet the problem with retribution, as anyone who tries to quash gang warfare in modern cities will tell you, is that the death toll quickly mounts up. If you believe in an eye for an eye, you end up with an awful lot of blind people before honour is satisfied. According to retributive justice in the Bronze Age, Clytemnestra's two remaining children, Orestes and Electra, must then avenge the death of their father. Orestes kills his mother and her lover, and is then pursued by the Furies, who appear whenever someone incurs blood-guilt, i.e. has killed his father or mother.

No one had really questioned the rights and wrongs of this system until Aeschylus. The first play of his trilogy, *Agamemnon*, deals with the king's murder. Clytemnestra slaughters him with an axe, while he is in the bath. The whole thing is eerily predicted by Cassandra, a Trojan priestess he has brought back from Troy as his prize. She has been cursed by Apollo (after spurning his affections – always a dangerous pursuit in Greek myth) to see the future but never to be believed. Clytemnestra kills her too. In the second play, *Choephoroi*, Clytemnestra tries to placate Agamemnon's spirit. She encourages Electra, along with the libation-bearers (from whom the play takes its title), to pour libations on his tomb. Electra meets up with Orestes at the tomb, and Orestes promptly kills their mother.

In the third play, *Eumenides*, Orestes is chased all over Greece by the avenging Furies, or, as they are called in the play's title, the Eumenides – 'Kindly Ones'. If you call something terrifying by a nice name, goes the theory, it might be better disposed towards you. The Furies are about to kill Orestes when the goddess Athene steps in and decides there must be a trial. And Orestes is tried in Athens, Athene's home town, before an Athenian jury. When their judgement is tied, with half the votes going to Orestes, and half to the Furies, Athene sets him free, saying that he must be acquitted of the charge 'ison gar esti tarithmema tōn palōn' – 'for the number of votes is equal'. And so art imitates life: Aeschylus captures a vital aspect of Athens' civic pride in this play. The distant Bronze Age – of myth and gods and heroes and monsters – is the source of his inspiration, but the Bronze Age is no more; Aeschylus lives in Athens, in the fifth century BCE, and society has advanced beyond retribution killings and blood-guilt. Orestes, in Aeschylus' play, is treated as a foreign citizen should be in Athens (although not all foreigners would agree, as we shall soon see in *The Murder of Herodes*). Orestes is subject to the same laws, the same juries, the same courts as an Athenian. And because of that, the endless destructive cycle of retributive killing, where each new death incurs another, is finally brought to an end. Reason, laws and the values of a city have conquered the brutal, unruly world of myth.

Aeschylus' play, therefore, shows us how things were supposed to work in principle. The reality, of course, was a little different. Luckily, we have some excellent examples of legal speeches from both ancient Greece and Rome. The speeches were kept long after the cases were won or lost, as learning aids for aspiring public speakers. And really, you couldn't do better than read the speeches made by Cicero, Demosthenes, Antiphon or Lysias, if you wanted to learn how to win a case. Cicero could destroy a man's character with a few well-chosen phrases. And his speeches against Lucius Sergius Catiline are a case in point.

Cicero spoke out against Catiline for fomenting a rebellion in 63 BCE. The final years of the Roman Republic were ripe for plotters and schemers, and the only real difference between the men history records as criminals, such as Catiline, and the eventual emperor, Augustus, was the failure or success of their respective endeavours to undermine the Republic. And Catiline picked his fight with Cicero, a man with a profound love of Rome's political status quo and a point to prove: that first-generation senators were as good as or better than any aristocratic reprobate. This is an excellent example of history being written by the winner; it is Cicero's words that survive today.

Cicero used rhetorical flourishes like an Old Master wielded a paintbrush: his speeches are full of techniques that we recognise in those of politicians or lawyers today. He loved to use apophasis, an allusion to something by promising not to talk about it. 'Quod ego praetermitto et facile patior sileri' – 'I make no mention of this, and readily allow it to be passed over in silence' – he says, of the unproven accusation that Catiline had killed both his wife and child. And just to be sure you noticed, he says he won't mention it twice. He used lists, to enormous effect, especially the tricolon (or rule of three: the emphasis always falls upon the third and final part of the phrase, hence *The Good, the Bad and the Ugly*). So, on the subject of Catiline remaining at large in the Senate, Cicero declares, 'non feram, non patiar, non sinam' – 'I won't bear it, I won't endure it, I won't allow it.' He also omits all conjunctions, which gives the list extra speed and impact – a rhetorical device called asyndeton.

Cicero used every trick in the book to win his cases: repetition, hyperbole and litotes (deliberate understatement for extra effect). A terrific example of this in modern culture is the character of Patrick Nice, played by Mark Williams in *The Fast Show*, who is persistently underwhelmed by his good fortune: 'And I was rummaging round in the attic, and I found the original copy of the Bible, signed by God. Which was nice'. By the time Cicero had finished demolishing Catiline's character, accusing him (by saying he wasn't going to accuse him) of killing his wife and child, who would vote against him? Not that they needed to: Catiline wisely made a run for it the following night.

Cicero learned his rhetorical techniques from the great Greek orators. An orator needed to be able to write wonderful, memorable phrases. He needed to construct a complex and winning argument (especially if he was in the wrong). He needed to be able to remember it, as speaking from notes was decidedly not the done thing. And he needed to be able to perform it, in front of a large crowd of rowdy Roman senators or Athenian jurors. Ancient rhetoric had to strike a fine balance for its audience: confident but not cocky, humble but not deferential, persuasive but not tricksy.

Lysias, a Greek orator in the fifth and fourth centuries BCE, wrote legal speeches that ticked all these boxes, and he wrote these speeches for other people to deliver. If you were charged with, say, murder in Athens, you had to defend yourself; no hiding behind a lawyer. This was demonstrably unfair. Quite aside from the fact that the wealthy could afford to pay Lysias to write their speeches while the poor had to produce their own, a man's freedom was dependent on his capacity for public speaking. If you were nervous, shy or softly spoken, what chance did you have in a court of a thousand jurors? Lysias couldn't train his clients to sell themselves, but what he could do, brilliantly, was write speeches that sounded as though the clients had written them themselves. In other words, he got into character.

Euphiletus delivered Lysias' speech in his defence, for the killing of a man named Eratosthenes. Eratosthenes had spotted Euphiletus' wife at her mother-in-law's funeral, and liked what he saw. He followed her servant girl and sent messages to her; they soon began to have an affair. Eratosthenes began to neglect another girlfriend, who promptly sent an old crone (all the best stories should have one) to tell Euphiletus what was going on behind his back. Euphiletus then found Eratosthenes: 'katakeimenon para te gunaiki ... gumnon' – 'lying beside my wife ... naked'.

Eratosthenes begged for his life and offered financial reparation to Euphiletus, knowing that an Athenian man had the legal right to kill anyone he found in bed with his wife. But Euphiletus chose to reject the cash offer and killed him instead. He was taken to the Areopagus when Eratosthenes' relatives brought a case against him for this execution. They claimed it was premeditated murder, which was illegal. Euphiletus needed to prove that he had killed the man in an act of justifiable homicide. Lysias provided him with a masterful speech, which tells us a great deal about how a legal case was argued. Firstly, we see that there are breaks in the speech, where a relevant law is read out, in one instance, from its inscription on a pillar in the Areopagus itself. Lysias wants Euphiletus' audience to be in no doubt that he had a legal right to kill Eratosthenes: imagine the impact of hearing this law read aloud from the very fabric of the building in which you were judging a case.

But Lysias' real skill is revealed in the presentation of the case. Euphiletus does not attempt to deny that he killed Eratosthenes. Instead Lysias presents him as an ordinary Joe, the kind of man, jurors, who behaved just as you would behave, in the same circumstances. He reminds the jury that if a man can't trust his wife to be faithful, he can't believe that his children are his own. He refers them to the law which states that rape is less serious than seduction. This may (and should) seem crass to us, but in a world where women had no rights, it makes perfect sense. A rapist, as Euphiletus explains, is hated by his victim. But a seducer corrupts souls, as well as bodies, and a man ends up unable to trust his wife at all.

We can only marvel at the sleight of hand that Lysias employs to spin the morality of this case on its head. In a few thousand words, Euphiletus goes from being a man accused of undeniable murder to a man who has acted on behalf of the public good. If the jury finds him guilty, he suggests, they are ensuring that any burglar will soon claim to be an adulterer, as the penalties for adultery have become non-existent, and wandering round other men's houses has been deemed perfectly fine. The jury must acquit him, or run the risk of undermining its own laws, established to keep the city safe. In his final flourish,

Lysias goes one step further still. Euphiletus concludes his speech by saying, 'I am now in danger of losing my life, and my possessions, and everything else, because I obeyed the laws of the city.' He isn't just protected by the law, he's upholding it. The jury can hardly do otherwise. We don't have a record of the verdict, but unless the prosecution had a hell of a speechwriter on their side, it's hard to imagine Euphiletus losing his case.

It's frustrating that only one speech tends to survive from cases such as this and not a pair. The prosecution's speech against Euphiletus would be an extremely interesting read. And the verdict would be even better. But at least we know defendants and prosecutors received the same amount of time to impress their version of events on the jury. Athenian courts used a clepsydra (literally 'water thief') to keep time in their cases. This was a pot of water with a small hole near the bottom. The water dripped out while the speeches were made, ensuring that each side had the same opportunity to make their cases. Whenever laws were read out, or witnesses gave their evidence, the hole would be stopped up, temporarily, and reopened when the speechifying began again.

But even if the timing of the case was equal for both sides, it didn't mean things were going to be fair. Antiphon, another great speechwriter, produced a defence for a man called Euxitheus, from Mytilene. Euxitheus appeared in court in Athens, charged with the murder of an Athenian man named Herodes. What happened to Herodes remains shrouded in mystery: the two men, who did not know each other before they happened to share a voyage, set sail from Mytilene, on the island of Lesbos. A terrible storm forced them to put in at Methymna, so they could be transferred to a more appropriate ship for the weather. During this interlude at Methymna, Euxitheus and his companions began drinking. At some point, Herodes disappeared. A cursory search was conducted the following morning, but he wasn't found. Euxitheus presents witnesses to corroborate all this. When Herodes could not be found, Euxitheus set sail again for Aenus, his intended destination.

However, Herodes' relatives suspected foul play. They decided that Herodes must have been murdered on the shore, or perhaps on a boat, and they accused Euxitheus of the crime. They investigated, but found no evidence for his murder. Then they investigated the ship from which Herodes had disappeared, where they found bloodstains. In a *CSI*-style twist, however, the blood turned out to have come from a sacrificial sheep. They had no evidence. So they tortured two men to try to acquire some.

The first man they tortured said nothing incriminating. According to Euxitheus, the second man, a slave, was kept waiting for a few days. He initially agreed that Euxitheus had done nothing wrong. Then, after being tortured, he changed his story. And here, we come back to the problem with evidence obtained through torture: its reliability is suspect. As Euxitheus says, 'Probably he was persuaded to make false charges against me by both considerations: he was hoping to gain his freedom, and he wanted the immediate end to this torture.'

Once again, it is important to bear in mind that Euxitheus is not anachronistically opposed to the idea of torture itself, far from it. Rather, he feels he has been denied the chance to set the record straight by torturing the slave himself. And denied it by the prosecution, who executed the slave before Euxitheus could question him. One hardly has to be a campaigner for fair trials abroad to see that these aren't ideal conditions for justice to prevail. Even so, Antiphon has a good stab at righting the balance: Euxitheus points out, extensively, that the man initially backed up his version of events. Then he was tortured, so said whatever the prosecution wanted to hear. Once it became clear that he was then going to be executed, he reverted to his original story, now having nothing to gain from lying. Even if one doesn't take an ideological exception to torture and death, it's still hard to see what the prosecution has achieved, other than a discredited, dead witness.

So, once all these cases had been heard by the jury, and the verdict had been delivered, then what? Well, the ancients weren't big on prisons. They had holding cells, where you might be kept while you waited for your trial. But it was hardly a maximum security facility: even if one allows for a little literary exaggeration, while his trial and appeal were pending, Socrates seems to have spent his final days in prison having high-minded discussions with his many followers, some of whom even urged him to escape. Bribing the prison guards seems to have been perfectly acceptable (to everyone but Socrates. We'll hear more of his trial in the next chapter).

The Greeks had a range of alternative penalties, as we have already seen: monetary reparation, exile and execution. And the Romans used the same kind of punishments, crucifixion being the one for which they are probably least fondly remembered. Mass crucifixions, like those that followed the revolt of Spartacus, memorably brought to life by Kirk Douglas in the eponymous film, were unusual only for their scale. The Romans had a casual brutality towards human life that would make the most rabid modern right-winger pause and suggest quietly that it might be a bit much.

Even crucifixion, for example, doesn't seem too bad in comparison with the traditional penalty for parricide (the murder of a close relative, a parent or sibling). If you were convicted of this charge, you would be scourged, then sewn into a bag with a dog, a rooster, a snake and a monkey. Which, frankly, would be pretty grim without scourged skin. Then the Romans threw the bag into the Tiber. You drowned helplessly, being attacked by panicking animals. And the poor monkey hadn't killed a soul. This punishment wasn't simply a statute-book anomaly, either. In Britain, for example, we technically retained the death penalty for thirty-four years after our last prisoners were hanged. Only when parliament ratified the 6th Protocol of the European Convention on Human Rights, in 1998, did the death penalty become properly void. However, the traditional parricide punishment was not simply a barbaric oversight, on the books but not in use. Cicero chastises his brother, Quintus, for putting two Mysians 'into the parricide's sack'. As so often in the ancient world, you were much more likely to be on the receiving end of something ghastly if you were foreign. Men from Mysia (in modern-day Turkey) had far fewer rights than Roman citizens. But even citizenship couldn't save a man from the threat of the parricide's doom. One of Cicero's most famous criminal trials was also one of his first: the defence of Sextus Roscius of Ameria, a man prosecuted for the murder of his father.

Sextus Roscius the Elder was walking home in Rome one night in 80 BCE. He was set upon by unknown assailants and killed. If we believe Cicero's version of events (and it is mightily persuasive), Sextus Roscius was killed by two distant relatives who had conspired with a former slave named Chrysogonus. Chrysogonus was fabulously wealthy, and a favourite of Sulla, the recently retired dictator of Rome, whose lists of the proscribed (those sentenced to death by the state for picking the wrong side in the civil war) had cut a swathe through the upper classes of first-century BCE Rome. When a proscribed person was killed, their property could be confiscated and sold at auction for a fraction of its true worth (hence the enormous wealth of some of Sulla's friends). Chrysogonus and his cronies, according to Cicero, added the elder Roscius' name to the proscription lists, and split the booty between them. Sextus Roscius the Younger found himself fatherless, and penniless.

Questions began to be asked about the proscription. It became clear that Sextus Roscius was on no list: he had been murdered in the streets of Rome, and his name had then been inserted so his handsome property could be divided among his killers. Not wishing to give the property back, when the fake-proscription was uncovered, Magnus and Capito (Roscius' kinsmen, on to whom Cicero tries to pin this crime) came up with a better plan. They accused Sextus Roscius the Younger of killing his father. This was, of course, an extremely clever wheeze: kill a man, pretend it was a political execution, nick his stuff. If anyone complains, say he is the killer and take him to court (something you can easily afford to pay for, having swiped his inheritance. Conveniently, this has the added advantage of making it very difficult for him to be able to afford to pay anyone to defend him). So you get the money, and a patsy takes the fall for your dirty work. The perfect crime?

Well, it might have been, if Roscius' friends had been less loyal or less wealthy, and if his lawyer had been less brave and less ambitious. Cicero hit out with everything he had. He demolished the case against his client with a systematic refutation of the prosecution's speech (which sadly doesn't survive). He annihilated the suggestion that Roscius and his father did not get on. He pointed out that Roscius was on the family farm on the night of the murder, and nowhere near Rome, where the crime occurred. He made snide comments about the prosecutor not knowing who his own father was. Crucially, he provided his audience (for this was a performance as much as a trial) with an alternative narrative of the crime: he threw suspicion on to Magnus and Capito, and revealed Chrysogonus as the shadowy Mr Big behind the whole affair.

He also used the very nature of the parricide charge to his advantage. Another lawyer might have tried to gloss over the word, to ensure the jury didn't start to link his client with this terrible crime. But Cicero was never happier than when he was standing atop moral high ground, hurling accusations in every direction. The jury had no choice but to dwell on the awful punishment that awaited the tragic Roscius if they found him guilty, because Cicero came back to it over and over again: 'insutus in culleum per summum dedecus vitam amittere' – 'sewn up in a sack, Roscius [would] lose his life in the most degrading way.'

Cicero looked back on this case fondly, and with good reason. Roscius was acquitted, and did not die the vile death that he feared. Cicero took on the big money, and won. And an innocent man walked free. It contains the features of all the best courtroom dramas. On which topic, one final note. The ancients loved a celebrity trial just as much as we do. And in a way, that is unsurprising. The Greeks had two big drama festivals each year, the Lenaia and the Dionysia. The Romans had the theatre, gladiatorial games and chariot races. But who wouldn't want a bit of real-life courtroom drama to spice things up during the rest of the year? Think how greedily we have gobbled up the trials of O. J. Simpson and Michael Jackson, or the courtroom divorce proceedings of Paul McCartney and Heather Mills. We were hooked, and we have a vast array of entertainment alternatives at our fingertips. Nothing beats a real-life drama.

Socrates might be the most famous casualty of the Greek courts, but he certainly wasn't alone: as previously noted, the Athenians also charged Thucydides, the historian, for military incompetence. They took the comedian Aristophanes to court for insulting them, and they prosecuted Euripides, the tragedian, who ended his days in voluntary exile in Macedonia. The Romans exiled poor Ovid, the love poet, to Tomis (Constanta) in Romania. The five books of poetry that he wrote there are so miserable that they are called the Tristia, meaning 'sorrows'. He described his crime as 'carmen et error' – 'a poem and a mistake'. The poem was the *Ars Amatoria*, a smart guide to urban love affairs, which turned out to be an extremely unpopular work with the emperor Augustus, determined as he was to create a morally upright society. And the mistake? An affair with Augustus' daughter Julia, who was also exiled (to a different island from Ovid's). Sex and crime have been a compelling combination for 2,000 years.

3

Thinking Allowed

The word 'philosophy' encompasses plenty of meanings. If it's a degree subject, it's rarefied, impractical – the epitome of what goes on in those ivory towers, presuming the betowered intellectual can make a well-argued, ethical case for ivory. But at the other end of the spectrum, how often does a tiresomely drunk person feel the need to explain their philosophy to us, using that very word to describe it? It usually comes in the form of an epigrammatic saying: you've got to work to live, not live to work; anything for a quiet life; plenty of time to rest when you're dead. We may not all be students of philosophy, but we're certainly practitioners of it.

And we shouldn't be scornful of a philosophy that can be distilled into a few short words, either. The Delphic Oracle was located in Apollo's temple in ancient Delphi, central Greece, just north of the Gulf of Corinth. It was a hub of gnomic utterance, often too opaque for ordinary people to understand. But two phrases were inscribed in the foretemple that were easily understood by all. Pausanias, a second-century CE travel-writer, says they were dedicated to Apollo by the Seven Sages, men whose wisdom was renowned throughout the ancient Greek world. Who knows which of these men, if any, came up with the actual phrases? The Greeks, certainly, considered the words to be so wise that attributing them to the brainiest men of their time seemed only appropriate. And these two pearls of concentrated wisdom were *mēden agan*, 'nothing to excess', and *gnōthi seauton*, 'know thyself'.

As sage-like wisdom goes, these are pretty unarguable. 'Nothing to excess' is still the best advice for a healthy life: people who drink a glass of wine a day are usually healthier than those who drink a litre of it. Those who walk a few miles each day are less likely to suffer from shin splints than the champion marathon-runner. Extremes, as the Greeks realised, are uncomfortable things. There is something intrinsically, if mildly, hedonistic about this saying, too. No ordinary Greek would have dreamed of depriving himself of the good things in life (bonkers religious and philosophical sects notwithstanding. The Pythagoreans, for example, weren't just vegetarian, which is a perfectly sensible lifestyle choice; they also didn't eat beans, perhaps believing humans could be reincarnated as them, and not wishing to practise transmigrational cannibalism). And *mēden agan* sums this hedonism up perfectly: no one needs to be teetotal, or abstain from sex, food or anything else. They can take their pleasures where they find them. They simply need to indulge to a restrained degree. And as for *gnōthi seauton*, self-knowledge is surely one of the ultimate goals of philosophy. 'An unexamined life,' Socrates declared, during his trial, 'is not worth living.' And while one hesitates to decide for others what constitutes a liveable life, perhaps he was right. When a patient loses the capacity for thought, and self-examination of any kind, doctors refer to him or her as 'brain-dead'. But the physically paralysed are never called 'body-dead'. It's the loss of reason that creates the halfway state: essentially alive, but functionally dead.

In philosophical terms the Greeks were the real big-hitters, and this chapter will focus far more on them than the Romans. If you need convincing, it is worth pointing out that of the fourteen philosophers mentioned in Monty Python's legendary 'Bruces' Philosophers Song', which decries the greatest philosophers in history as a bunch of drunks ('There's nothing Nietzsche couldn't teach ya 'bout the raising of the wrist, Socrates himself was permanently pissed'), three of them are Greek, none is Roman, and only Socrates is mentioned twice.

Not that ancient Greek philosophy began with Socrates. He had plenty of predecessors: Thales, Heraclitus and Parmenides, to name just a few. The works of Heraclitus of Ephesus, who was born in the later part of the sixth century BCE, have survived only in fragments, one of which is another two-word spectacular: *panta rhei*, 'everything flows'. Heraclitus believed that the world and everything in it was in a constant state of flux, a philosophy with which students of quantum mechanics would probably agree. Heraclitus expresses things in enigmatic ways, but we can see what he's getting at when he says a man never steps into the same river twice. Evidently, I can go and put my foot in the River Seine any number of times, and it is ostensibly the same river, with the same name. But the river itself will be different: different fish might be present, certainly different molecules of H_2O. I won't be stepping into the same river twice, because everything, as Heraclitus observed, is changing all the time. And Heraclitus wasn't especially hard-line on this issue. His pupil Cratylus criticised him for what he considered was underselling the case. According to Cratylus, Heraclitus should have said that you couldn't step into the same river once, because it's changing even while you're putting your foot into it.

Heraclitus' younger contemporary Parmenides disliked the idea of constant change. And who can blame him? If everything is shifting around us all the time, how can we do anything, or comprehend anything? Nowadays we understand that constant change is happening, but at a minuscule level, so that we barely perceive it at all. But if we lived before molecules and atoms had been identified, we might share Parmenides' disquiet. 'Everything changes' is a terrifying philosophy. Who is to stop things from suddenly changing beyond recognition? The world takes on a nightmarish Daliesque quality, where certainties can suddenly slide away, like a molten pocket watch.

Parmenides, therefore, decided that the opposite was true. Everything did not change. In fact, nothing changed. Because for things to change, they have to become, even temporarily, not what they are, and that is impossible. Take water, for example, becoming steam. Steam is not a liquid, it's a gas. If water turns into steam, there must be a moment when it is both liquid and not-liquid. It has to be something, and not be it, at the same time. And that is impossible. So obviously nothing changes, and nothing is created. People challenged Parmenides by pointing out that his theory was a fallacy. Look at the real world, they said. It's full of change. Children grow up. People die. Water freezes. Not one to let a little thing like empirical evidence disrupt his thinking, Parmenides drew the rather huffy conclusion that if we perceive change, which his theory disallowed, then we cannot trust our senses at all, and would do better to disregard them. Again, a logical enough position to hold, until a runaway horse comes thundering towards you, whereupon the wise, and indeed only, course of action is to believe your eyes and make a run for it.

Parmenides founded a school in Elea, a Greek colony in Campania, southern Italy. The Eleatics embraced his philosophy that one should renounce the senses and use only argument and reasoning to come to conclusions. One of his most celebrated students was Zeno of Elea, who was born around 490 BCE and died around 430 BCE. Zeno was renowned for his ability to start with a reasonable proposition, then follow it through, with perfect logic, to an utterly illogical conclusion. His famous paradoxes can still tax us now.

Aristotle tells us of the Dichotomy Paradox – dichotomy meaning something split into two – with which Zeno could prove that motion was impossible. According to the terms of the paradox, if I am in Paris, and I wish to travel to Berlin, I must first cover half the distance between the two. Before I can do that, I need to travel a quarter of the way. Before I get there, I need to move an eighth of the way. Before that, a sixteenth. And so on, and so on. Motion is impossible, according to Zeno, because I must travel an infinite number of ever tinier distances to reach my destination, and doing an infinite number of things is impossible. Aristotle tried to resolve the paradox by concluding that something which is infinite in scale is different from something which is infinitely divisible. A cheesecake is infinitely divisible, if you can cut it into small enough pieces, especially now we know how to split the atom (which means, literally, 'uncuttable' or 'indivisible', so is a rather out-of-date name these days). And I, at least, don't feel too intimidated to embark on a cheesecake. Zeno might have been clever, but with his fondness for proving the commonplace to be impossible, it's hard to imagine he wasn't also annoying.

These late-sixth- and early-fifth-century philosophers did not live in the same place or form a single school of thought. They are grouped together under the name of their most celebrated successor, and called the Pre-socratics. Pre-socratic philosophy was a mixture of what we might now call philosophy with natural science. Then Socrates began to ask the questions that shaped Western thought for two and a half millennia, about truth, goodness and beauty. There can be few individuals who have had such a considerable, and lasting, effect on human thought, without writing a single word.

The Socrates we know appears to us through the pages of his fans and detractors alike. Xenophon, the right-wing historian, wrote a few Socratic dialogues, detailing conversations between Socrates and friends in which they discussed philosophical matters. Like most of Xenophon's writing, they are sadly dull. Fortunately, Socrates had another fan who had a better way with words: Plato. Philosophers have argued for centuries about the words Plato puts in Socrates' mouth. How much of what we read is Socratic philosophy, and how much is Platonic? Plato was Socrates' pupil, and devoted to his master. Is he slavishly accurate, therefore, or does he edit Socrates to seem a bit more likeable, consistent or dazzling? It's impossible to know, and our ignorance in no way detracts from the quality of the texts we have. Luckily, we also have Aristophanes' play *The Clouds*, which is a relentless mockery of Socrates and the various types of philosophical teachings that took place in Athens during the later part of the fifth century BCE. None of these sources is likely to be 100 per cent accurate, or to come even close, but the composite picture gives us a better idea of the real Socrates.

So, what do we know about him? He was the son of a midwife, and he was born in Athens around 470 BCE. He was not exactly handsome: in Plato's *Symposium*, a discussion on the nature of love, Alcibiades, the Athenian playboy, suggests that Socrates resembles Silenus, a mythical figure and friend of the god Dionysus. Silenus is a balding old man with a squashed nose. Alcibiades also compares Socrates to Marsyas the satyr, half-man, half-goat. If these descriptions sound rather unflattering, then take a look at the head of Socrates in the Louvre, in Paris. For a start, everyone else will be trekking round to see the Mona Lisa, so you will avoid the crowds. And secondly, you can see that Alcibiades had a point: according to this statue, Socrates had a snub nose, receding hairline, long moustache and beard. There is certainly something more than a little goaty about him.

Socrates was unusually impervious to physical hardship. Alcibiades tells us that when they served together in Potidaea, Socrates outclassed not just him but the whole army when it came to endurance. He could go without food with no complaint. Even the cold did not bother him, 'barefoot, he walked over ice more easily than men with boots on'. But Alcibiades is quick to explain that Socrates was no steely ascetic. Whenever food and drink were plentiful, Socrates tucked in with more gusto than most. But as much as Socrates drank, 'no one has ever seen Socrates drunk'. Like James Bond, Socrates could, apparently, quaff any amount of alcohol and remain unimpaired. Given that they are at a drinking party when this claim is made, Alcibiades can tell his audience that they will soon see proof of this assertion. Suffice it to say that Eric Idle's characterisation of Socrates as 'a lovely little thinker but a bugger when he's pissed' seems rather unfair.

According to Plato's version of his trial speech, *The Apology*, Socrates was impoverished and unpopular. We have no idea how he made money: he appears to have had no job, and prided himself on the fact that he never accepted a fee for teaching, because he didn't believe he taught anyone anything. He was married to a woman named Xanthippe, who is traditionally viewed as rather shrewish. Given what she had to put up with, however – bringing up their three sons with little money while her husband argued the toss with strangers all day – it's hard not to think she might have earned the right to occasionally pursing her lips.

At the age of seventy, Socrates was eventually put on trial, in the Heliaia, on three charges: impiety, introducing new gods and corrupting the young. He gave an impassioned speech in his own defence, peppered with anecdotes and perhaps ill-advised sarcasm (at one point, he suggests an alternative punishment to the death penalty, should he be found guilty, of a 100-drachma fine. It's hard to correlate ancient money with modern, given how much our world has diverged from theirs, but that's about three months' salary for a skilled worker in fifth-century Athens. It was almost certainly seen as an insulting suggestion by the jurors, if their subsequent decision on his punishment was anything to go by). He was sentenced to death by the Athenians: he famously drank hemlock, which paralyses you from the feet upwards, until you eventually suffocate when your lungs can't expand enough to give you sufficient oxygen. It was not a very glorious end.

Societies have often sought to quash their revolutionaries by accusing them of corrupting the young, especially when the society itself is in danger. And in 399 BCE, when Socrates died, Athens was certainly weak. She had finally lost the debilitating war with the Spartans in 404 BCE. The democracy had been overthrown, temporarily, and replaced with a murderous oligarchy known as the Thirty Tyrants. Indeed, Socrates tells his trial jury that the Thirty sent him, along with other Athenians, to fetch a man, Leon of Salamis, for execution. They were ordered to do this on pain of death. Socrates made a simple decision: he wasn't afraid to die; he was afraid to do something morally wrong. So he went home instead, fully expecting to be executed himself. The Thirty were overthrown before they could carry out their threats, but Socrates was dead five years later anyway.

We shall see below why Socrates might have peeved a few people sufficiently for them to bring a case against him. But he was an old man: why did a jury of his peers vote for him to be killed? The answer is, surely, the charge of corrupting the young. Athens was a city in fear: the democracy had fallen once, and it was still at risk. They were suddenly afraid of Socrates, their gadfly, when before they had been only exasperated by him. A parallel might be drawn with the case of the celebrated Russian tenor, Vadim Kozin. After a successful early career, Kozin was asked by the police chief Lavrentiy Beria why he didn't write songs about Stalin. Kozin replied that songs about Stalin weren't suited to tenor voices. Shortly afterwards he found himself sentenced to five years in a prison camp in Magadan, in the far east of Siberia. The charges against him, as against Socrates, included corrupting the young. The young, it appears, are never more corruptible than when they listen to individuals of whom their elders disapprove.

Socrates had an inner voice, a *daimonion*, which told him when he was about to do the wrong thing. It was only ever negative, discouraging Socrates from pursuing the wrong course of action. It never chipped in with a ringing endorsement when he was doing something well, so must have been rather like having an especially hard-to-please ethics teacher lurking within. He certainly believed it was divinely inspired: the voice of some god, keeping him from going astray. One wonders how he would be viewed in today's world, where any deviance from the norm is considered a medical condition: sadness, boisterousness and shyness becoming depression, attention deficit disorder and social phobia. It's hard not to suspect that we might view him as a paranoid schizophrenic: hearing voices inside your head might be less risky now than it was for Socrates then (his inner voice was almost certainly the reason his accusers could claim he was trying to introduce new gods), but it is certainly not without peril.

It would be reasonable to wonder why Socrates asserted that he could not teach anyone anything. He is, after all, one of the most celebrated philosophers of the Western world. Doesn't that, by definition, make him a teacher? Why would Plato have written so extensively about Socrates, if he learned nothing from him? It is here that we begin to get a sense of just how slippery a customer Socrates could be. He embraced a paradox of ignorance. Socrates tells the story in Plato's *Apology* of an oracular pronouncement. A friend of his, Chaerophon, went to Delphi one day and asked Apollo if anyone was wiser than Socrates. The priestess replied that there was no one. Socrates was thrown into confusion: he made no claim to wisdom 'oute mega oute smikron' – 'either great or small'. But Socrates knew that the god wouldn't lie, so he set himself the task of questioning men who had an impressive reputation for brains, to find one cleverer than him, and thus prove the oracle wrong.

And now we can see why Socrates, a man of no wealth or political ambition, might end up on trial for his life. He interrogated a politician with a reputation for having the smarts. But Socrates discovered that, although this politician was well regarded in the wisdom stakes by other people, and especially by himself, he was, in fact, not wise at all. Socrates left the encounter realising that neither of them was very knowledgeable, but that he, Socrates, was cleverer in one crucial regard: he knew that he knew nothing. This is the Socratic paradox that comes up many times in Plato's writing. No one is wise, because none of us knows anything. But Socrates knows that he doesn't know a thing, which makes him wiser than the rest of us. It seems like a fallacy – how can he literally know nothing when he knows one thing, namely his ignorance? It's rather like the fallacy when someone says, 'I am telling a lie.' Are they lying? If they are, they're telling the truth, which means they can't be lying. But equally, they can't be telling the truth, because that would mean that they are simultaneously telling a lie. If you can contemplate this without feeling a little bit like crying, you are a better person than I am. It's enough to make one long for Zeno, and his infuriating paradoxes of motion. At least if you sit still those ones don't affect you.

But if we try to set our upper lips to stiff and ignore the paradoxical nature of the statement 'I know that I know nothing', it gives us a great insight into Socrates' character and behaviour. Embracing a lack of knowledge is a powerful thing: if you don't believe me, try pretending at a party that you are acquainted fully with the films of, say, Ingmar Bergman. Read up on them, memorise details, talk about them constantly. Then try another party where you cheerfully admit you've never seen a minute of Bergman, and only watch romcoms. I guarantee that the latter will be the more fun evening, unless you bump into a romcom nerd. Socrates is empowered by his professed ignorance, because whenever he wishes to discuss love, beauty, equality or whatever, he can always play the role of questioner, and force his interlocutor to do all the work. If you want to know how much fun that is, find someone at a party, admit you only watch romcoms, and ask them to tell you all about Bergman, of whom they have rashly claimed to be a fan.

Socrates is playing both sides of the game: he's ignorant, so won't you please enlighten him with your views on a subject? But when you offer your opinions, he crushes them, with brutal efficiency, by asking you loaded questions, and getting your agreement before proving that you have contradicted yourself. There's nothing like being beaten in an argument by someone who keeps telling you how ignorant they are: it's the intellectual equivalent of a supermodel saying loudly that she really needs to lose a pound or two while she's sitting next to a fat girl. And Socrates did this over and over again: no wonder a few people wanted him dead.

One of Socrates' best tricks was to refuse to discuss the nature of say, piety, until his interlocutor had defined it. When his friend Euthyphro, in the Platonic dialogue of the same name, defines piety as 'that which the gods love', Socrates reminds him that he believes the stories in which the gods are always falling out with one another. Euthyphro agrees: how can he not? *The Iliad* and *The Odyssey*, for a start, are full of scenes where one god goes behind another one's back to advance his or her particular favourite. Aphrodite loves Paris, so she helps the

Trojans; Achilles has the support of his mother, the nymph Thetis; Hera supports the Greeks because she hates Paris; and so on and so on. There are factions, schemes and duplicities among the gods to rival those of any family wedding.

So, if Euthyphro accepts, as he does, that the gods are often in disagreement, his definition of piety cannot stand up. 'That which the gods love' is a nonsense if they all love and hate different things. So Euthyphro has to refine his definition of piety to 'that which all the gods love'. But even that is not enough of a definition for Socrates. He wants to know if something is pious because the gods love it, or the opposite: do the gods only love it because it's pious? He and Euthyphro agree eventually that it is because things are pious that the gods love them, rather than the other way round. But although Socrates and Euthyphro were happy with this definition, as, presumably, was Plato, theologians haven't been satisfied at all. So the dialogue has given rise to an enduring problem called the Euthyphro Dilemma, which is invariably, and inaccurately, attributed to Plato. If we say that something is pious, or moral, because God loves it, then we are allowing for an arbitrary moral code. What if God decides one day to love murdering innocent children? Would it then become a moral, pious course of action? Surely not. But the alternative definition is not much better. If God loves something only because it is pious, then God is making the same decisions we make, since we also tend to love moral behaviour, such as kindness, and hate immoral behaviour, such as murder. If God is just doing exactly what we do, what is the ethical difference between us and him? In the ancient Greek world of anthropomorphic gods, who are immortal but certainly not omniscient, omnipotent or omnipresent, this is an even trickier question to answer.

One can quite legitimately be critical of Socrates for this obsession with defining something completely and utterly before being prepared to discuss anything else about it. It is, after all, both annoying and rather simplistic. Many of us couldn't define (certainly not to Socrates' satisfaction) love. Romantic love is different from maternal love, for example, and Socrates would doubtless have us tangled up in knots trying to work out whether a teenage crush is really the same thing as the love we might feel for our husbands or wives. Is it only love if it's reciprocated? Surely not, given that a newborn baby doesn't feel the same kind of love for her mother that the mother feels for her. What about unrequited love? And can you still love someone after they have died?

We would – or at least I would – struggle to define love; to find the one common element in all these disparate situations, without the definition being so broad that it becomes worthlessly banal. And Socrates is surely wrong on this point: just because I can't define love doesn't mean I don't understand it. I know what it means when I tell someone I love them. And I know what my friends mean when they talk about their lovers, too. We have all managed to say that we love you but, sorry, we aren't in love with you, at some time or another. So our inability to define the concept of love doesn't stop us from talking about it, thinking about it and behaving according to it.

One point to note, though, is that Socrates' obsession with definition may be tiresome, but it may also be more important now than ever. We live in a time when language is tortured beyond sense. Who hasn't received a letter from their bank telling them that for their convenience, the bank will now open later on Wednesdays to provide staff training? There is a glib, corporate expectation that no one will question the misuse of the word 'convenience', when in fact its antonym would be more appropriate. We are unlikely to receive leaflets telling us that because of its total contempt for our time and money, the bank will open whenever the hell it feels like. Which is rather a pity, really, as a bit of honesty would make a refreshing change. And it's not just the corporate world that has forgotten how to tell the truth and use words to mean what they actually mean. The inability of virtually every politician to say he or she was wrong has created the most baffling political discourse of any generation. When the prime minister calls cuts in spending 'investments', and no one simply pelts him with eggs until he tells the truth, we are all in jeopardy of losing track of reality.

And this isn't just a rhetorical issue, either. When words are misused, or misdefined, we all end up in trouble. Take the word 'bullying'. Most of us think we know what we mean by bullying. We have an image of a school bully, either from our own experience or from reading a book, or watching a TV show set in a school. It's usually a boy, he's mean, everyone avoids him, his school uniform is messed up, but the teachers are too scared to tell him off, and he has a couple of henchmen who do his bidding. Draco Malfoy, in J. K. Rowling's books, is a perfect example. This definition is so pervasive that it is hard to shift. And that makes it very much harder for us to take claims of bullying seriously enough: after all, we have all felt bullied at some point or another. Our mental picture of the bully means that we tend to assume that if you stand up to him, he'll back off and everyone will grow up safely. So when we hear of children, or adults, driven to suicide by relentless hate campaigns, we're shocked. When a child is stabbed by another child with a kitchen knife in a classroom, we're appalled. How can they have been bullied to death? The simple answer is that we have allowed dangerously aggressive behaviour to be called 'bullying', and not noticed that it is also assault, grievous bodily harm, attempted murder. If we had thought more about the real definition of the actions we described as 'bullying', things might have worked out differently.

But when Socrates spent his time needling his fellow Athenians about their sloppy definitions, did they view him as a teacher? Were they taken in by his false modesty? The short answer is no. As his trial revealed, an Athenian jury was perfectly able to believe him capable of corrupting the young, and that wouldn't have happened if they had believed his protestations of ignorance. One of the most celebrated portrayals of Socrates is in Arisophanes' play *The Clouds*. It depicts Socrates as a teacher, the owner of the Thinkery, an academy where ordinary people can learn the dark arts of sophistry. For Aristophanes, these are either dishonest, useless or both. So the Thinkery encourages its students to learn the Wrong Argument, which is always able to prevail in law courts or debates, even though it is (morally) wrong. They study the height a flea could jump, in its own feet. And they memorise tortured etymology and sneaky debt-dodging techniques.

This play is funny and vulgar, like all Aristophanes' work, but it's also incredibly revealing. Firstly, Aristophanes lumps Socrates in with the sophists, a bunch of largely non-Athenian teachers who came to Athens, made their fortunes educating the well-to-do and were not very popular with ordinary Athenians. Socrates-in-the-play is obsessed therefore with the gender of nouns: we can't use the word 'chicken' to apply to both a male and female bird, as the Greeks did. We need to say 'chickeness' for a female chicken and 'chicker' for a male one. This Socrates is, of course, full of nonsense. But the joke that Aristophanes is making is probably to link him with Prodicus of Ceos, a sophist who specialised in teaching etymology. The idea that Socrates could teach rhetorical trickery, and give someone the ability to use a morally bankrupt argument to defeat a better one, is also a fudge: Socrates didn't teach rhetoric, but a Sicilian sophist, named Gorgias, did. Then, as now, a person could be considered too clever. When Socrates-in-the-play is exclaims that 'There is no Zeus', he offers an argument that would sound pretty convincing to Richard Dawkins's fans. The hapless Strepsiades, his would-be pupil, points out that thunderbolts are conclusive proof of Zeus' existence and the mechanism he uses to punish perjurers, but Socrates is ready with a rebuttal: don't thunderbolts sometimes hit Zeus' own temples, or even oak trees? When did an oak tree last commit perjury?

Aristophanes didn't just link Socrates to the sophists therefore, he made him the über-sophist. And the joke is very powerful: Strepsiades is soon claiming that he doesn't believe in Zeus either. So is this a harmless comic portrayal, or (as Plato believed) a character assassination of Socrates that contributed to his conviction almost twenty-five years later? The play shows Socrates corrupting young and old alike, refusing to accept the existence of traditional gods and introducing his own, all charges of which he was eventually convicted.

It is tempting to think that jokes have considerable power to affect popular perception. Anyone who was watching *Spitting Image* during the premiership of John Major will find it hard to think of him as anything other than grey. David Steel, then joint leader of the SDP-Liberal Alliance, believed that the programme, which portrayed him as a miniature, fawning sidekick to his fellow leader, David Owen, cost him his political career. And who could forget the sight of Tina Fey's eerily accurate pastiche of Sarah Palin, declaring brightly, 'I can see Russia from my house!' Caricatures are extremely effective, precisely because they appeal to prejudices we already have. Once fixed in the mind, they prove difficult to shift.

So Socrates was the victim of a theatrical stitch-up. But he seems not to have minded too much: he and Aristophanes are portrayed as friends in Plato's *Symposium*, and he continued to badger anyone who would listen for a quarter of a century before it caught up with him. Yet if his goal, from his conversations with the wisest men of his time, was to prove that they, like he, knew nothing, how does he avoid being seen as a nihilist? The answer is simple and complicated at once: Plato wrote the Socratic dialogues, portraying Socrates as a brilliant interrogator. But Plato was no scribe, he was a great philosopher in his own right (he also warrants a mention in the Monty Python number: 'Plato, they say, could stick it away/ Half a crate of whisky every day'). Plato, incidentally, was not his given name, according to his biographer Diogenes Laërtius. Diogenes tells us that Plato was actually called Aristocles, named after his grandfather. Plato was a nickname, given for one reason or another. Perhaps it was because he was so clever: *platon* means 'broad', and might apply to the width of his head, or the breadth of his eloquence. Alternatively, Diogenes suggests that his wrestling coach, Ariston of Argos, named him Plato because he was so chunky. Try as one might, it's rather difficult to get past the fact that one of the most influential figures in the history of Western philosophy may have been known for 2,500 years by the Greek equivalent of Fatso.

Scholars have spent lifetimes trying to work out where Socrates ends and Plato begins, and this isn't the place to add to the debate. Let us assume that Plato was like everyone else: at the beginning of his career, he was probably keen to share what he'd learned from his beloved mentor; and as he got older, he began to formulate more of his own ideas.

Plato learned a great deal from Socrates about questioning assumptions and unpicking lazy beliefs. But he wasn't satisfied with the conclusion that we should all accept we know nothing. He wanted answers as well as questions. And Plato's answers were the Forms.

Forms, also called Ideas, are idealised forms of things we see in the world around us. So, for example, whenever we see someone behaving justly, we know they are behaving in a just manner; however, they are not the perfect embodiment of justice: they are human and fallible. There is a Platonic form, or idea, of justice, which exists separately from us. There are forms of all kinds of abstracts – beauty, equality and so on. And things that we think are beautiful or equal here on earth are only pale imitations of the perfect forms.

Along with the theory of forms comes Plato's theory of knowledge and understanding. Before we are born, our souls (the best part of us) have total understanding of the forms. When we're born, we lose that knowledge. We spend our learning lives not trying to acquire knowledge for the first time, but trying to recollect what we once knew. This may sound bonkers. But actually, it's quite a plausible explanation, millennia before psychology existed, for some aspects of the learning process. When a child is given two large pebbles and a small pebble and asked which ones are of equal size, he or she will pick the two large pebbles. They are, of course, not perfectly equal: they're pebbles. But children have a sense of what equality means, in this context. Similarly, if I draw a circle, a triangle and a square, and ask the child to identify which is which, she wouldn't struggle. Even though I am a terrible artist, and incapable of drawing a perfect shape, I could get near enough for her to identify what I was trying to convey.

Plato looked at this kind of phenomenon, and he produced a theory that explained it: the child has prenatal understanding of the Forms, which she remembers when she sees my hapless attempt at a circle. Obviously, it isn't a very convincing theory to us now, because we understand a great deal about innate potential, something Plato knew nothing about. We all learn to recognise shapes and words because we are born with highly advanced brains, into which we imprint all kinds of stuff as babies and young children. We learn incredibly fast, not because we're remembering prenatal knowledge, but because we are born with the potential to learn.

Nonetheless, there is something alluring about Plato's Forms. Visually, especially, they can feel irresistible: we have all looked at a piece of furniture, an item of clothing, a longed-for painting or yearned-for shoe and known, utterly and completely, that it is the most perfect specimen of its kind. Indeed, marketing and advertising depend on precisely this part of our psyche. If we can be made to feel dissatisfied with what we have, we will spend our money on something new. So each new car, laptop or mobile phone has to be shinier, sleeker, slimmer. Suddenly, the old phone looks like a brick, the old computer (which was once the fastest thing on any desk) now seems sluggish and tired, the old car seems lumpy and insufficiently aerodynamic. If we remembered the theory of forms, and its central tenet that nothing on earth can replicate the beauty of the ethereal ideal form, then each time Apple tried to flog us an ever cuter iPod, we might be a little more resistant to its charms. The Platonic form of MP3 player will always be superior to the ones in the shops.

Plato had none of Socrates' issues with calling himself an educator. In the mid 380s BCE he set up a school, of sorts, in an olive grove in Athens, called Akademia. Plato's Academy didn't charge fees, but it was an organised location where men could come to exchange ideas and arguments. It lasted for hundreds of years, and produced countless other intellectuals, of whom the most famous is Aristotle.

The educational lineage is remarkable. Socrates was mentor and inspiration to Plato. Plato was mentor to Aristotle, and Aristotle went on to be the tutor of Alexander the Great. For a professed ignoramus, Socrates certainly cast a long shadow. Aristotle is sometimes referred to as the last (and perhaps first) person who could and probably did genuinely know everything there was to be known during his lifetime. We've become so used to the fracturing of knowledge, to the idea that a clever, well-informed person won't feel in the least self-conscious telling you they are terrible at maths and can barely add up. But the term 'Renaissance Man' might well have been retroactively applied to Aristotle, who inspired so many thinkers during the Renaissance and beyond. His interests were incredibly diverse: politics, drama, astronomy, physics, metaphysics, anatomy, ethics. And his writing is incredibly dense. The works of Aristotle that survive today are in such condensed form that they are often thought to be lecture notes or study aids. Even his biggest fans probably wouldn't think of him as a fun read.

But while Aristotle may lack Plato's literary charm, he is worth the effort, if only because he was the first person to ask questions that have shaped our thinking ever since. Even if you only read Aristotle to disagree with him, he's important. And often, you wouldn't disagree with him. In the *Poetics*, for example, he formulates the rights and wrongs of constructing a tragedy. He discusses how plots should work, coming down heavily in favour of a story in which one action entails another, in which the hero's actions cause his own downfall, in which friends wittingly or unwittingly hurt one another, and so on. His reasons are perfectly argued: of course a story is more engrossing if one event entails the next. It is a symptom of so many bad dramas or novels that things happen episodically with little cause or effect. And the idea of the tragic hero, whose mistake (*hamartia*, in Greek) causes his tragedy, is one that remains incredibly powerful to us now. There is surely no more potent sense of human failure than the moment when we realise that if we had simply done one thing instead of another, our sorrows could have been averted.

Again, he is right on the money when he explains that friends or relatives hurting one another is where tragedy really resides. If two strangers meet in a dark alley and fight, and one kills the other, there is no tragedy. We might feel sorry for the dead man, for his family and loved ones, but that is all. Aristotle knew that if the street lamp suddenly flickers on and the killer realises that he has unknowingly picked a fight with his long-lost brother, whom he was hurrying to meet at the station, but has instead killed, that's a tragedy. There isn't just grief at your loss, there is the awful realisation that you are responsible for your own bereavement. That had you been earlier, later, more polite to passing strangers, less quick to anger; if you had been too lazy to visit the gym and develop that right hook, too tired to walk to the station and had got in the car instead, too nervous to meet up with someone you hadn't seen for ten years, you would not have become the architect of your own inconsolable misery. Tragedy, the perfect tragedy, as Aristotle realised, must depend on a million 'if only's.

Some of Aristotle's obsessions seem more curious to us now. His ethical views were teleological; in other words, he believed that ethical actions were defined by their goals. In the *Nicomachean Ethics*, his most celebrated text on the subject, Aristotle argues that the highest goal of human life is *eudaimonia* – a word so untranslatable that undergraduates have written entire theses on what word or phrase might be used to try to explain it. *Eudaimonia* means, among other things, 'happiness', 'success', 'prosperity'. To have a good *daimon* also means you are blessed, so there is a religious meaning there, too. And this kind of happiness is not the transitory state we might be accustomed to thinking it is. Aristotle is quick to point this out, and in so doing gives us an unexpected aphorism: 'One swallow does not make a spring, and nor does one fine day. Similarly, one day or a short time of happiness does not make a man blessed and happy.'

This idea, that true happiness cannot be transitory, lures us back to another piece of sage-like wisdom, quoted again and again in Greek literature: call no man happy till he's dead. The example often given is that of Priam, king of Troy, father to dozens of sons and daughters, wealthy, happily married to Hecabe and safe in the knowledge that his kingdom will pass on to a wise and responsible son, like Hector. But then, of course, comes the sorry saga of Paris and Helen, and the Trojan War. Priam sees his sons killed on the battlefield or slaughtered when the city is overrun by the warriors stashed within the Trojan horse. He ransoms the body of his son Hector from Achilles, after Achilles has killed Hector and dishonoured his corpse, tying it to his chariot and dragging it three times around the city of Troy. He knows his wife and daughters will be enslaved, become spoils of war, Greek concubines. Priam is eventually slaughtered by Neoptolemus, Achilles' son, even as he clings to an altar claiming sanctuary. A salutary lesson indeed, for those unwary enough to consider themselves happy in old age.

But what of the other philosophical descendants of Socrates? The line through Plato and Aristotle to Alexander the Great is so pleasing that one can easily overlook the other schools of philosophy that sprouted up in Socrates' wake. But they, too, played a pivotal role in the development of Western thought. Socrates had another pupil, Antisthenes, who had little patience with Plato and his representation of Socrates. According to Diogenes Laërtius, Antisthenes thought Plato rather conceited, and compared him to a frisky horse. It's not a description of Plato that can be found in his own prose, that's for sure. And Antisthenes was fiercely loyal, too, taking revenge on the men who prosecuted Socrates and demanded his execution: 'It was Antisthenes himself who seems to have been the cause of Anytus' banishment and Meletus' death.'

Antisthenes founded an altogether different branch of philosophy from Plato's. But he also wished to live what he believed was the virtuous life, and he associated that with Socrates' ascetic tendencies: he obviously didn't see Socrates as the bon viveur Plato allows Alcibiades to describe in *The Symposium*. Rather, he embraced Socrates' poverty and self-denial, and was the founder of a philosophical movement called Cynicism. This word sounds unquestionably strange to our ears. We all know what a cynic is, and it isn't someone who denies himself a stiff gin and an iced bun. It's someone who expects the worst, has little faith in his fellow man and sees self-interest everywhere. But a Cynic was once someone who eschewed worldly pleasures like money, power and influence, and lived a life of simple purity, eating little and sleeping outdoors. 'Cynic' in Greek means 'doglike', and it's easy to see how the connection could be made in a time when dogs slept outdoors and didn't fit into a handbag. The celebrated Cynic Diogenes of Sinope (confusingly a different Diogenes from the biographer Diogenes Laërtius, who lived some 600 years later), was often called the Dog. He took his life of asceticism very seriously, and lived in a barrel or tub rather than a house. The Cynic doctrine involved giving up possessions and living in poverty, and it was an alluring proposition for ordinary people living in deeply unsettling times. After all, if you refuse to own things, you can't lose them if your fortunes suddenly take a turn for the worse. Complete self-sufficiency is a refusal to participate in the greater social model, and when the world around you seems chaotic, and you don't know who will invade your city next, that's quite a tempting idea. It's no wonder that historians have linked the Cynics with that other great enthusiast for relinquishing worldly goods, a man who also lived in politically charged times, Jesus Christ.

The Hellenistic period, which followed Aristotle's death in 322 BCE, offered many different paths to a virtuous life. The Cynics may have chosen barrel-dwelling, but the Epicureans took a more pragmatic approach to things. Epicurus was a man whose name has been taken in vain just about every time it is ever used in modern times. Like the word 'cynic', 'epicurean' has acquired a totally different meaning from its original one. Epicurus believed that the virtuous life was one of pleasure. But his embracing of hedonism has led to the mistaken conviction that he was a gourmet and a gourmand, in thrall to the sensual pleasures of excessive eating and drinking. Actually, he was neither. The Epicurean ideal was a life of ataraxia – tranquillity. For that to be achieved, a person needed to be free from pain. And for Epicurus, freedom from pain was the same thing as pleasure. In other words, you don't need a feather bed to lie on to feel pleasure. You just need to stop lying on a bed of nails. In this light, it becomes clear that a true life of pleasure is a very simple one, because that gives you the best chance of being free from the pain of wanting what you can't have. If you can't be happy without a very expensive wine, for example, you are in jeopardy of having that wine taken away from you: you might run out of money, or your supplier might stop stocking it, or someone else might buy up the entire year's vintage and leave none for anyone else. If, on the other hand, you are happy with any old plonk, or indeed a glass of water, you stand a far better chance of achieving ataraxia. So next time you prod someone repeatedly in the arm just so that they can have the pleasure of you stopping, try to remember that you are embodying the teachings of Epicurus.

The virtuous Epicurean was pitted, in philosophical terms, against the virtuous Stoic. Stoicism was founded by Zeno of Citium (again, confusingly, not the same Zeno as the one from Elea with the paradox obsession) in the early third century BCE. He taught at the Stoa Poikile, 'the Painted Stoa', which was a colonnade overlooking the Agora, or marketplace, in Athens. Stoicism was the philosophy of choice for many of the ancient world's biggest names: Seneca, Epictetus and, of course, the philosopher king, Marcus Aurelius. The virtuous Stoic needed to have the four primary virtues: prudence, moderation, justice and courage. In addition to these, according to Stobaeus, a fifth-century CE compiler of extracts from Greek authors, were secondary virtues of lesser importance: good sense, good calculation, quick-wittedness, discretion, resourcefulness, good discipline, seemliness, modesty, self-control, endurance, confidence, high-mindedness, cheerfulness, industriousness, piety, honesty, equity and fair dealing.

The Stoics believed, in essence, that one should suffer the vicissitudes of life with a calm, accepting attitude. One sees this with the imposed suicide of Seneca, who was implicated in a plot to overthrow the emperor Nero, in CE 65. Tacitus describes Seneca calmly attempting several different methods of suicide, as one after another fails, like a masochistic Rasputin. Eventually, after surviving poison and wrist-slitting, he suffocated on the steam from a hot bath he was hoping would enable him to bleed to death more swiftly. He was then cremated with none of the usual funeral rites, in accordance with his will. Stoics didn't need the consolation of a big, showy funeral.

The meditations of Marcus Aurelius are packed with platitudes to enable a Stoic to live a life of total acceptance: 'That men of a certain type should behave as they do is inevitable. To wish it otherwise were to wish the fig-tree would not yield its juice.' 'Let it make no difference to you if you are cold or warm, so long as you are doing your duty.' And certainly acceptance of what we cannot change is a recurring theme in religious and philosophical thought, even if it is, frankly, a bit pious and tiresome. Accepting things may be the sensible, calm way to behave, but it will hardly result in anyone changing the world for the better.

Which brings us to one of the trickier parts of Stoic philosophy. Stoics didn't need to think about railing against the system and demanding change, because they didn't believe in free will. They were determinists, who thought everything was fated to happen. This was in stark contrast to the Epicureans, who couldn't stomach a world where nothing we do is of our own volition. Stoic determinism is certainly not a very appealing doctrine: most of us choose to believe that we have at least some control over the lives we lead, or how can we have any notion of moral responsibility at all? Diogenes Laërtius sums the whole thing up: 'The story goes that Zeno was flogging a slave for stealing. "I was fated to steal," said the slave. "And to be flogged," was Zeno's reply.' It's a great epigrammatic story, but ultimately reveals how very unsatisfying Stoicism can be – lacking free will, we become little more than organic robots. Nonetheless, Cicero gives us an impassioned defence of Stoic ethics: 'It is a peculiar characteristic of the wise man that he does nothing which he could regret, nothing against his will, but does everything honourably, consistently, seriously and rightly; that he anticipates nothing as if it were bound to happen, is shocked by nothing when it does happen ... I can conceive of nothing happier than this.' And it's hard not to agree, at least in part, with his assessment. The Stoic life doesn't sound exactly riveting, but neither is it painful or cruel. Yet most of us, surely, would plump for Epicurus instead, just so we can decide whether to be good or bad today.

So, what use was all this philosophising put to in the ancient world? Well, ancient philosophers weren't all like Socrates, refusing to charge fees and living off the kindness of friends. The sophists, at least, charged hefty fees for sharing their wisdom. And, given the breadth of learning these philosophers often had, there was good money to be made by the pragmatic. Aristotle tells a story about Thales of Miletus, the first of all the pre-Socratic philosophers. People had been telling Thales that philosophy was useless, a mug's game. But one winter, Thales deduced from his knowledge of the stars that there would be a good olive crop the following year. He hired all the olive presses in Miletus and in nearby Chios. There were no other bidders, so he paid peanuts. When the bumper olive harvest came around, he hired the presses out for a huge sum, demonstrating that philosophers could make a ton of money if they wished, but that wasn't their objective. And just in case they got too big for their boots, there is another story about Thales. So engrossed was he, on one occasion, in studying the stars – either for purely philosophical purposes, or because he had olive-harvest investments to protect – that he failed to look where he was going, and fell down a well. So perhaps philosophers did need a little help with the practicalities of life.

And the practical implications of ancient philosophy don't end in the ancient world, but resonate in our world, too. An intellectual debate that raged in fifth-century BCE Athens was the nomos–phusis question. *Nomos* means a man-made law, or custom. *Phusis* is natural law, the basic order of things. So, a stop sign on a deserted coast road is an example of nomos. You'll stop, but only because society's conventions say you should. But if, two feet behind that sign, the road disappears over the edge of a cliff, that would be an example of phusis. You'll stop, because otherwise you'll plunge to an early death. So, which should take priority, nomos or phusis? Nomos tells us that we shouldn't kill, phusis says to go right ahead. Just as a lion can bring down a wildebeest, why shouldn't we enslave, torture or kill those weaker than ourselves?

This may seem like mere intellectual posturing – the equivalent of a pre-Montgolfier-brothers balloon debate – but to the ancient Greeks it was deadly serious. And its effects were felt not just in the arguments of students and teachers, but in the real world. The Melian Debate, related by the historian Thucydides, illustrates just how deadly the practical consequences of philosophical belief could be. In 416 BCE, the Athenians decided that they needed some extra allies. They demanded that the previously neutral island of Melos should join their side in the Peloponnesian War. The Melians replied that they wanted to remain neutral. But they were faced with the Athenians' chilly pragmatism: 'You know as well as we do that, when these matters are discussed by practical people, the standard of justice depends on the equality of power to compel, and that in fact the strong do what they have the power to do, and the weak accept what they have to accept.' In other words, the Athenians were arguing that phusis trumps nomos. The power to do something is the only consideration that matters. There is no independent moral question of right and wrong; to put it succinctly, might is right.

The Melians tried to apply the nomos argument in return: 'In the case of all those who fall into danger, there should be such a thing as fair play and just dealings.' You might have the power to crush your opponents like bugs, but just because you can, doesn't mean you should. What about the basic rules of society? They even used a simple altruism argument: if the Athenians demolish their enemies when they can, what is to stop those enemies destroying Athens, if she eventually falls from supremacy? If you want to be treated well by others, you need to treat others well, ergo altruism is in your own best interests.

The Melians proved unable to defeat the Athenians, either in debate or in battle. The Athenians besieged them, they executed the men and enslaved their women and children. Melos was repopulated as a colony and given as a new home to a few hundred Athenians. The Athenians had used a philosophical argument to justify wiping out a whole island race. And this is why philosophy is still so important to us today. The Melian Debate foreshadows the concerns of everyone who worries about the strength of modern superpowers compared with that of their neighbours, for example. When people protest about the behaviour of China towards Tibet, they are arguing against the phusis stance.

So we still use and need ancient philosophy today. Our physics, biology and zoology may have superseded Aristotle and his predecessors, but there can be few times in history when we have had to think so hard about what kind of world we want, and what kind of behaviour is right. When it comes to ethics, we have spent decades failing to really formulate arguments about moral relativism or cultural supremacy. The instinctive liberal response has been to believe that modern Western ways are no better than any others, until we come across things we can't tolerate: female genital mutilation, the killing of children because they are 'possessed', the execution of dissidents, academics or homosexuals. We should be thinking about the arguments and ideas posed by Aristotle, Plato, Socrates and other philosophers – ancient and modern – or we condemn ourselves to self-contradiction and lazy thinking. There are worse things to be than argumentative.

4

In the Lap of the Gods

To suggest that religion is a vexed issue in this century is rather to understate the case. If the twentieth century was divided by big politics – fascist or communist? Socialist or capitalist? – the twenty-first shows every sign of being divided by religion. This phenomenon is all the more remarkable when it is married to the fact that fewer of us (at least in Britain, where I am writing, and in much of Western Europe) than ever are what might be called practising believers, that is, go to a place of worship other than at funerals or weddings when one doesn't really get to choose. Religion is at the heart of a Middle East/West conflict which seems set to drag on for the foreseeable future. And quite aside from this global divide between religions, factional disputes also prevail within religions, whether it is the Sunni versus Shia conflict in Iraq, or the schism of the Anglican Church over a gay bishop in America. And just when it seemed like there were quite enough faith-related battles for now, non-believers stepped up and declared their own agenda: the war on God, which has pitted Richard Dawkins, Christopher Hitchens and the ghost of Charles

Darwin against any and all deities, has begun. While many of us seem to live cheerily from one day to the next with virtually no thought of theology at all, the passionate few have seized the headlines from the apathetic many. In 1843, Karl Marx wrote that religion was the opium of the masses. He couldn't possibly have foreseen that after a century and a half religion would, instead, be the cocaine of the few.

But is religion simply an issue which has to create conflict? After all, if adherents to a certain faith believe that they have the only true knowledge of how the world really is, isn't it rather naive to think they might be prepared to accept that theirs is just one belief with no more validity than anyone else's? And that's quite aside from the whole burning-in-hell issue. If you genuinely believe that anyone who has sex outside of marriage, or with someone of the same gender, or using contraception, or that involves any one of a number of other deviancies – which many of us have done, sometimes more than once, often several at a time – is going straight to hell, why would you keep quiet? Hell, if you believe in it, is an eternity of endless suffering. You would try to save those you care about, perhaps even those you could take or leave. After all, it's one thing not to fancy getting lumbered with someone dull at a party, but quite another to condemn them, by means of your refusal to encourage them back to the straight and narrow, to ceaseless damnation. And if that means you end up being the crazy person standing in a shopping precinct, hollering at those who prefer retail therapy to keeping the sabbath holy, well so be it. The problem is, essentially, a culture clash: religion doesn't have modern sensibilities. Quite the reverse: all major religions date back to a time when you didn't need to respect the lifestyle choices of those you didn't agree with. You could wage war on them, slaughter them or convert them. Or, if they were more powerful than you, you could be a victim of your faith, martyred, a saint. The idea of everyone agreeing to differ and simply getting on with things is, surely, a decidedly modern ambition.

Well, perhaps. But, actually, with some exceptions, ancient Rome often did a pretty good job of letting everyone get on with things, religiously speaking. One of the Romans' more cunning tricks, when conquering a country, was to synchronise gods with it. When they invaded Britain, for example, and arrived in what is now Bath, they could easily have demanded that the indigenous population stop worshipping their local goddess Sulis, and worship the Roman goddess Minerva instead. They could have fought pitched battles over it. But why bother? The ever-practical Romans simply declared that Sulis was the British version of Minerva, and stated that the goddess should now be known as Sulis Minerva, as though she had recently married but wished to retain at least some of her own identity. Merging sets of gods was an extremely efficient way of eliminating at least some of the differences between the Romans and those they conquered. And Roman priests weren't precious about their beliefs; they made no pretence to be humble servants of the gods. They were wealthy men (or women, in the case of the Vestal Virgins), and serving as a priest could be a crucial step on the path to political success. In 63 BCE, for example, Julius Caesar campaigned hard to be elected Pontifex Maximus – the chief priest of the Roman state religion. He knew it would give him an advantage in the vipers' nest of Roman political machinations.

So it's a pity that one of the facts everyone knows about the Romans is just how religiously intolerant they were, because of their persecution of the Christians. It is seen as a measure of their inhumanity. Firstly, they killed Christ, unless you decide to pin that one on the Jews. Secondly, they threw Christians to the lions. Thirdly, they martyred Christians at every opportunity, even when the lions were full to bursting and couldn't eat another thing. Yet, like so many widely held truths about the ancient world, the idea that the Romans were religiously intolerant is considerably less factual than one might believe. Which isn't to say that there's no truth in it at all. The Romans certainly did crucify Christ. That, sadly, is how they treated huge numbers of criminals and prisoners of war at the time. No historian can help but blanch when faced with a particularly lifelike crucifixion, or gruesome Stations of the Cross. Even if you don't believe in the divinity of Christ, you can't deny the reality of a man in agony. In fact, in many ways the pain of Christ is much harder to bear if you don't believe he was the son of God. The thought of anyone being tortured to death without the prospect of redemption at its end is truly awful. And that, of course, is how every Roman crucifixion, with the possible exception of one, played out. In other words, from a purely historical perspective, the Romans treated Christ no worse than they treated huge numbers of people every day. This isn't to belittle the suffering they inflicted on one man, but merely gives it a context: crucifying Jesus didn't make him special, to the Romans. It wasn't a sign of persecution or unique intolerance. It wasn't even because he was a dangerous political subversive who had to be degraded and slaughtered to discourage any others. It was, simply, the commonplace treatment of those who were deemed guilty of crimes in the Roman world, and weren't Roman citizens. Being a foreigner or a slave in the Roman Empire could only end well if you kept your head down. Antagonising anyone, especially anyone who had the ear of the Roman governor of your province, was an extremely risky undertaking. The Jewish historian Josephus tells of the brutal crushing of an uprising in Judaea in 4 BCE, for example. Augustus' general, Varus, didn't hesitate to use crucifixion as a mass punishment there: 'He crucified those that were the most guilty, about two thousand of them.'

The province of Judaea was a particularly troubling one for the

Romans. Mass crucifixions didn't have the crowd-calming effect they expected, at least not permanently. The Jews rebelled again in CE 66, and Vespasian was sent by the emperor Nero to quell them. By CE 70, the Romans had lost patience entirely. Vespasian, who was now emperor himself (thanks in no small part to his military record in Judaea), sent his son Titus to finish the rebellion off once and for all. The siege of Jerusalem was, even by ancient standards, a bloody and horrifying war. And unusually, we have a first-hand account from a non-Roman: Josephus, who was initially fighting the Romans, then captured, whereupon he became a negotiator for them and a chronicler of the war. His capture, incidentally, has provided a mathematical problem to delight modern-day computer programmers and maths puzzlers. Josephus was cornered in a cave, after the siege of Jotapata (or Yodfat, in Hebrew), a city in Lower Galilee. The Romans wanted him to surrender, but the forty or so men who were holed up with him said they would kill him before that happened. Then they wondered if they should kill themselves, too. Eventually, Josephus lighted upon a plan that pleased everyone. No one would commit suicide, because it was religiously unacceptable: 'The souls of those whose hands have acted madly against themselves are received in the darker part of Hades.' Instead, they would stand in a circle and draw lots to commit suicide by proxy: the one who drew the first lot would be killed by the one who drew the second lot, and so on. Luckily for future historians, Josephus was left till last, so he didn't have to die at all. He could now surrender to the Romans without fear of being cut down by his own men. The Josephus Problem, inspired by this story, requires you to calculate where you'd need to be standing in any given circle of people, taking into account the number of those participating and the interval between killings – every third person, for example – to ensure that you would be the last man standing. Josephus doesn't claim to have done the maths, however: he credits his survival either to chance or the providence of God.

Titus besieged Jerusalem for six months. Once the populace was starving, he used battering rams and fire to defeat them. Josephus gives us figures: 97,000 captives, 1,100,000 killed, most of whom were Jews. These figures are, of course, open to debate. It's another problem that arises whenever we consider the Romans and religion. Anyone who cares enough to record anything about a religious group is usually a biased source. And anyone who doesn't care very much may be less biased, but is correspondingly more ignorant. So, for example, we get a mangled description from Suetonius about Jews making constant trouble at the instigation of Chrestus, resulting in their expulsion from Rome. He means Christians, of course, but to the Romans, at this point in history (Suetonius is writing in the early second century CE), Jews and Christians were pretty much the same thing: Judaism had numerous cults and sects, as the writing of Josephus illustrates. Christianity came from Judaea, its early adherents were Jews, ergo for the Romans it was a branch of Judaism. But although Josephus can give us a much more detailed and careful chronicle of the siege of Jerusalem than any Roman author would, he was necessarily biased. Firstly, because he was a Jewish leader, he was a Jewish apologist. Secondly, because he was a Jewish leader, he was pretty intolerant of Jewish leaders of other factions with whom he did not agree. And thirdly, as a Jewish leader, he was a survivor of the Judaean wars only because the Romans allowed him to be. He was hardly likely to criticise Titus, the son of the emperor, a future emperor himself, and the man who had allowed Josephus to live. So, Josephus tells us that the Romans burned the temple of Jerusalem against Titus' wishes. He even puts an impassioned speech into Titus' mouth, during which he promises the Jews that he, Titus, will try to protect their holy temple. When the temple burns down, in Josephus' version, it's a mistake: the flames jump from the temple gates to the temple itself.

We get quite a different story from the Christian author Sulpicius Severus, who was born in the fourth century CE. Obviously, he wasn't an eye-witness, and we can't know exactly which earlier sources he used. But he was quite certain that Titus was to blame for the burning of the temple: 'Titus himself thought the temple should be destroyed, to destroy more thoroughly the religion of Jews and Christians.' But while Sulpicius disliked the Romans for their behaviour during the siege of Jerusalem, don't think for one minute that he was a fan of the Jews. He cheerily suggested the reason why the Romans had particular success during the siege of Jerusalem at Passover: 'No doubt it pleased God that this impious race should be given over to death, at the same time of year as when they crucified the Lord.'

Unpicking the rights and wrongs of this region is no easier for historians of ancient conflicts than it is for journalists trying to balance white phosphorus against suicide bombing. It is a truism to say that historians are biased: they can't help but be so. History is full of characters to whom we relate, causes we espouse, dictators we despise. But nowhere do we need to tread more carefully than when trying to establish the objective truth of religious conflicts. Each claim is the historical equivalent of Schrödinger's cat: both true and false until we open the box and render it one or the other. If nothing else, the wars in Judaea should remind us that the Jews, in purely simplistic terms – looking at the relative numbers of Jews and Christians killed by the Romans – had a far tougher time of things than the Christians did. Yet even simple statements prove impossible to accept: the modern dismissal of Titus, like that of Hadrian, is invariably that he was an anti-Semite. In the first place, this is a painfully anachronistic description: the Romans didn't hate Jews. They didn't hate anyone who opposed them. They simply obliterated their opponents until opposition was abandoned, and then they tolerated them. But the anti-Semitic label fits Titus less well than most for a second reason. As previously noted, the one scandal that stuck to this popular emperor was his taste in women. Instead of a good, Roman wife, he wanted to marry a Jewish queen, Berenice, with whom he conducted a public affair for about ten years. The relationship began while he was on campaign in Judaea. Only the disapproval of the Roman people (who feared Eastern queens getting involved with Roman leaders, after Cleopatra almost brought the Roman world to its knees) dissuaded him.

And what of the Romans throwing Christians to the lions? Again, this is one of those half-truths. Christians were persecuted, sporadically, under a few emperors. They were a natural target for persecution: like many belonging to cults that came from the East, Christians were, to quote Tacitus, 'per flagitia invisos' – 'hated for their disgraceful behaviour'. Most Eastern cults were, like Christianity, periodically banned. They were seen as being secretive, taking place only in the dark and in hidden locations. One could, of course, argue that the cults might have been less secretive had they been less despised, but whichever way round the cause and the effect worked, worship of Eastern gods, such as Isis, Mithras or Cybele, was often seen as worryingly deviant. Rumours about what really went on behind the closed temple doors abounded. Isis-worshippers believed that she had restored her dead husband, Osiris, to life. In some versions of the story, his body had been chopped up into numerous parts, not all of which could be found. Isis had to make him a new penis using magic, when it transpired that fish had eaten his original one. One can see why an ordinary Roman chap might feel uncomfortable with this kind of myth. Mithras-worshippers were like early Masons – all male, they met in secret temples, and had several different stages of initiation.

And like the Masons, their secrecy means we know little about them, although you can visit a Mithraic temple at Hadrian's Wall, or in the City of London. But worshippers of Cybele, the Great Mother, were strangest of all: her most devoted male followers would castrate themselves in a frenzy of religious fervour. Even the Romans, with their cheerful acceptance of animal sacrifice and entrail-reading, found self-castration rather hard to stomach.

And it wasn't only that Christianity was from the East. People suspected that any religion which had a criminal as its founder was probably full of criminality. Incest and cannibalism were only a couple of the unpleasant things the Romans believed Christianity entailed. It's easy to see how those rumours could start, too: if someone listening at a door overhears the Eucharist, what else are they going to think? Eating Christ's body and drinking his blood is a little weird, even if you've replaced it with some wine and a wafer. So the Christians were, indisputably, unpopular in ancient Rome. And they were persecuted. But certainly not constantly, and not very effectively, either, if anyone was hoping to destroy the religion.

The most famous persecutions took place under Nero. Tacitus tells us that, under Nero's orders, Christians were dressed in wild-animal skins, torn apart by dogs, crucified, or used as human torches. Tacitus is no fan of Christianity, but he still writes, 'Although these criminals were worthy of the harshest punishment, pity arose for them, because they were being obliterated not for the public good, but because of the savagery of one man.' There is something rather touching about this. By this stage in his reign, Nero was, according to all the accounts we have, a monster. The behaviour Suetonius accuses him of (incest with his mother, Agrippina, for a start) would make even a cult-worshipping cannibal blush. Nero's treatment of the Christians was vicious and cruel, all the more so because he needed a scapegoat for the Great Fire of Rome in CE 64, to divert suspicion from himself. But ordinary people, in spite of their dislike of Christianity, were moved to pity rather than lynching. Tacitus' account of the Roman world hardly suggests a consistently Christian-annihilating society. And, once again, we have to be wary even of attributing specific, anti-Christian sentiments to Nero. He needed a scapegoat and the Christians, being generally unpopular and sufficiently numerous, fitted the job description. But that doesn't mean he had a particular axe to grind against them. Suetonius tells us that Nero 'despised all religious cults, except the Syrian goddess. And he eventually scorned her too, by pissing on her image.'

And what of the third charge levelled against the Romans – that they martyred Christians at every opportunity? Again, this isn't a very fair assessment. Certainly, some Romans martyred some Christians sometimes. Christians, as discussed above, were an unpopular group. But we need to put things into perspective. Official, empire-wide persecution happened under very few emperors, such as Septimius Severus and Decius in the third century CE, and most notably under Diocletian and Galerius in the early fourth century. And while many Christians lost their lives during these periods, the actual numbers have often been exaggerated. The Christian scholar Everett Ferguson, for example, has suggested that more Christians have been martyred in the past fifty years than in the first 300 years of the church.

It's easy to see how the figures might have been massaged by early writers. Surviving accounts about martyrdoms tend to be written by Christian authors (quite understandably – who else would have an interest in documenting the trials and deaths of unpopular cultists?). And if you were a Christian author trying to defend your religion, you would have a vested interest in describing the poor souls who were crucified, burned or tortured, but kept their faith. You would have an equally strong interest in not mentioning those Christians who renounced their faith rather than being burned alive. No one wants to celebrate the quitters. So the texts we have are extremely one-sided: if they were an accurate representation of reality, then there would have been virtually no Christians left by the end of the Diocletianic persecutions. Yet these ended in CE 311, only fourteen years before the emperor Constantine would summon the Council of Nicaea and establish the first uniform Christian doctrine across the Roman Empire. Eusebius, the Christian historian and biographer, reckons that more than 250 bishops were present at the Council. Add their assorted deacons and acolytes, and you can see how he could describe those attending as innumerable. And that was just church officials attending this council – ordinary Christians remained at home. So, as persecutions go, Diocletian's was pretty ineffectual. To give an example of scale, only a small minority of the total number of bishops went to the Nicaean Council, and still more than twice as many attended it as there are in the Church of England today.

We do have one excellent, non-Christian source for martyrdom, however, and that is Pliny the Younger. Pliny was governor of Bithynia, in modern-day northern Turkey, during the reign of the emperor Trajan, in CE 110. He wrote to Trajan with queries about administrative issues in his province. In one particular letter, he asked Trajan's advice on how to deal with Christians. It's a long letter, full of detailed questions. Pliny hasn't attended interrogations of Christians in the past, so he doesn't know how to proceed himself. He wants details: should he treat them differently if they're young, rather than adults? What if they retract their beliefs – can he pardon them? And, most interestingly, should he punish somebody for being a Christian, even if they haven't committed any of the crimes associated with Christianity, or is professing Christianity a crime in itself?

Pliny explains his modus operandi, in detail. First he asks someone charged with Christianity if they are Christian. If they admit it, he asks them again, a second and third time, reminding them that they will be executed if they maintain their position. If they refuse to recant, he has them executed because, he feels, 'pertinaciam certe et inflexibilem obstinationem debere puniri' – 'their obstinacy and unbending stubbornness ought to be punished'. Pliny, it seems, finds mulishness a more unforgivable crime than Christianity. Conversely, if the alleged Christians brought before him are prepared to invoke the Roman gods, offer wine and incense to the emperor's statue or revile the name of Christ, he dismisses the charges. He has done some research into Christianity, too, and dismisses it as a 'superstitionem pravam et immodicam – 'a wicked, immoderate cult'.

Trajan wrote back with his customary patience, congratulating Pliny on doing things correctly. His one criticism is that Pliny has been responding to an anonymous list of Christians, which has been circulating in his province. Trajan remonstrates with him, 'These people [Christians] must not be hunted out ... Anonymous pamphlets haven't any place in criminal accusations. For they set the worst type of precedent, and they are not in the spirit of our age.'

It's an interesting distinction to make. Christianity is clearly a crime, punishable by death. But under Trajan's principate, there appears to be a 'don't ask, don't tell' policy in place. He isn't looking to make things difficult for Christians on religious grounds. Rather it seems to be the secrecy of their meetings that tends to get Christians into trouble. Secret meetings – ratted on to the authorities by a slave or other discontent – might be a harmless, private affair, but they might equally be a sign of political plotters at work, which couldn't be ignored. The conflation of these two groups – political and religious – is clear: the Christians whom Pliny pardons have given up their prayer meetings since he issued an edict banning political societies. But still, there is no impetus from Rome to seek out Christians and kill them. If anything, the existence of anonymous pamphlets suggests that sporadic anti-Christian sentiment is welling up among ordinary Bithynians, rather than among the Roman governing class. Pliny's letters give us a much more coherent idea of how Christians survived, increased and thrived under Roman rule: something that never makes sense if you believe all the tales of endless martyrdoms and persecution. Again, we need to remember who's telling the story before we can decide to what extent we can believe it. And we need to remember the temporal distance between Nero's persecution of Christians in CE 64, and the next major persecutions in the third century. There are almost 150 years between Nero's rule and that of Septimius Severus, during which time things probably ticked along like Pliny's letters suggest, with far fewer, far less frequent martyrdoms than we might initially have believed.

There is one more reason why Jews and Christians were viewed with suspicion by Rome's ruling class. The Romans didn't have a problem with people believing in different gods from theirs. They didn't pick religious battles, if they could avoid it: they were pragmatists, not fanatics. But, whichever gods you believed in, if you lived under Roman rule, you needed to view the emperor, and his ancestors, as occupying a space between ordinary men and gods. People poured libations as offerings to the emperor's genius (meaning his divine spirit, rather than his intellectual prowess). Once an emperor died, unless he had behaved shockingly (like Caligula), he was deified. And this would be memorialised in coins and on buildings. So one of the things the Romans wanted from their provincial residents was a commitment to the imperial cult. Again, it was a pragmatic choice – if you pour offerings to your ruler, and commemorate his divine predecessors, that will gradually affect the way you think about him. Are you really going to consider rebellion if you're reminded frequently that you are ruled by someone with gods running in the family? Many parts of the Roman Empire would have seen nothing unusual in deifying a leader; the Egyptians, for example, had long viewed their pharaohs as divine. So the Romans slotted their leader into an existing cult structure, or imposed a new one, and everyone learned to live with it. Apart from the Jews and the Christians.

Pouring offerings to a man was, obviously, something monotheists weren't going to find easy. Pliny, in his letter to Trajan, mentions that he uses the acid test of pouring offerings to the emperor as a way of deciding whether someone is a true Christian or not. He believed that a genuine Christian couldn't be persuaded to make such an offering. So again, we see why Christians might have seemed dangerously seditious. If they didn't acknowledge the imperial cult, how could the Romans be sure they wouldn't persuade others to follow the same belief? This was how rebellions started.

Meanwhile, the Jews compromised as best they could. Josephus tells us that they made sacrifices 'peri men Caesaros kai tou demou tōn Romaiōn' – 'on behalf of Caesar and the Roman people'. The key word in that sentence is the preposition, *peri*, which means 'near, around, about'. The Jews weren't sacrificing *to* Caesar, as though he were a god. They were sacrificing *for* him, on his behalf, as though they were saving him the effort of doing some sacrificing himself. The distinction may seem finicky, but if you have to choose between an early death or breaking your divine laws, finicky is a good place to start.

And the Jews did get more latitude from the Romans than the Christians did, because their religion was already so old and revered. So the Romans accepted this kind of compromise, for the most part. One exception, however, was the emperor Gaius Caligula, who decided that he would have his statues put up all over the empire, no matter how religiously insensitive that might be. And no matter how crazy it made him look. The Romans had no problem at all, during the reign of Caligula, with coins that were inscribed to 'The Divine Augustus', for example. They worshipped an imperial cult that depended on the idea that the emperor had a spark of divinity in him, and full-blown gods among his ancestors. But the emperor's divinity was a finely nuanced affair: a living emperor was not yet a deity. So it was seen as a measure of Caligula's madness that he wished to be viewed as a god while he was alive, and have his statues erected across the empire, among those of other gods. He sent the legate of Syria, Petronius, to Judaea to erect these statues in the temple in Jerusalem. The Jews appealed to Petronius, and reminded him that it was against their religious laws to have a graven image of God in their holy temple, let alone one of the emperor. Petronius resisted their pleas, pointing out that Caligula would simply have him killed if he failed to carry out his orders, and that the Jews would still end up with statues they didn't want in their temple, either way. The Jews reminded him that they made their sacrifices on Caesar's behalf every day, and that they would all die, women and children too, before the statues went up. Petronius, according to Josephus, was so moved by their fervour that he wrote to Caligula and tried to dissuade him. Caligula wrote back, threatening him with death if he failed to comply. But bad weather delayed the messenger for three months, during which Caligula was assassinated. And the messenger carrying the news of Caligula's death had a much easier journey, arriving twenty-seven days before his initial death threat turned up. For Petronius, and for those who might have had to endure Caligula's legendary threat to scorn the Roman political system by making his horse, Incitatus, a consul, Gaius died in the nick of time.

One of an emperor's titles was Pontifex Maximus – the chief priest.

The word 'pontifex' originally meant 'bridge-maker', so the role of chief priest had its origins in the idea of bridging the gap between people and their gods. But there is undoubtedly a difference between being the bridge to the gods and being one of them. Emperors were believed to undergo apotheosis at their death, and turn into fully fledged gods only then. But we have evidence of this whole notion being taken less than seriously by Seneca, the Stoic philosopher and tutor to the emperor Nero. After Nero's accession to the imperial mantle, he made sure that the senate deified his stepfather, Claudius (who had probably been bumped off by his fourth wife, Agrippina, Nero's mother). Politically, this was clearly a wise move for such a young emperor: Nero was only sixteen when he became the most powerful man in Rome. He needed people, especially people who might be coveting power for themselves, to believe that he was the natural successor to the Julio-Claudian emperors and gods. But within a year of Claudius' death, Seneca wrote a comic pamphlet, called *The Apocolocyntosis*. It's a made-up word, playing on the Greek word 'apotheosis'. But instead of turning Claudius into a god, Seneca has him turn into a pumpkin. Take that, Cinderella.

The Romans took the imperial cult seriously enough to impose it across the empire, and to threaten with death anyone who failed to participate in it. But this pamphlet mocks the very idea that the previous emperor might become a god, and no one appears to have been executed: Seneca was forced to commit suicide a decade later, but not for blasphemy. Rather, he was implicated, perhaps unfairly, in a conspiracy to assassinate Nero. So maybe there was a risk in allowing someone to mock divine imperial ancestors: if someone can mock a dead emperor, is it possible he might find it easier one day to plot against a living one. But *The Apocolocyntosis* is another piece of evidence suggesting that Roman state religion was entirely political rather than religious in its purpose. A bit of harmless mockery from a close friend and tutor could be tolerated. But if a province started getting uppity about the emperor's divinity, things might quickly develop into a political problem, so it had to be dealt with. It's worth bearing in mind, though, that even the emperors themselves weren't always entirely convinced by their potential apotheosis. According to Suetonius, the emperor Vespasian's final words were, 'Vae, puto deus fio' – 'Uh oh. I think I'm turning into a god.'

One question that bears asking, though, is whether the Greco-Roman gods would have been good company for, say, the weak, stammering scholar and emperor, Claudius. Our notions of what makes a god godly are not necessarily relevant here. The Romans, like the Greeks before them, had a very different set of expectations of their deities. Jupiter, Juno, Venus and Mars were immortal, certainly. They were powerful. And there, the resemblance to gods as we might perceive them ends. Venus – or Aphrodite, to give her her Greek name – wasn't all-powerful. She couldn't do a thing unless Jupiter, or Zeus to the Greeks, permitted it. She might go behind his back to try to get away with something, though: in Virgil's *Aeneid*, Venus and Juno conspire to make Dido, the queen of Carthage, and Aeneas, the Trojan prince, fall in love. They know Jupiter won't allow it – he wants Aeneas to set sail to Italy and start a new dynasty there – but they behave almost exactly as you would expect unusually powerful and articulate toddlers to behave. Petulance, pettiness, grudge-bearing and sneakiness were all skills that these gods had in spades, along with an eternal life to indulge in their back-biting and revenge. But omniscience, omnipotence, omnipresence: not so much. And let's not even get started on forgiveness. Greco-Roman gods were anthropomorphic, in so far as they looked like humans. But they lacked humanity. If a god or goddess had an axe to grind with you, you really were in trouble. Look at poor old Odysseus, who spent ten years getting home from Troy because he'd annoyed Poseidon by blinding Polyphemus, the Cyclops, who happened to be Poseidon's son. No one wants to incur the enmity of any god, but if you were a seafaring hero, falling out with the god of the sea was a particularly tough break.

Greek and Roman poetry and plays are littered with examples of the gods behaving in ways that would make a grown man weep – particularly if that grown man was Hippolytus, who ends up caught between the rival goddesses Artemis and Aphrodite. In Euripides' play of the same name, Hippolytus prides himself on his chastity, his total imperviousness to the opposite sex. He reveres Artemis, and spurns Aphrodite. As invariably happens in tragedy, hubris comes before a fall. These gods aren't characters who could learn to live with someone not being a particularly devout worshipper. Aphrodite sets her mind on revenge when she doesn't get her own way: she makes Hippolytus' stepmother, Phaedra, fall in love with him. Phaedra tries to resist her unhappy urges, but she speaks of them to her nurse, whom she has sworn to secrecy. The nurse reveals all to Hippolytus, who is revolted. Phaedra hangs herself in shame. Theseus, her husband and Hippolytus' father, returns home to find his wife dead and a letter blaming Hippolytus for her suicide. Theseus jumps to the conclusion that his son must have raped Phaedra, and exiles him. He calls on Poseidon to enforce his curses against Hippolytus. And as Hippolytus rides his chariot away, a bull rushes out of the sea (a Poseidon-sent curse-enforcer, if ever there was one), causing the horses to bolt in terror. Hippolytus is dashed on the rocks. Theseus only accepts that he has made a mistake when Artemis herself appears and explains exactly what has happened. It is a classic sequence of god-wrought havoc. Aphrodite is a spoiled brat: she takes revenge on a mere mortal because he doesn't fancy kissing anyone, and doesn't care who knows it. She doesn't hesitate to destroy the blameless

Phaedra as part of her scheme, although Phaedra has never shown her the slightest disrespect. Collateral damage is all part of the game with these gods. Artemis could, surely, have arrived a bit sooner on the scene and saved the life of her favourite, Hippolytus, but she comes too late, just in time to tell Theseus that he has killed his son in vain. Even Poseidon doesn't check with Aphrodite or Artemis before he puts Theseus' curse into action. He acts first and thinks never, killing a perfectly innocent, if sickeningly pompous, young man. And Theseus is Poseidon's son, so Poseidon causes the death of his own grandson. But none of the gods learns a lesson from the wanton destruction they have caused, and the play ends with Artemis swearing to kill whichever man Aphrodite loves above all others. So we can assume that this saga will be replayed some time in the near future.

Looking back with the smugness of hindsight, we might wonder why on earth anyone would believe in such capricious gods. They hardly seem to offer an enlightening world view. Well, we might again try to remember that most religions could be less than humane at this time. The Book of Samuel, in the Old Testament, countenances geno-cide, for example, 'This is what the Lord Almighty says ... "Now go and strike Amalek and devote to destruction all that they have. Do not spare them, but kill both man and woman, child and infant, ox and sheep, camel and donkey."' Or there is Psalm 137, which begins, 'By the rivers of Babylon, we sat and wept when we remembered Zion.' The weeping is soon over, though, and a few verses later, 'O Daughter of Babylon, doomed to destruction, happy is he who repays you for what you have done to us – he who seizes your infants and dashes them against the rocks.' Talk about visiting the sins of the parents on their children. While it is tempting to dismiss Greco-Roman gods as anathema to the values we now hold, we can't afford to forget that Judaeo-Christian tradition has some dark corners too.

So, what did these old, polytheistic religions offer to the Greeks and the Romans over the many hundreds of years they were the predominant belief systems? Well, for a start they provided social cohesion, and a sense of belonging. The Spartans, for example, had a particular fondness for the Dioscuri – the twins Castor and Pollux. As indeed they might, since Castor and Pollux, the mythical brothers of Helen of Troy, were born and raised in the Peloponnese. They were heroes, demigods, and they personified many characteristics that the Spartans admired: they were brave, warlike, adventurous. Plus, there were two of them, which was a convenient echo of the Spartan system of dual kingship.

The Athenians, meanwhile, knew that the goddess Athene was their protector; they had a huge temple dedicated to her: the Parthenon, on the Acropolis. The word *parthenon* means 'maiden', so the temple honours that particular aspect of Athene: her unmarried status. She was also the goddess of war strategy (Ares, or Mars to the Romans, was the god you wanted for brute force; Athene for tactical cunning), so the image of her as the city's guardian was very powerful. All ancient religious worship involved offerings. The Athenians would pour libations to their gods, spilling a little wine for Athene, and sharing a drinking cup among themselves. They would sacrifice animals at their temples. The internal organs of the sacrifice would be burned, as the god's portion. The willingness of the sacrificial victim (bulls were less docile than the average sheep, for example), the darkness of its blood – these things were seen as omens. Then the rest of the animal would be cooked and eaten by those attending the sacrifice. The religious experience was therefore actually a social one. It may be rather bloodier than we're accustomed to, but setting that aside, it's rather reminiscent of the version of the Church of England we see in an Agatha Christie novel: arranging the church flowers is often more important to Miss Marple's neighbours than believing in anything. The social commitment is what really counts.

The Athenians were also careful to ensure that they had a god for every occasion. According to Diogenes Laërtius, in the 46th Olympiad (595 BCE), Athens was afflicted by a pestilence. Not knowing how to get rid of it, they asked the philosopher Epimenides for help. He found some sheep, black ones and white, and took them to the Areopagus. They were freed to wander where they chose, and wherever they stopped, a sacrifice was made to the local god. Some of the sheep stopped in places to which no god was attached, so the Athenians set up altars there to the nameless or unknown god. Best to err on the side of caution when you're trying to shift a pestilence. Pausanias, too, mentions altars to the 'theōn onomazotōn Agnostōn' – 'the gods named "Unknown"'. St Paul tried to claim this god as the Christian deity, but it seems rather a shame to spoil the Athenian version; there is something very touching about naming a god 'Unknown' because you are trying to get rid of a plague, have sacrificed to all the gods you can think of, but don't want to run the risk of offending any you haven't yet come across.

The polytheistic gods also provide a comprehensive world view that has many parallels with other religions before and since. If a Greek or Roman believed in Zeus or Jupiter and the other occupants of Mount Olympus, he believed in a great deal. Firstly, these gods had specific areas of expertise. If you were a blacksmith, you might well feel a special affinity to Hephaestus (Vulcan, to the Romans), the blacksmith to the gods. A sailor would probably be more concerned to pray to Poseidon, or Neptune, in the hope of having fair sailing weather and good fortune. There is something very appealing about this division of labour and specialities among the gods. If you pray to one god in charge of the whole world – war, disease, famine – in the hope that the deity will help you find a boyfriend, you might end up feeling rather trivial and frivolous. But pray to Eros (Cupid) or Aphrodite (Venus) and you're pursuing your particular interest and being pious at the same time. You're not distracting them from curing the sick or fighting a battle – love is their only passion.

And the myths that are told of these gods are ones we see in most religions. Obviously, we're accustomed to the notion of sinners being sent to hell, according to many branches of Christian theology and tradition. Some sins are worse than others; some areas of hell are worse than others. Behave well and you could go to heaven. Behave badly and you will burn in hell. Die in a state of insufficient purity and you'll wander hopelessly in purgatory. The Greco-Romans had similar ideas. They had an underworld – Hades – and a god who ran it, also called Hades, although unlike the Devil, with whom he has often been associated, Hades wasn't evil or especially to be feared. The world was divided into three, and allotted to three gods: Zeus/Jupiter had the skies, Poseidon/Neptune had the sea and Hades/Pluto had the realm of the dead. If you were heroic during your life, you might end up in the Elysian Fields, a paradisal area of the underworld. If you offended the gods in some way – usually by means of a hubristic crime, such as comparing yourself to them, or pinching something that was previously theirs, like fire – you would end up in Tartarus, being punished for all eternity. This is where you would find poor old Sisyphus, endlessly pushing his rock up a hill only to watch it fall back down to the bottom, forcing him to start again. It's where Tantalus, forever hungry and thirsty, reaches for grapes and water, only to see them disappear before his eyes. His name is now a byword for this particular type of torment: we get the verb 'tantalise' from him.

There is something very alluring about the idea of an underworld that is only removed from our own world by geography. In Book Six of *The Aeneid*, Aeneas visits it: he has to go to Cumae, not far from Naples, to find the Sibyl, who leads him into the netherworld. He sees Charon, the ferryman, punting the souls of the dead across the River Acheron. He's shocked to see souls thronging on the banks of the river, begging to be rowed across, but waiting there in vain. The Sibyl explains that these are the unburied, those who didn't have a coin placed on their mouths or dirt thrown over them when they died. They must wait on the shore, homeless, for a hundred years. Aeneas finds answers to some of his questions, too. He soon meets the man who was his helmsman when he set sail from Troy, but who had disappeared from their ship. Palinurus explains that he was holding the tiller when it broke off, and it dragged him into the sea, where he drowned. Eventually, after travelling through the underworld, Aeneas finds his father, and can ask him for advice. It's a touching scene, and one that helps us see why Greco-Roman theology and myth might have lasted like they did: wouldn't we all wish to be reunited with our loved ones this way? The notion that the dead are only temporarily separate from us, the other side of a door through which we too can pass, is incredibly enduring in many cultures. Isn't the death of a beloved parent or friend easier to understand if we believe there's a possibility that they and we might speak again some time? Only those of considerable emotional sturdiness can resist the idea; the consolation of afterlife myths is extremely powerful. So much of our longing for supernatural beings – gods and ghosts alike – and a world view which includes them, surely derives from this: many of us want to believe that death is not the end, either for our loved ones or for us. And if we fear death now, after a couple of hundred years of enlightenment, we can only begin to imagine how the Greeks and Romans must have felt, facing a shorter life expectancy and with limited medical knowledge.

So, why then, if the Greeks and Romans sought the same things from religion as the adherents of any other faith, did they not pick rather nicer gods? Why have a king of the gods who persistently rapes women? A consort for him who is fuelled by petty jealousies? Well, the ancients needed a way to make sense of a world that was, in many ways, unknowable to them. If you have no meteorologists, how can you possibly predict when a hurricane will appear, destroying lives and property in its wake? How can you know to protect your crops from unseasonal bad weather, and save your harvest? When every trip through the mountains or over the seas was fraught with danger, what were you supposed to think? Human beings have an intense desire to impose order on the world. That's why we still develop rituals and beliefs, even now. We have all that science and reason have taught us, yet we still see grown men turn away from a television showing a football match in which they have an interest, because they believe their team plays less well when they are watching. We long to believe, instinctively, that we have control over our destinies. But the natural world is arbitrary. So even the irreligious (insurance companies among them) tend to refer to natural disasters as acts of god. It seems the only way many of us can comprehend the scale of a tragedy. How else do you cope with a world where a tsunami can wipe out a quarter of a million people in a day? Do you shrug and say that bad things happen sometimes? Do you try to set up an early warning system to prevent such a loss of life next time? Do you take legal action against the governments that allowed residential areas to be built on a potentially dangerous coast? Or do you decide that god was punishing the wicked and that there's nothing more to be said about it? We respond to natural tragedy in many different ways, depending on what kind of explanation or consolation we need.

The ancients were no different from us. There was just more of the world that they couldn't understand using rational explanation;

consequently they had more acts of god. Earthquakes cause havoc now, even with our knowledge of tectonic plates and the seismologists who work all over the world. It takes only the smallest leap of imagination to think how it must have felt to live somewhere as quake-ridden as Italy, and have no idea what caused them or when they were going to happen next. Why wouldn't they have believed that Neptune had smashed his trident on the ground somewhere, with the information they had available?

Hand in hand with religion comes superstition. Indeed, for critics of organised religion, they are the same thing. And ancient peoples were certainly deeply superstitious. They performed sacrifices, and read omens, horoscopes and entrails. Haruspices were professional entrail-readers in the Roman world – they would poke their noses into the intestines of a sacrificial victim and declare that the omens were good or ill, depending on what they saw. And perhaps on who was paying. The more powerful someone became, the trickier it was for them to ignore superstition: Croesus, king of Lydia (in modern Turkey) in the sixth century BCE, was desperate to know which of many competing oracles could be relied upon to tell him the truth, so he sent messengers to test them. When the messengers reached the oracle, they asked it what Croesus was doing. According to Herodotus, it was the Delphic oracle that nailed it. At the exact time of their asking the oracle what the king was doing, it stated correctly that he was boiling a tortoise. Croesus then sent messengers with golden gifts to the oracle, and asked if he should invade Persia. The oracle gave one of its famously enigmatic replies: if Croesus invaded Persia, a very great empire would be destroyed. Croesus saw this as a ringing endorsement, and promptly attacked the Persians. He soon found his expedition demolished and himself taken prisoner. The great empire that had been destroyed was his own. Oracles could be decidedly tricksy.

And Roman emperors could be just as fearful as Lydian kings. In the first century CE, Tiberius banished all the astrologers from Rome early in his principate, seeing them as a pernicious influence. But as an old man, paranoid and afraid, he consulted Thrasyllus, an astrologer, extensively. Proximity to death made him far more nervous that he might be hurried into it before his time. And it's not as though we don't see examples of this type of behaviour in the modern world. After an assassination attempt was made on Ronald Reagan in 1981, his wife Nancy consulted the astrologer Joan Quigley over several years, trying to establish which days were good for him and which were not, so as to curtail his riskier activities on the bad days, in the hope of keeping him from being shot. Fear often makes even the otherwise rational superstitious, whether we're afraid of unlucky numbers, black cats, broken mirrors or solitary magpies.

Again, it's a question of trying to exert order over a disordered world, and the ancients lived in a world that had considerably less order than ours. If you're standing next to a chap who gets struck by lightning, it's obviously more tempting to believe that he hadn't performed the proper sacrifices, and so deserved his fate, than accept that you were simply luckier than him today. For if you believe the latter, you also have to accept that you might be the unlucky one tomorrow. And human beings are so desperate to be able to shape their own futures. Most of us don't want to live in a deterministic world, where what is written in the stars decides our fate. We believe that we are individuals, that we can't be lumped in with other people who simply happened to be born in the same month, or on the same day. Yet horoscopes didn't die out with the invention of the telescope and the understanding of what stars really are. We live in a time when men have walked on the moon, when we know the sun is just another star in a crowded sky. But even broadsheet newspapers print a daily or weekly horoscope. We want things both ways: we demand free will, and the belief that our actions shape our lives. But plenty of us believe simultaneously that Taureans are obstinate because, apparently, bulls are too.

The more vulnerable we feel, the more we tend to want to throw our fates into others' hands. If you read nothing else classical this year, you should make time to read the fourth book of Virgil's *Aeneid*. There are many excellent reasons for doing this, of which only one is that it is the most brilliant book of verse ever written, and it's your own time you're wasting if you decide to read something else instead. But mostly you should read it for Dido, the Carthaginian queen who died for love of Aeneas, another broken consequence of the gods' involvement in human affairs. Dido has loved before, her husband Sychaeus, who was killed by her brother in an attempted coup. She flees Tyre, her city in Phoenicia (modern Lebanon), and sets up a new city in Carthage. Then Aeneas turns up, another refugee, this time from Troy. Jupiter has already decreed that Aeneas will go to Italy and found what will eventually become Rome. But his ships were blown off course in a storm, and he lands at Carthage first. Dido receives him and his men, and allows them to stay in the city while they repair their ships and the weather improves. Juno, who loves Carthage and wants it to prosper and become a rival to Rome, and Venus, Aeneas' mother, conspire to make Dido and Aeneas fall in love. They enlist the aid of Cupid, to fire his arrows into Dido's breast. She is ruined by this love. She can't concentrate on anything else, even the construction of her new city: 'Towers begun then fail to rise ... all building works were interrupted, both the huge threatening walls and the cranes as tall as the sky.' Infatuation is bad enough, but Dido is also racked with guilt, believing that she is betraying her late husband. She immediately resorts to superstition to try to find out if the gods can give her guidance, little knowing that they are entirely responsible for her unhappiness. She becomes obsessive about the whole process, choosing the sacrificial victim herself (instead of letting the priest do so), pouring the wine on its face, peering into its still-breathing entrails. This, we realise, is an excessive practice of superstition, the deviant behaviour of someone maddened by the gods. Not that the priests can tell her that, for they know nothing about the gods' real ambitions. Virgil, at least, isn't taken in by them: 'heu vatum ignarae mentes!' – 'Alas for the unknowing minds of priests!' But is poor Dido so very different from her modern counterpart, sick with love and poring through every available magazine in the hope of finding just one horoscope that tells her things will all work out well?

The Romans had a very business-like attitude to their gods, a relationship that can best be described with the Latin phrase *do ut des*, 'I give, so that you may give'. In other words, a Roman would offer a sacrificial gift to the gods in the expectation of getting something in return. No wonder the idea of sacrifice was so integral to ancient polytheism: how could you expect some help or favour from a god if you hadn't killed an animal or poured some wine for them? You can't get something for nothing. The Romans would even offer up a defixio – a curse tablet – with an expression of desire and a promise of payment scratched in lead (sometimes backwards for extra magical impact): *I'll sacrifice two goats if you punish the man who stole my wife and pinched my tunic*. Roman religion really was a place of give and take.

The Romans weren't offering prayers of humility. They were, essentially, consumers of gods' good or bad will. Again, it is a mindset that is easy to dismiss, but impossible to deny: who hasn't promised to be good, in a silent prayer, if only their test results are negative? The ancients had far less foresight than we do. We can forecast the weather, the election results, the financial markets. We have computer-modelling, statistics, measurements. The future is not a mystery to most of us, most of the time. And we keep trying to demystify the bits of it that are. We can test our DNA to find out if we'll develop a debilitating disease, try to take steps to avoid it before it's too late. The Romans, meanwhile, could sacrifice to Aesculapius, the god of medicine, in the hope that this would work instead.

Amid all this belief – deities, sacrifices and martyrdoms – we shouldn't lose sight of the unbelievers. Suetonius wrote of the emperor Tiberius, 'He lacked any deep regard for the gods, or other religious feeling.' It isn't an especially critical passage, just an observation that Tiberius' belief in astrology made him too deterministic to believe that anything could be changed, hence his lack of passion for the gods. The idea that a ruler in some parts of the modern world could be so casually godless seems unlikely: a Gallup poll taken in 2007 asked Americans if there were any qualities a person could have that would prevent them from being an acceptable presidential candidate. Ninety-four per cent of respondents said they would vote for a black candidate, 88 per cent would vote for a woman, 72 per cent would vote for a Mormon, while only 57 per cent would consider a candidate if he or she were seventy-two years old. And coming in last place, with only 45 per cent of the electorate considering candidates voteworthy if they possessed this characteristic, was atheism.

Not all ancient godlessness was treated as lightly as Tiberius', however. We can't forget that Socrates was put to death over his perceived failure to honour the traditional Greek gods, though it wasn't a charge he accepted. Indeed, after he had been sentenced to death, he gave a final speech to the courts. The last thing he said, to the jury of Athenians who had condemned him for heresy, was, 'It's time for us to be going, me to die and you to live. And which of us faces the better prospect is unclear to anyone but God.' When you are about to be executed for dishonouring the gods, closing your speech like that is pretty classy.

Questioning the gods' existence and form was a very philosophical pursuit. Xenophanes, a sophist from Ionia born in the late sixth century BCE, once wrote, 'If oxen and lions and horses had hands like men, and could draw and make works of art, horses would make gods like horses, and oxen like oxen, and each would draw pictures of the gods as if they had bodies like their own.' This is an extraordinary statement for its time, suggesting that gods are made in man's image, rather than the other way around. The scepticism of Richard Dawkins and Christopher Hitchens goes back a great deal further than we might have imagined.

Perhaps the final word on religion should go to Protagoras, another sophist. 'About the gods,' he wrote in a book introduction, 'I do not know whether they exist or not, nor of what sort they might be. There are many obstacles to such knowledge, including the obscurity of the subject, and the brevity of human life.' Protagoras was a proper agnostic in the real sense of the word: he believed that any kind of understanding of the gods was literally unknowable. Agnostics are a tolerant bunch, by and large, which is lucky, because otherwise they would surely have thumped at least one of the many people who feel that need to tell them they should make their minds up and decide whether they believe in a deity or not. Agnostics, just like Protagoras, know exactly what they believe; they aren't indecisive at all. At least, not about gods.

Protagoras was a rationalist; he had none of the conviction of the religious zealot. And none of the conviction of the irreligious one either. Yet even his unexceptionable statement may have provoked horror among his contemporaries. According to Cicero, writing several hundred years later, it was because of Protagoras' introductory sentence to his book 'that he was banished by a decree of the Athenians from their city and lands, and his books were burned in the Assembly.

This, in my opinion, made many people less keen to profess this view, after a case in which even the expression of doubt had not been able to escape punishment.' We have no contemporary evidence for this treatment of Protagoras' work, however, and enough of his books survived for Cicero to be able to quote the offending sentence confidently. But book-burning often attends those who question the gods, even if it rarely manages to snuff out their work entirely. The Athenians certainly weren't very tolerant of those philosophers who asked religious questions. But Athenian intolerance was easily eluded, if you were prepared to leave Athens for a while, like Protagoras. Modern religious intolerance can be harder to avoid. The Bebelplatz in Berlin, site of the Nazi book-burnings in 1933, displays a quotation from the German poet Heinrich Heine. The Holocaust Museums in both the United States and Jerusalem display the same line. It reads, 'Where books are burned, in the end people will burn.' All of us, religious or otherwise, might bear it in mind. Our gods, if we believe in them, can surely cope with unbelievers. They can't all be like Hippolytus' Aphrodite, pettily offended by the rejection of a paltry human. If we can't learn to tolerate each other's religious choices, perhaps we could at least learn to believe that any god which has retained the belief of millions across centuries doesn't need us to kill, maim or fight on his behalf. The idea that gods have nothing better to care about than individual people is rather demeaning to them, surely? As the philosopher Epicurus wrote, 'It is not the man who denies the gods worshipped by the multitude, but he who affirms the gods to be what the multitude believes about them that is truly impious.'

5

Frankly, Medea, I Don't Give a Damn

It may seem rather unfair to have a chapter just for women. Precisely the kind of positive discrimination that raises hackles. There isn't a chapter for men, so how can this be right? Well, women are, of necessity, excluded from large chunks of this book. When we've looked at politicians, orators, soldiers and philosophers, women have had to take a back seat. And often that seat has been many rows back. Women were missing from a great deal of ancient public life, and consequently they're missing from a large number of these pages. So it's time to redress the balance a little, and look at the role women did play in the ancient world, rather than focusing solely on the roles they couldn't play. The women in this chapter will, with very few exceptions, be refracted through male eyes, however – almost all ancient authors were men, and the fragments we have of, say, Sappho are few. Even those probably only exist now because Sappho was deemed a great lyric poet by male readers and scribes. So don't feel that men are really missing from this chapter: they are crucial to it. They just aren't so much in the spotlight this time round.

Let's start in Athens. In the fourth century BCE, Demosthenes wrote a speech for a man named Apollodorus, 'Against Neaera'. Apollodorus, responding to what he viewed as unreasonable litigation from a man named Stephanos, had decided to hit him where it hurt. He brought a case against Stephanos for being married to a foreign-born woman, Neaera, and a hetaira at that. The word 'hetaira' is usually translated, with customary tact, as 'courtesan', and means an educated foreign woman who you might well pay for sex, but with whom you could probably also discuss the respective qualities of Aeschylus and Euripides. This is as opposed to a *pallax*, which is routinely, and rather politely, translated as 'concubine'. The divide between low- and high-class call girls is as old as the oldest profession. There were also flute girls, who turned up at parties, played the flute and were usually open to other offers.

In his summing up, Apollodorus uses a phrase that would chill the heart of any right-minded modern girl, but which gives us an incisive snapshot of the status of different types of women in Athenian polite society. 'For this is what living with a woman means: to have children by her ... We keep hetairai for the sake of pleasure, concubines for the daily care of our bodies, and wives to bear us legitimate children and be trustworthy guardians of our households.'

It seems that Athenian women lived a pretty unenviable life: they stayed indoors most of the time, in women's quarters, segregated from all but their closest male relatives, because it was the only way their husbands could be certain that the children their wives bore were theirs. As so often in primitive societies, ancient and modern alike, women's rights were suppressed by an all-encompassing male fear that somehow a man might end up with another man's children sitting at his table. This very real terror is what lies at the heart of another legal speech we have already looked at: Lysias' *The Killing of Eratosthenes*.

Euphiletus explains to the jury that early on in their relationship, his wife was 'pasōn ēn beltistē', 'the best of all wives'. But when his mother died, Euphiletus' wife went to the funeral, and was spotted by Eratosthenes, who went on to seduce her. As the cornerstone of his defence, Euphiletus (or rather, Lysias) really milks the jury's belief that this kind of thing could happen to any one of them. It is the same deeply depressing view that now lurks beneath demands that women keep their hair, faces and bodies covered in some societies. The dispiriting subtext of these requirements is surely that women are, first and foremost, amoral seductresses, and men are nothing more than priapic scoundrels. The notion that women and men could simply be friends, acquaintances or colleagues seems to be missing entirely.

So, the life of an Athenian-born wife was not a very alluring one. Pericles summarises the role of Athenian women thus: 'The great glory of a woman is not to fall short of your natural character. And the greatest glory of a woman is to be least spoken of by men, either in praise or censure.' Pericles' idealised vision of women, as slightly less seen or heard than Victorian children, would seem pretty miserable even if we lived in an era when fifteen minutes of fame wasn't the single most desirable thing anyone could achieve. It's good to know, therefore, that Pericles didn't even come close to practising what he preached. Divorced from his first, Athenian wife, he shacked up with Aspasia, who was easily the most notorious woman in fifth-century BCE Athens. Not only was she talked about in the usual, gossipy sense, she was mentioned on stage at a dramatic festival, in front of the whole city. She was a foreign-born woman (not Athenian, in other words), and is often described as a hetaira, certainly by Aristophanes. In fact, he goes even further. In his play *The Acharnians* he calls her a brothel-keeper, and suggests that a conflict between the Athenians and Megarians was caused by some reciprocal whore-thieving: a few Athenian men kidnapped a Megarian woman, Simaetha, so the Megarians swiped a couple of Aspasia's prostitutes in return. As always with Aristophanes, we have to work out how much of what he says is fantasy and how much is real. The conflict between Athens and Megara is the true part. The idea that it was caused by men stealing prostitutes is a joke. But on which side does the description of Aspasia as a brothel-keeper fall? I think it's there for comic effect, and therefore untrue, but plenty of stories about Aspasia from the ancient world suggest that others believed it. It's very hard to unpick facts about someone's character when the only source we have is comedy: imagine trying to define the real Barbra Streisand if your sole reference to her is in the *South Park* episode 'Mecha-Streisand', in which the titular evil robot version of Streisand tries to destroy the town.

Aristophanes isn't our only source for Aspasia, but the others are just as awkward. We find a reference to her in Plato's *Menexenus*, where Socrates suggests a woman is the finest teacher of rhetoric around. 'Who is?' asks Menexenus, before answering his own question. 'Oh, it's clear you mean Aspasia.' Is Socrates kidding, as commentators have often believed? Is the joke at Aspasia's expense, because her regular salons had made her too big for her boots? Is it at Pericles' expense, as behind every successful man there must be an oratorical mistress? Or is it a genuine compliment – that while Aspasia wasn't a proper teacher of rhetoric, in so far as she didn't take payment and teach classes, she was nonetheless an excellent coach of her close circle of male friends?

Aspasia gave her name to a couple of philosophical dialogues too, which sadly haven't survived. But her fame wasn't short-lived: Cicero, some 400 years later, translated one of those dialogues in his *De Inventione*. We can see Aspasia taking on the role Socrates usually took, asking Xenophon and his wife if they would prefer to have their neighbour's property if it was better than their own. By using the same inductive reasoning as Socrates used, she has soon persuaded them both that if they would rather have a neighbour's superior gold, they would also prefer that neighbour's superior husband or wife to their own. Xenophon and his unnamed wife are quizzed into an embarrassed silence. Let's assume no one went to Aspasia for marriage guidance.

All these sources suggest that Aspasia was sharp, clever and more than a little mischievous. For a man who praised the unspoken-of woman, Pericles certainly liked a celebrity mistress. And other men liked her too: according to Plutarch, the Persian prince Cyrus renamed his favourite concubine Aspasia in her honour. Even the ordinary Athenians eventually managed to find it in their hearts to overlook her foreign birth. Pericles' son, by Aspasia, would not have been an Athenian citizen: for that, you needed two Athenian parents. It was a law that Pericles himself had proposed in 451 BCE. But after his two sons by his first wife died in the plague of 430 BCE, the Athenians were moved to pity, and voted to allow his son by Aspasia full citizenship, so that Pericles wouldn't die without leaving an heir.

And Aspasia wasn't the only hetaira who wielded profound influence over powerful men. Thaïs was an Athenian woman who lived in the fourth century BCE. She was a favourite of Alexander the Great, and the lover of Ptolemy, who had been a general in Alexander's army, and later became pharaoh. Thaïs went on campaign with Alexander, the very opposite of respectable behaviour for most Greek women. In 330 BCE, when they reached the palace of Xerxes in Persepolis, she made a speech, partly (according to Plutarch) to praise Alexander, and partly to entertain him. She said that she would like to burn Xerxes' house, in revenge for the fact that he once burned Athens, in 480 BCE. She must have been quite a speaker, because Alexander's friends were soon encouraging him too, and they did indeed burn it down.

According to Diodorus Siculus, Thaïs was the first person, after Alexander himself, to hurl a torch into the palace. It was most remarkable, said Diodorus, that the burning of the Acropolis should have been repaid by 'mia gunē' – 'one woman'.

So if Aspasia and Thaïs were everything a woman in Athens wasn't supposed to be, what about the women who behaved as Athenian men thought they should? The majority must have played their role appropriately, as Aristotle described when he wrote about the division of labour in an Athenian household: 'Men and women have different tasks in the household; his job is to acquire property, hers is to look after it.' We're lucky to have Xenophon's Socratic dialogue *The Estate-Manager*, or *Oeconomicus*. Well, lucky in some ways: after Plato's Socratic dialogues, Xenophon is leaden stuff. Nonetheless, he gives us a valuable insight into the organisation of a well-to-do Athenian home. The word *oeconomicus*, incidentally, gives us our word 'economy', which is why you should never trust a financial adviser who has an overdraft: the ancient Greeks knew perfectly well that if you couldn't manage your own money, there's no way you should be looking after anyone else's. In the linguistic sense, at least, financial management really does begin at home.

In the case of this dialogue, that home belongs to Ischomachus, a man whom Socrates interrogates because he has a reputation for being 'kalos k'agathos' – 'fine and good'. Socrates wants to know where his reputation comes from, and Ischomachus gives him an extensive lecture on his domestic arrangements. He has trained his wife, whose name (as so often) is lost to us, in the art of household management. She is in charge of the household goods, in much the way Aristotle envisages a woman should be. She looks after the household slaves, ensures that everything they have is kept neatly and securely, and generally behaves like the perfect housekeeper. Socrates is hugely impressed by her enthusiasm, and perhaps her patience with her rather pompous husband. When Socrates hears that she believes it is pleasanter for a sensible woman to look after her possessions properly than to neglect them, he pays her the ultimate compliment: 'And hearing that she had given him this answer, I exclaimed, "By Hera, Ischomachus! Your wife has a mind as good as a man's!"' Hera was the appropriate goddess for Socrates to swear by, too, for she was responsible for matrimony (separated, by the pragmatic Greeks, from Aphrodite, who dealt with love rather than marriage). And Ischomachus, with his sensible wife who preferred to put things away carefully rather than chuck them on the floor, had a lot to be thankful for, in his view. We also see, in this dialogue, the role of other wives of men in Socrates' social circle. Socrates asks Critobulus two questions that reveal the ancient Athenian attitude to their womenfolk perfectly: 'Anyway, Critobulus, since we're among friends here, you should be completely honest with us. Is there anyone to whom you entrust more important matters than to your wife? – No one, he replied. – And is there anyone to whom you speak less than to your wife? – No one, or almost no one, he said.'

The temptation, of course, is to believe that all women in the ancient world lived like this: in a strange hinterland between trust and mistrust, looking after the house but not allowed to leave it. But not all ancient societies were the same, any more than all modern ones are. So women had a very different life in Sparta from the one they would have had in Athens, at least according to Plutarch. Plutarch wasn't a contemporary source for classical Greece, writing as he did in the first century CE, but he was a magpie, acquiring anecdotes and proverbs the way it steals shiny buttons. And he devotes some considerable time to the lives of Spartan women. Sparta ran itself on militaristic lines: the men slept in dormitories, and ate in mess-halls. When they married, it was a decidedly fetishistic business. The bride's head was shaved, and she was dressed in a man's cloak and sandals. Then her husband had dinner in the mess, before he came and carried her to bed. Fearless in the face of a euphemism, Plutarch explains what happens next: after spending a short time with her, he went back to the mess. The couple would continue to live and sleep apart, and see each other only briefly. Anachronism isn't a healthy indulgence, but one still cries out to know what Freud would have made of all this. Even Sparta's unmarried girls were comparatively liberated: 'The girls made jokes at the young men's expense, and helpfully mocked them when they made mistakes.' Poor Spartan boys – helpful mockery really does sound like the most debilitating kind.

Plutarch also records a set of Spartan sayings, legendary quotations attributed to various Spartan women. It's inconceivable that he could have written a set of Athenian women's sayings, even if he'd been able to track down their names. But Gorgo, the daughter of the Spartan king Cleomenes, in the fifth century BCE, was impressively pithy. So, Plutarch tells us, when the Ionian leader Aristagoras was badgering her father to make war on the Persian king and offering him a hefty sum of money as an incentive, Gorgo piped up, 'Father, this grubby little foreigner will completely ruin you if you don't chuck him out of the house at once.' Gorgo, in Plutarch's version of her at least, sounds like an imperious Mitford sister: having been asked by an Attic woman (i.e. from the area around Athens) why Spartan women were the only ones who ruled over their men, Gorgo replied, 'Because we're the only ones who give birth to men.' It's hard not to think that Plutarch has a sneaky fondness for these rude, brash women, so cheerfully does he record their blunt, epigrammatic words. Aristotle is less approving of the Spartan way of life, and its effect on women: 'For the lawgiver, wanting the city to be strong ... neglected the women. So they live licentiously and in every kind of luxury.' Plutarch corrects Aristotle on this, and it's not difficult to see why. Nothing about the Spartan way of life makes it seem luxurious for anyone involved in it. For a start, they practised eugenics. When a baby was born, the elders of a man's tribe would have a look at it. If it appeared a bit puny, they would chuck it off Mount Taygetus rather than have it live on as a weak Spartan. It's hard to reconcile that attitude with a life of untrammelled luxury for anyone.

Of course, we can't even consider women in ancient Greece without discussing the most famous one of all, Sappho. She was a lyric poet, born in the seventh century BCE on the island of Lesbos, and our knowledge of her is frustratingly vague. Only fragments of her poetry survive, and the guesses we make about her personal life are only that, guesses. She may have had a mother and a daughter, both called Cleis. She once wrote a poem which began, 'The man who sits opposite you seems to me to be like a god.' It was translated into Latin in the first century BCE by the Roman poet Catullus, who knew a good love poem addressed to an idealised woman when he saw it. For all that Sappho has given us the word 'sapphic', and indeed the word 'lesbian' in its non-topographical sense, we have no idea if she was a lesbian, if she jumped to her death for the love of a ferryman, if she ran a girls' school like a smutty Jean Brodie, or indeed if any of the myths about her are true. Sappho was and remains an enigma. But she is an enigma who transcended her time and place, and was regarded by the ancients as one of the finest lyrical poets that the Greek world had produced. So, even though we don't have many facts about her, we can at least embrace one: she was a woman of formidable talent, whose gender and perhaps sexuality were not enough to hold her back, writing at a time when women writers were not exactly commonplace. Like Aspasia, and Gorgo, she was a much talked-about woman in the best possible way.

Life was different again for women in ancient Rome. For a start, they weren't cloistered away in a women-only section of their homes. They could and did move about the Roman world without a husband or father in tow to keep them from misbehaving. Read Juvenal's Sixth Satire, and you'll discover they did a lot more than that. Juvenal isn't a kind man: he's misogynistic, xenophobic, bigoted and cross. He is also hilarious. His sixth satire is one long screed about the awfulness of women and why no one in his right mind would ever marry. Juvenal is the first stand-up comedian, a man who wrote long, angry, absurdist rants against what he hated, which was pretty much everything. And the subject of women was especially inspiring, as this satire is twice the length of any of his others. Juvenal's women are genuinely ghastly: they have crushes on hideous, mangled gladiators or gay dancers. They're all whores. Except the ones who are frigid. They're greedy and want whatever the neighbours have. They're uneducated and stupid, or over-educated and boring. Don't even get him started on mother-in-laws. Women spend too much or they're stingy. They have affairs with eunuchs, so that they don't have to worry about getting an abortion. Your wife will commit adultery at any opportunity. Sure, you can try to lock her up. But – and this is, perhaps, the most quoted and reused epigram in all Latin literature – 'quis custodiet ipsos custodes?' 'Who will guard the guards themselves?' It's worth noting that Juvenal didn't coin the phrase because he was worried about a police state, about the encroaching power of government or the inherent grubbiness of authority figures (although he would no doubt have hated all those things too), in spite of the fact that it's quoted so often that way today, usually by a po-faced man on the news with an abiding, if understandable, dislike of CCTV cameras. He was writing about the impossibility of keeping immoral women chaste. Even the guards would be screwing them, given half a chance. And how are you supposed to guard against that? Try to bear this in mind next time the quote appears. If nothing else, it adds a little frisson to the civil liberties debate.

Roman women were, assuredly, not as licentious as Juvenal claimed. But they certainly had the potential for a more exciting life than their Athenian predecessors. They could even travel to the furthest reaches of the empire: the earliest example of a woman's handwriting in Britain comes from Vindolanda – a Roman fort near Hadrian's Wall – pretty much the northernmost point of the Roman Empire. Claudia Severa was the wife of a fort commander there, Aelius Broccus, and she wrote a letter to her sister, Sulpicia Lepidina, asking her to a birthday party. Although the main part of Severa's letter, like those of most people at the time, was written by a scribe, she adds a closing message herself, exhorting her sister to come. Not only does this show us that some women travelled across the known world, but it also proves that they were educated. Severa has basic literacy skills; even if a scribe does most of her writing for her, it isn't because she can't write, but rather because she can afford an amanuensis. When she wants to say something from the heart, however, 'Goodbye my sister, my dearest soul', she ignores the secretary and writes it herself.

Roman women could earn their way out of perpetual male guardianship, too. Women would be under the guardianship of their fathers, or other nearest male relative, although it was more a technical hindrance than anything else. While some women undoubtedly had very strict, inflexible guardians, many more would have responded to the guardianship of a father or brother in much the same way teenagers now respond to the rules their parents might have: with limited obedience. Nonetheless, a woman couldn't officially conduct business transactions, inherit money or free slaves without a guardian to transact these affairs on her behalf. What she could do, however, was have three children, whereupon she would be freed of guardianship. This was a law introduced by the emperor Augustus, the *ius trium libero-rum*, or 'right of three children'. Give birth to three Roman kids, and a woman could inherit and make transactions whenever she liked, without a guardian to interfere.

The correlation of female responsibility and childbirth has a long history, and continues today: how many times do we see people claiming moral authority over a contentious issue – from the serious, such as publicising the home addresses of paedophiles, to the comparatively trivial, such as demanding that no one cycles in a park in case children are accidentally injured – because they are parents? The subtext of these sentiments is surely not that parents care more, while non-parents would cheerfully see a child mown down by a passing cyclist, pausing only to admire the tyre marks. Rather, it seems to suggest a belief that a certain gravitas only exists among those with children: the childless, or those whose children are safely grown up, cannot be expected to have a proper understanding of how a park should best be organised.

It's worth mentioning that most of the women we've looked at in Athens, Sparta and Rome have been comparatively well-to-do. The wife of a fort commander, the daughter of a Spartan king and the long-term partner of the most influential man in Athens are hardly representative of the ordinary women of their times. Don't the less well off deserve a few pages, too? Again, we come up against a problem with understanding these periods in time: the history, the plays, the philosophy and everything else was written by comparatively rich men. And while Horace might wish to commemorate his beloved Chloe, Catullus his Lesbia and Propertius his Cynthia, there isn't any love poetry to lower-class women. When we read Cicero's letters, we find out about his wife, Terentia, and his daughter, Tullia, but not about his laundry-woman, or the woman who ran the local bar or brothel.

We know that a Roman matron could run a business, such as Coelia Mascellina, who imported wine and oil in the second century CE. We see bricks and pipes stamped with women's names because they owned a brick-making factory. And Eumachia, a Pompeian woman, was even the patroness of the local fullers: they erected a statue to commemorate her. However, these women weren't impoverished, they were respectable businesswomen.

We just don't know very much about very many middle- and lower-class women from past ages. The washerwoman and her lover, even if he wrote her reams of exquisite verse – even if he could write at all, when education had to be paid for – are lost to us. Whenever we are despairing of the ceaseless need to communicate that characterises our time – text messages, emails, status updates and all the rest, however banal – we should at least try to think about this: for the first time in history, there is a record of what millions of ordinary people – boring and fascinating, rich and poor – think and do with their time. This may not be very interesting to the rest of us. We may tire of reading people's poorly spelled, cliché-riddled descriptions of their tedious days at work. But we shouldn't forget that trying to piece together ordinary people's lives at almost any period in history is incredibly hard, precisely because they didn't have anywhere to register their views. Future historians might well find us grindingly banal, but at least they should have some material with which to judge us.

But ancient Romans of the lower orders are hard to pin down. And women all the more so. The latter were, of course, politically irrelevant because they had no vote; and so, to all intents and purposes, they didn't exist. Roman consuls or emperors often tried to curry favour with the plebs with food programmes, doling out grain to the poor. If that sounds charmingly paternalistic, think again. It was, of course, pure politics: no one cared on humanitarian grounds if the unwashed poor keeled over from starvation. But even poor men had votes, and they could often be bought for the price of a few loaves of bread and a day out. One of the best-known phrases in all Latin literature comes again from Juvenal, who described the cheap price of the masses with his customary fury: 'The people, who once had in their power military command, civil office, legions, everything, now restrains itself, and prays anxiously for just two things: bread, and circuses' – 'panem et circenses'. But the grain dole wasn't for everyone: each man received enough grain for himself. Women received nothing: no vote meant no free lunch. Children were included in separate doles; predictably, boys received a larger allowance than girls. The boys could grow up to be soldiers, so they were worth a greater investment.

When we are thinking about the lives of Rome's poor, and its slaves, we should also remember that women formed a minority of them. Girls might be exposed as babies, because keeping them was too expensive and produced no long-term benefit. They might simply die sooner than boys from disease, caused by malnutrition. Certainly, large households tended to have a majority of male slaves, perhaps about 60 per cent. Girls were very often considered literally worthless. And before we pat ourselves smugly on the back at how very far we've come, this is still true in many parts of the world today. Figures in *Half the Sky*, a book on modern gender inequality by Nicholas Kristof and Sheryl WuDunn, are just as chilling. China has 107 men for every 100 women, Pakistan has 111 men for every 100 women. Across the world, 2 million girls a year disappear: they are abandoned at birth, or not treated when they are ill, or worse. Certainly poor citizen women in the Roman world were treated less well than its slaves, male and female: at least the slaves were property, and therefore had a monetary value. So let us try to bear all this in mind next polling day. Not being bothered to exercise your right to vote is a privilege that many women still don't have. Dismissing politicians as all the same is a luxury. Our votes may not seem very important to us, but our lives without them would be immeasurably worse. For we needed universal suffrage to be firmly and unarguably in place before we could demand equal rights. And while it may be tempting for people to mutter that feminism is old-fashioned, boring and a fight already won, we only have to look at the statistics to see that what is true for some women is a very long way short of being true for us all.

So, let us return to the women we know a little more about. Girls married young in Rome, although they were probably a couple of years older than their Athenian counterparts. Calpurnia, for example, became Pliny the Younger's third wife when she was about fifteen, and he was about forty. He praises her qualities in a letter to her aunt, Calpurnia Hispulla: 'She is highly intelligent, and thrifty. She loves me, which is a sure sign of her virtue. In addition to these qualities, she has an enthusiasm for literature, which began with her affection for me. She has my books, she reads them, she has even learned them by heart.' Poor Calpurnia, she must have been either terribly polite or wholly infatuated with her husband to be such an enthusiast of his prose. Schoolchildren of her age have, for generations, read Pliny's letters without being moved to reread or learn them by heart, even (in my case) when faced with an exam on them. So perhaps Calpurnia was deeply in love with her husband. Either that or she had more salacious reading matter stuck between the pages of his sensible books. One rather hopes for the latter.

Marriage was often a business arrangement in ancient Rome, as indeed it can still be now. The emperor Augustus, for all his commitment to moral rectitude, didn't hesitate to use his daughter Julia as a political pawn. Julia was married off to Agrippa, with whom Augustus needed to cement an alliance. Then Agrippa died, and Livia, Augustus' wife, pushed her son Tiberius towards centre stage as Augustus' eventual successor. Julia found herself in the hot seat once again. She was soon married to Tiberius, her stepbrother, and when Augustus found out that she was less than a model of wifely fidelity, he exiled her to a prison island for five years and, according to Suetonius, even considered executing her. Being the emperor's daughter didn't necessarily mean having a good life.

But many women in the imperial household wielded considerable power. Livia certainly did more than the weaving, which was the archetypal woman's work. For example, Suetonius mentions her requesting that Augustus grant citizenship to a man from Gaul. Augustus wasn't moved to do so, but still we can see that Livia is no meek Roman matron: she is quite comfortable getting involved in detailed political and social matters. Indeed, she may have been comfortable with a whole lot more than that: Tiberius only made a public announcement of Augustus' death, and his own succession, after getting rid of Agrippa Postumus, Augustus' grandson (the son of Julia and Agrippa). Postumus was killed by a tribune who had received a written order to do so: 'It was in doubt whether Augustus had left the order, as he was dying, to prevent civil war after his death, or whether Livia had issued it in Augustus' name, with Tiberius' knowledge or not.'

Suetonius, it must be remembered, was the ancient equivalent of the gossip pages of a tabloid: no claim was too salacious for him to omit. He was chief secretary to the emperor Hadrian, and so presumably had access to confidential imperial paperwork. But he was writing a century after Augustus had died, so we shouldn't view his work as reportage. He certainly couldn't have spoken to any eye-witnesses of these events, so he was presumably reporting rumours, gossip and scandal, following the no-smoke-without-fire principle. Perhaps he was right about Livia, and she really was a monster, determined to see her son, Tiberius, succeed Augustus, rather than any of his numerous blood-relatives. Perhaps she didn't hesitate to have those killed who stood in her way. Certainly Robert Graves – who translated Suetonius in addition to writing the historical novel *I, Claudius* – viewed her that way – although the success of the latter, and its television adaptation, can make it hard to remember that it is fiction, based on the biographies of the biggest gossip in the ancient world. But whether Livia was a murderous psychopath or simply the wife of the first Roman emperor and mother of the second, she was a woman of enormous influence. Tacitus describes her friendship as an extremely valuable commodity, when he remarks upon 'Urgulania, whose friendship with the Augusta raised her above the law'. The Augusta (as Livia was known after Augustus' death) couldn't keep her friend from being summoned to court in this instance, but she did pay off Urgulania's accuser, and Urgulania remained, in Tacitus' view, excessively influential in Roman society purely because of her intimacy with Livia.

Livia was the first in a long line of imperial women who wielded unofficial but considerable power. Claudius managed to have four wives, the latter two of whom at least were not women you would wish to cross. Messalina, Claudius' third wife, was a serial adulterer, according to Tacitus. So much so that she eventually married (albeit bigamously) one of her lovers, Gaius Silius. At which point, Tacitus says, 'domus principis inhorruerat' – 'the emperor's household shuddered'. Messalina was no longer indulging in an overblown affair, but was seen to be making a very real threat to Claudius' principate. In other words, people feared that the emperor's wife could be the mechanism of succession, and with good reason, in Tacitus' view: 'Without doubt, fear rose up when they thought of how obtuse Claudius was, and how uxorious, and when they considered the many murders carried out on Messalina's orders.' Once Claudius had been told what

Messalina was up to, he panicked that Silius might be making a bid to take over as emperor: 'Full of fear, Claudius kept asking if he was still the emperor, if Silius was still a private citizen.' So it wasn't just his servants and freedmen who were afraid that Messalina had the power to orchestrate a coup, it was the emperor himself. Messalina's power, however, melted away, once Claudius moved against her; she begged for her life, but to no avail. She was too afraid to commit suicide, so one of the Praetorian Guard took a dagger from her hands and ran her through. Threats to the emperor were dealt with in much the same way, whether the conspirators were ambitious senators or unloving wives.

The modern view of Claudius is that he was nothing like the idiot most ancient writers considered him to be, but that he was misunderstood and denigrated because he had mild disabilities; that we are a more sensitive audience nowadays, and realise physical deformity and mental incapacity do not go hand in hand. But Claudius' tendency to leap from marital frying pan into nuptial fire suggests that, if not an idiot, he was certainly more than usually unlucky in his choice of wives. To have one wife who plots your downfall is unfortunate, but to have two transcends carelessness and begins to look like masochism. Messalina was swiftly replaced by Agrippina, great-granddaughter of Augustus, mother of Nero, and Claudius' own niece. Perhaps the moral of this tale is that if you have to change the law on incest in order to marry your niece, your story may not have a happy ending. As far as Tacitus was concerned, the marriage didn't even have a happy beginning: 'All of Rome was now obedient to a woman ... It was a strained, almost masculine despotism.' Even conquered kings could see that Agrippina was a virtual equal to Claudius. When Caratacus, a rebellious British king, was captured and brought to Rome in chains, Claudius pardoned him, his wife and his brothers. 'And they, released from their chains, paid homage to Agrippina, who was seated nearby on another dais, with the same praise and thanks as they had offered the emperor.' No wonder conservative writers like Tacitus were appalled by Agrippina; this was certainly not how a Roman *matrona* was supposed to behave.

Soon Agrippina's ambition was not sated by being the emperor's wife. Agrippina wanted to be the mother of the next emperor, too, and she could see that Claudius was gradually becoming disenchanted with her and her son Nero, and turning back to his own son, Britannicus, as his intended successor. She decided to have Claudius poisoned, and turned to another woman of dubious morality, Locusta, to help her. Locusta found the appropriate poison to dispatch Claudius without making it look too obvious that he had been murdered by his wife. No wonder she warrants one of Tacitus' bitchier epithets: 'Agrippina chose an expert in such matters, a woman called Locusta, who had recently been sentenced for poisoning, and who had a long career in imperial service ahead.' The poison was administered, according to Tacitus' sources, on a plate of mushrooms. When it appeared that the poisoning had failed, Agrippina didn't panic. The contemporary accounts on which Tacitus based his own history said she had an accomplice: the imperial doctor. He put a feather down Claudius' throat, to help him vomit up whatever had made him sick, and thus hasten his recovery. But the feather was dipped in poison, and Claudius swiftly died.

But if Agrippina thought that her son would be a puppet king, easily controlled by her, she underestimated him. Nero was only sixteen years old when he became emperor, and for a while he was susceptible to her influence: 'Every honour was publicly heaped upon her, and when the military tribune asked for his usual watchword, Nero gave "The best of mothers".' But sixteen-year-old boys aren't amenable for ever. Nero soon found a girlfriend, Acte, of whom Agrippina thoroughly disapproved. Agrippina became highly critical of Nero, and started suggesting that she might have backed the wrong horse. After all, Britannicus was growing up quickly, and he was Claudius' real heir. At this threat to his principate, Nero proved he was truly his mother's son: he called in Locusta. But Britannicus was trickier to poison than Claudius, employing a taster who checked all his food and drink. That was no problem for Nero and Locusta, however: 'A harmless drink, which had been tested by the taster and was very warm, was handed to Britannicus. He refused it because it was too hot. Cold water was added, along with poison, which spread through his whole body. Speechless, he stopped breathing.'

Agrippina knew her days were numbered. The confidence needed to murder a stepbrother was not very far short of the confidence needed to murder a mother. She tried everything, according to one of Tacitus' sources, Cluvius Rufus, to get back into Nero's good books, even incest. But Nero had his eyes on someone else, a mistress named Poppaea, who 'had every quality, except virtue'. Perhaps it seems appropriate that Agrippina's downfall should come at the instigation of another woman. Poppaea needled Nero, knowing her own power could only grow if Agrippina was off the scene. And sure enough, Nero was soon arranging to have his mother killed. He considered poison, but Agrippina took a range of prophylactic antidotes: you can't poison a poisoner. Nero's final scheme differs according to various authors, but Tacitus' version tells of a ship with a collapsing ceiling, designed to kill her apparently by accident. As Anicetus, Nero's fleet-commander and partner in crime suggested, 'Nothing produces accidents like the sea.'

The collapsible ship almost worked but not quite. And even with the shoulder injury she acquired, Agrippina was a good swimmer.

Nonetheless, she might still have been killed, had not her friend Acerronia intervened. Failing to read the subtleties of the situation, Acerronia assumed that help would most swiftly be brought to one of the imperial family. So she cried out that she, Acerronia, was Agrippina, and that the ship's crew should help her, the emperor's mother. The men beat her to death with their oars.

Agrippina knew her time was up, and she waited for Nero's next attack. Anicetus arrived at her house with two other men, one of whom promptly clubbed her round the head. Realising this really was the end, she told them to strike her womb, which had once nurtured her son and killer. They stabbed her there repeatedly. And as if this story wasn't full enough of symbolism, Poppaea didn't live long enough to die of old age, either. Six years later, in CE 65, she was kicked in the stomach by Nero while pregnant with his child, and she too died. Wombs weren't always a metaphor for life-giving, in imperial circles.

It may seem like there are no good women in the whole period of imperial Rome. This, of course, isn't the case. There were plenty of good empresses, such as Faustina the Elder, wife of the second-century CE emperor Antoninus Pius, and Faustina the Younger, wife of his successor, Marcus Aurelius. Both emperors established grain doles exclusively for girls (who traditionally got less food than boys, remember) in memory of their virtuous wives. But there's no doubt about it, the conservative, salacious historians and biographers of the ancient world did love a female villain. We must turn to the less gossipy Pliny the Younger for a story where a woman is a hero instead. Caecina Paetus was invited to commit suicide during Claudius' reign. These invitations could not be refused: if you were asked to commit suicide and did, your family could usually inherit your property, and continue to live as they had when you were alive. But if you waited until the courts convicted you on some charge, and you were executed, your property was then forfeit. So suicide really was the only way to avoid bringing disgrace and ruin on your family. But Paetus was afraid of dying, and couldn't bring himself to do it. Arria, his wife, showed him the way: 'That deed of hers was glorious, when she took a dagger, drove it into her breast, and pulled it out again. She offered it to her husband with the immortal, almost divine words, "It does not hurt, Paetus".' Even female heroes didn't always die a natural death.

All these women, the monstrous wives and mothers, and the heroic ones too, are constructs, however. We don't really know what Agrippina was like; we don't even know the truth of half the stories that are told about her. Biographers and historians construct their characters, just like novelists do. They choose what to include and what to leave out. If an author is a contemporary of their subject matter, they'll be subject to bias: common sense tells us that a historian won't write a warts-and-all biography of a powerful figure if it could cause trouble. Even the historians who write some decades after the events they describe are biased. Take a writer like Tacitus, for example. Having lived through the violent days of the emperor Domitian, Tacitus is no fan of the imperial system: he has a sort of survivor's guilt, which means he loves those who stand up to corruption (and often die for it), and hates the servile masses who accede to an emperor's whims. And it's hard for him to be dispassionate about an emperor when he doesn't think there should be emperors in the first place. Then there's the issue of verification: Tacitus only tells us about his individual sources when they disagree. But what happens when they are all in perfect harmony, yet still wrong? Rumours didn't start becoming facts with the dawn of the Internet; it has happened for millennia.

Rather than wring our hands at how impossible it is truly to know anything, we must view history on its own terms. By reading, for example, Tacitus' account of the reign of Nero, we may not be learning the objective truth of everything that happened during the years CE 54 to 68 (quite aside from everything Tacitus chooses to leave out, or simply doesn't know); however, it is a fantastic story, some of which is verifiably true. We're also reading something written only a few decades after Nero, based on contemporary sources, some of whom at least must have had extraordinary access to their subject. And by looking at what he mentions and what he misses out, we learn about Tacitus, as well as the people who played a major role in an extraordinary time in history.

But that isn't the only way to find out about, say, women in the ancient world. The ones who really existed, as we've established already, aren't always well recorded. But there are authors who give us a different type of insight into the ancient role and view of women: poets, playwrights, satirists and comedians. The women who populate the pages of Homer, Euripides, Juvenal or Virgil may not be real, in the sense that Agrippina was a real, historical figure. But they are a different kind of real: real female characters that men dreamed up and put on a page, or in a song, or on a stage. And that tells us something about the role of women in the societies that created these characters. After all, if women couldn't be police officers, then we wouldn't see female police officers in our television drama. All women police officers may not be like the ones in *CSI*, but if you were trying to understand our society from a point far in the future, the cultural prominence of detective fiction and drama would certainly be interesting. It might give you a rather inflated idea of the crime figures of our age, but if you were an astute reader, it would reveal a great deal more than that.

Literature's first women are those in Homer's epic poems, *The Iliad* and *The Odyssey*. They are both stories of men: *The Iliad* covers a chunk of time during the Trojan War, and *The Odyssey* describes the return journey to Ithaca of Odysseus and his men after the Trojan War. They are, however, thick with extraordinary female characters. Goddesses such as Athene, Artemis and Aphrodite are able to jump in and direct the action, at least until Zeus notices that they are plotting against him. Aphrodite is keen to support Paris, who, after all, became her favourite when he declared her the most beautiful of all the goddesses. And lesser goddesses, such as Thetis the sea-nymph, play a part too. Thetis is on the side of the Greeks, encouraging her son, the warrior Achilles, and comforting him after the death of his beloved friend Patroclus. These supernatural female characters are in the middle of the action in a way that the ordinary women of epic poetry can't be.

There are devoted wives and mothers in both poems: Penelope, who waits patiently for her wandering husband in *The Odyssey*; and Andromache and Hecabe in *The Iliad*. In Book Six of *The Iliad*, Hector leaves the battlefield outside Troy and returns home. He meets Andromache, his wife, on the city walls. She reminds him that her parents are dead: her father killed by Achilles, her mother by Artemis. She has only Hector left, he is her everything: 'Hector – you are father and mother to me, brother and husband too.' We, the readers, know that Achilles will have killed Hector before the war is over, before the book is finished, even. So Andromache gives a name and face to the losses of war. These aren't just soldiers being killed, but husbands, brothers, fathers and sons. Homer uses Andromache to clarify exactly what is at stake when a city loses a war. She, and the other Trojan women, will be enslaved by their husbands' killers when Troy falls. Andromache will become the slave-concubine of Neoptolemus, the son of Achilles, her husband's killer. In Euripides' retelling of her story, her baby son by Hector, Astyanax, is hurled to his death, to ensure he never grows up to avenge his father. Casualties of war aren't limited to the battlefield.

Although he has a respectable wife waiting for him at home, Odysseus' wanderings aren't purely geographical. And the women he meets aren't always the trustworthy kind: the enchantress Circe, for example, turns half of his men into pigs. When they arrive on Aeaea, her island, Odysseus divides his men into two groups, one led by him and one by his comrade Eurylochus. They draw lots, and Eurylochus' men go to explore the island, while Odysseus and his men wait on the shore. When Eurylochus' men reach Circe's palace, she invites them in and gives them food and drink in abundance. Only Eurylochus, suspicious of her motives, refuses her hospitality and waits outside. His suspicions are justified: in a scene echoed by Hayao Miyazaki's animé film *Spirited Away*, those who take excessive pleasure in eating and drinking strange food are rewarded by being turned into the dustbins of the animal kingdom, pigs. Only the suspicious outsider – Eurylochus in *The Odyssey*, Chihiro in *Spirited Away* – remains in human form. Eurylochus returns to Odysseus and explains what has happened. Odysseus then meets the god Hermes, who gives him a magic herb that will prevent Circe's poison taking its effect on him. He offers further advice: Odysseus must threaten Circe with his sword, at which point she will invite him into her bed. But he must make her swear to do him no harm, or she will render him 'kakon kai anēnora' – 'broken and unmanned'. Odysseus follows Hermes' instructions to the letter, and post-coitally persuades Circe to return his men to their pre-pig state. Once she has done so, Odysseus and his men spend a year in her palace feasting on meat and wine. His men eventually demand that they leave Aeaea and get on with their journey, and Circe sends them on their way with advice and gifts.

Circe is an archetypal witch: she casts enchantments over men, she is sexually alluring, she is dangerous. She is also physically weak: Odysseus has only to threaten her with harm, and she capitulates. But she is sneaky. If she isn't forced to do what's right, she will unman him. Women, and especially foreign women, are routinely defined by Greeks and Romans in these terms. We might consider it misogyny, or xenophobia, but there is more than a touch of the Bond villainess to these archetypes, a woman who will lure a decent man into her lair for sexual pleasure and danger combined: only the villainess's smutty name is missing. Odysseus is a Greek hero, whose Homeric epithet is *polumētis* – meaning 'of many counsels, crafty, wily'. But even he, the most ingenious man in the heroic age, the inventor of the Trojan horse, still needs the help of a god to best the cunning and dangerous Circe.

Virgil paints a rather more sympathetic portrait of a foreign woman who embarks on a relationship with an epic hero in Book Four of *The Aeneid*. Dido's doomed love affair with Aeneas is pure tragedy. At the start of the book, she is in an untenable position: having fled Tyre, and her homicidal brother, Dido is vulnerable in her new territory of Carthage. Various African princes have tried to persuade her to marry, and she must forge alliances somewhere: she is surrounded by hostile tribes. But she loves only her dead husband, Sychaeus. Nonetheless, Juno and Venus conspire against her so she falls hopelessly in love with Aeneas. He, for a time, reciprocates. Like Odysseus, he is perfectly happy to postpone his heroic journey while he has a love affair. But eventually Jupiter intervenes, and sends Mercury to tell Aeneas that he has spent long enough in Carthage. Aeneas' epithet is *pius* – 'dutiful'. He can shirk his duty (to travel to Italy and resettle the surviving Trojans there, the early ancestors of the Romans) no longer. He plans to leave Carthage, and orders his men to fit out the fleet. Dido, of course, realises what is happening, and corners him: 'Did you really hope to hide such a huge crime, you traitor? And leave my land without a word? Didn't our love hold you here, or your pledge to me, or is Dido doomed to die a cruel death?' she demands. Anyone who has ever been chucked would want to be as cleanly articulate in their fury and sorrow as Dido. Why are they leaving in winter? she asks. The storms will damage the fleet. She begs him to stay, in tears, reminding him of the vows they both made. Then she turns to the damage their relationship has done: by throwing her lot in with Aeneas, she has antagonised local tribes and rulers. If he leaves her, they will surely turn upon her. Her brother might come and destroy her city. She could end up the concubine of a local prince she despises. She doesn't even have a baby, 'parvulus aula luderet Aeneas' – 'a little Aeneas, playing in the halls', to remind her of him, once he's gone. He answers her accusations as best he can, remembering Jupiter's admonition that he must leave Carthage quickly. His apparent coldness finally breaks her, and she snarls insults at him: 'No goddess was your mother, nor was Dardanus your ancestor, you traitor. The hard rocks of the Caucasus gave birth to you, and Hyrcanean tigers suckled you.' She promises him that she will soon be dead, and even then she will pursue him as a shade. But he leaves anyway, and she is as good as her word: she reminds the gods that she would have been happy, even after the death of Sychaeus, if only the Trojans had never come to Carthage. Then she falls upon a sword. When she and Aeneas meet again, in the underworld, in Book Six, she won't even meet his eyes. She is, at least, reunited with her beloved Sychaeus.

Virgil creates an astonishing character in Dido. She is every bit the barbarian woman archetype – passionate, intense and dangerous. There is, after all, a real risk that Aeneas will abandon his divine mission to stay with her, and if he does that, the future of Rome itself is at stake. Again, the gods have to get involved to put our hero's quest back on track. And let's not forget when this was being written: Virgil began writing *The Aeneid* in 29 BCE, when the memory of Cleopatra

– who came so close to destroying everything the Romans held dear – was fresh in the minds of his audience. Dido is clearly meant to remind us of Cleopatra, and of the dangers of Roman men becoming embroiled with Eastern women. Virgil's audience might well be thanking Jupiter that Octavian was less susceptible to these barbarian charms than Julius Caesar or Mark Antony. Yet still, Dido is a hugely sympathetic, beautifully drawn character. She is no mere symbol; her death is just as devastating as it would be if she appeared in her own tragedy, rather than as an interlude in a hero's quest for a new home.

And women play the most extraordinary roles in Greek tragedy. The ultimate barbarian queen is, of course, Euripides' version of Medea. Medea was a princess, the daughter of Aeëtes of Colchis. She was the niece of Circe and shared many of her skills, witchcraft especially. Medea fell in love with Jason when he came questing for the golden fleece. She used magic potions to help him steal it away from her father. She fled with him to Corinth. They had two sons – a happy and productive marriage. But at the start of the play we find things have not gone well for Medea. Jason has left her for another woman. And not just any other woman, but Glauce, the daughter of Creon, king of Corinth. In other words, he is leaving his older wife, the mother of his children, for a new young bride. So far, so mid-life crisis. But there is more to Jason's treachery than that: he knows perfectly well that as fugitives in a foreign land, he and Medea have very little power. By marrying into Corinth's royal family, he is seriously improving his lot, which he feels has been sorely damaged by Medea's barbarian excesses. Sure, she helped him complete his quest for the fleece, but in doing so, she left a trail of bodies in their wake, not least that of her own brother. Medea, understandably, feels that while remarriage will help Jason's cause, it can only weaken her own, and that of her children. Why would a new wife look kindly upon Jason's sons from his first marriage?

She bemoans her situation in one of the most famous speeches of all Greek tragedy, explicitly listing the ways in which women have little or no control over their lives. A woman must buy her husband with a hefty dowry. She can't divorce him, or reject him. She has to learn to please her husband. If the marriage is a success, her life is enviable, but 'ei de mē, thanein chreōn' – 'if not, death is better'. Men can look elsewhere for partners if they get bored at home, but a woman cannot. Men tell women that they can stay at home out of danger, while men have to fight in battles: 'Fools. I would rather stand on the battle line three times than bear a child once.' This is an explicit comparison of male and female heroics. Men stand on the battle line, run the risk of an early grave and are called heroes. Women bear children, run the risk of an early grave and are left for a younger model. No wonder Medea is angry.

She rages at Jason, and plots her revenge. She pretends to be sweet, and asks him to keep their sons with him. She will go into exile alone. At least then their boys will have a chance for a happier future than their mother could offer them. The real surprise is that Jason is stupid enough to fall for all this. We've known Medea for twenty minutes and we know better than to trust her. He, sadly, does not. Medea sends the boys with a robe and a crown for Jason's new bride. She has coated them in a terrible poison, so that when Glauce tries them on, the dress and crown fuse to her flesh and start burning through it. Her father rushes to her aid, and he too dies, melted into her in agony. The children are rushed back to Medea, and she takes the ultimate revenge on Jason: she kills their sons. It is a truly horrifying moment. We often feel divorced from the participants of Greek tragedy: how many of us can relate to a story where someone accidentally kills his father and marries his mother? How many of us know how it feels to inadvertently kill our husbands with poisoned centaur's blood, which we have credulously believed is a love potion? Do we really know how it feels to be marooned on a desert island by our friends because we have a gammy foot? But *Medea* is a play that sings across the centuries: we all know how it feels to be abandoned. We know how it feels to hate someone we used to love. And we know how it feels to want revenge.

Most of us, happily, stop short of killing our children to spite our ex-partners. But not all of us: a Medea story, or its male equivalent (in that case, more a Hercules story, as he too kills his own children), appears in the news cycle every few months. Sadly, the desire to make someone suffer at the expense of a child's life still exists. Even those who stop short of physically harming their children often don't hesitate to use their children as weapons against their ex-partner. After all, who does it hurt if you tell people your partner used to abuse the children? The very person you hate most in the world. And also your children.

But Medea takes a more complicated revenge. She knows that when she kills her sons, she will inflict a greater pain on herself than she does on Jason. She loves them more than he does – he was, after all, fully prepared to see them rotting in exile. And she is by far the more emotionally complex of the two of them: loss, for her, is a much more brutal business than it is for him. But she also knows that the only real harm she can cause him is the destruction of his line. By exterminating both his offspring and his new wife (with her potential to create new offspring), she leaves him without an heir, cursed and unloved. It is the ultimate vengeance. It simply comes at an extortionately high price.

Nonetheless, Medea is a woman to whom cutting off her nose to spite her face seems positively easy. She can and will cause herself a lifetime's agony, just to cause Jason a moment of it. Is this any kind of excuse? Of course not: Medea is a psychopath. Children aren't weapons in an attritional war, they're people. Albeit small, noisy ones.

Her story doesn't excuse the destructive behaviour of people who don't get their own way and turn on their children with a shotgun, a knife or a pack of lies about their other parent. What it does, though, is help us to understand how easy, how reasonable, monstrous behaviour can appear to someone who feels wronged. We're so keen to establish ourselves as victims, knowing full well that once we have construed ourselves as put-upon and mistreated, it becomes markedly easier for us to behave abysmally. Self-justification is that much simpler if you start with the handicap that someone did you wrong and it isn't fair. Medea should remind us all that revenge wreaks at least as much havoc on its perpetrator as on its victim.

It's worth pointing out, however, that Euripides doesn't offer any criticism of her actions. Quite the reverse: she escapes all punishment for her deeds, other than her own suffering. She has an escape plan in place before she embarks on her homicidal spree, and she leaves the play on a winged chariot, belonging to her grandfather, Helios, the sun god. In other words, the gods themselves accept that Medea's punishment of Jason was appropriate, even though, to our eyes, it looks anything but. Jason, meanwhile, is left a broken man: no royal bride, no children. He doesn't even have their bodies to bury, and as she departs, Medea delivers one final blow: she foresees Jason's unheroic death, smacked in the head by wood from his own boat, the *Argo*.

Medea is staged with incredible frequency. It's a rare year that doesn't boast at least three productions at the Edinburgh Fringe Festival alone. The reason is surely that it feels so contemporary: the timeless battle of the sexes, the disintegration of a marriage, the need to wound those who have injured us. However much the play attracts modern theatre-goers, though, the Athenians didn't love Euripides' *Medea*. When it was first produced in 431 BCE, they gave it third prize

(out of three) at the Dionysia. Women killing children was as culturally taboo then as it is now.

Not all women in tragedies were murderous, however. Sophocles
gives us Antigone, daughter of Oedipus, sister of Polynices and Eteocles. Her two brothers fought over the Theban throne: they were supposed to share it in turns, but Eteocles refused to give it up at the end
of his year. Polynices massed an army and declared war on Thebes. The
brothers ended up killing each other in single combat. Their uncle,
Creon, buried the 'good' brother, Eteocles, and left the warmonger
to rot. This, we must remember, was a terrible fate: if a Greek wasn't
properly buried, if he didn't have at least a handful of dirt thrown
over him, he wouldn't be able to cross the River Acheron and enter
the underworld. So Antigone defies her uncle's law, and buries her
brother. Her uncle – even though Antigone is his niece and is engaged
to his son – promptly has her buried alive. By the time he realises his
mistake, it is too late. She has hanged herself with a linen noose.

Antigone is a very different creature from Medea: she is obsessed
with family loyalty, with preserving the cursed family into which
she was born. She prefers to be a sister than a niece or a fiancée, and
believes that doing her duty by her dead brothers is more than worth
dying for. She does, of course, still die, so we may choose to see her
story as less than empowering. Nonetheless, she offers an audience,
ancient or modern, a moral choice: is it more important to obey the
laws of the state, even when you believe they are unjust, or to obey
moral imperatives, even if that obedience will cause your destruction?

Antigone believes her religious duty is worth far more than merely
defying the law: so is she a freedom fighter, or a terrorist? Socrates was
prepared to give up his life rather than overthrow a law that unjustly
caused his death: preservation of the state was everything, personal
sacrifice was nothing. But Antigone overthrows the law and then dies:

she would rather preserve the family unit, broken and dead though her family is, than abide by the law.

We'll finish this chapter on a cheerier note: there are fictional women who neither kill their loved ones nor die walled up in a cave. Aristophanes comes to the rescue once again. His play *Lysistrata* is a fantasy. By 411 BCE, when it was written, Athens had been at war with Sparta for twenty years, and had recently suffered catastrophic losses on the Sicilian Expedition, an ill-advised campaign against Syracuse, in Sicily, which culled the best part of a generation of Athenian men. Somehow, Athens managed to stagger on in its other war with Sparta. But everyone was sick of it. And Aristophanes, so often able to catch the public mood, wrote a play in which the war was finally ended.

The men of Greece have done a lousy job of stopping the war themselves, so the women intervene. Lysistrata, an Athenian, calls her friends from Athens together, and arranges a meeting with Lampito, a gruff Spartan woman. They make an agreement: no sex till the war is over. Husbands and boyfriends will be teased and tortured, but the women won't give in until the men agree to make peace. Aristophanes has a great deal of fun with this: the women are all nymphomaniacs, so it half kills them to refrain from sex. The men walk on with huge erections, providing a visual clue as to how the women's plan is progressing. Eventually, the men capitulate, and the Greeks can finally make love not war.

I've mentioned before that Aristophanes cannot be taken at his word. The women of Athens and Sparta clearly had nothing like the influence required to bring an end to the war. Well-to-do Athenian women, remember, couldn't even leave the house unaccompanied. Nonetheless, these female characters are given all the good sense in the play: the men are weak and foolish. The women might be sex-mad, but they are practical and determined, and prepared to put aside short-term pleasure for long-term gain. It is, of course, important to bear in mind that these female characters were being played onstage by men in masks, so they weren't as female as all that. Still, if all the real women were cloistered away, classicist-feminists must take what we can get.

6

There's No Place Like Rome

It's time to put the people and politics of the ancient world into their proper context. We've looked at different societies in different periods: from the golden age of Athens to the final days of Rome, from the exotic east to the frozen north. But ancient peoples didn't live on the pages of an atlas, any more than we do. They lived in real towns, real houses, real farms. They lived in the city and longed to escape to the country. They had seaside boltholes that they could go to when the weather became too hot or the politics too oppressive. They had strong views on the most respectable ways to live, in a city-state, a provincial town or a rural idyll.

There was a far stronger connection between these different parts of their worlds, too. As they had to ride through countryside for days at a time to get from Rome to Naples, we can assume they picked up more than a glancing awareness of their surroundings on the way. It's a very different process from speeding through the countryside as most of us do now: driving along a motorway, or sitting on a high-speed train. The scenery moves past so quickly that it's hard to tell which part of a country you are in at any one time. The banks of trees by the train tracks and the fields near the arterial roads look much the same on one side of a country as they do on another. And we live on a small island: in larger countries people simply fly over the chunks they need to travel through. Even the flight information, which we used to see on television screens as we flew over the Rocky Mountains or the Great Lakes – reminding us of where we really were – is in jeopardy: terrorists can't blow up a plane over Detroit if they don't know when they're over Detroit, goes the theory.

For better or worse, we have become disconnected from those who live in the other parts of our world, our country and even our county. Many of us are suburban, by choice or necessity. We're persuaded by our newspapers to fear the inner cities, with their young, violent underclass. And we're encouraged by the newspapers' lifestyle supplements to aspire to the life of the country squire, or gentleman farmer. We're embarrassed by the ordinariness of where we live. Yet the country life that so many people wish to achieve is a chimera, an oasis of green, pleasant land that disappears when we look at it hard: no rural schools, impossible house prices, closing pubs and post offices. Does the rural idyll even exist? And did it ever, outside of costume dramas?

The first author to really attempt to document the countryside is Hesiod, a Greek poet who lived in Boeotia, in central Greece, in the late eighth century BCE. Hesiod wrote two poems that have survived to the present day: *Theogony*, an origin story of the gods, and *Works and Days*, which is rather more difficult to define. It is, among other things, a list of agricultural tasks, together with the best and worst times for these to be carried out. It is also an extended moan directed at his brother Perses, who has vexed Hesiod in a number of ways: firstly, he has pinched more than his fair share of their joint inheritance; secondly, he has bribed various local noblemen to enable him to continue in his life of petty crime; and thirdly, he is work-shy, and will soon be impoverished (if he isn't already), in spite of his thieving tendencies, because of his inability to carry out his landowning responsibilities on the appropriate dates. Indeed, to describe *Works and Days* as an extended passive-aggressive strop would not be inaccurate: 'Foolish Perses! Work at the tasks which the gods have ordained for men, lest one day when you have a wife and children, sickening in your heart you look for a livelihood among your neighbours, and they pay you no heed.'

Hesiod is full of advice for his brother and, by extension, other land-grabbing gentlemen farmers. He explains how to cut wood when it is least likely to be wormy. He knows how big a wheel should be, depending on the size of the cart. He has recommendations on the number of ploughs a man needs (two: one made from a naturally plough-shaped piece of wood, and one made from two pieces of wood joined together. That way, when one breaks, you don't need to give the oxen a day off). He is keen on self-sufficiency: 'Make all your tools and things ready at home, so you don't have to ask another for help, and have him refuse you, and while you're in need, the season change, and your work be wasted.' And he is not a man to procrastinate, either: 'Don't put things off till tomorrow or the next day. For a worker who puts things off isn't a man who fills his granary.' Amid the advice, however, lies a real love for the Greek countryside: 'When the artichoke flowers, and the chirruping grasshopper, sitting on a tree, fills the air with his piercing song from under his wings, in the season of wearying heat, that's when the goats are fattest, and the wine at its best.' It's worth noting that Hesiod wrote in hexameters, just like Homer did. Hexameter is the verse-form of epic poetry, which features gods, heroes and battles. So, to Hesiod at least, there is something heroic about farming your land, keeping your barn filled with grain, tending your crops and taking care of yourself.

The image Hesiod gives us is of a nation of small, self-sufficient farms. And this ideal persists to the fifth and fourth centuries BCE, when Xenophon was writing. Ischomachus, whom we have already met discussing what made his wife good, and who is presented by Socrates as 'kalos k'agathos' ('fine and good'), is exactly the sort of estate-owner that Hesiod is describing. He doesn't have a huge farm worked by dozens of slaves, but rather a smallholding worked by a few and organised by a slave overseer, which provides for him and his household. Again, the heroics of small-scale agriculture are explicitly drawn, this time by Socrates: 'If someone wants to serve his country in the cavalry, then agriculture is the most appropriate way of feeding a horse as well as himself; and if he wants to serve in the infantry, it's the best way to prepare the body.' Socrates goes on to explain that farmers make the best soldiers because they have the most at stake: it is, after all, their land and crops that will be ravaged by an invading force if they lose. And farming isn't purely the preserve of the middle-class landowners, either. 'Even the very wealthy aren't able to keep their distance from agriculture. For the practice of it seems to be both a luxury, and the means of increasing an estate, and of training the body to be able to do all that befits a free man.' While working the land may not seem very luxurious to us, we should probably bear in mind that a wealthy man would have plenty of slaves to do the really hard labour. And that wealthy people now spend a fortune on decent workouts at the gym and acquiring a golden tan, two things a bit of light land-working would quickly provide. The supremacy of agriculture is considered completely uncontroversial by Socrates' companion Critobulus: 'Well, Socrates, I think I've been sufficiently persuaded that agriculture is the finest, noblest and most pleasant way of making a living.'

The divide between town and country wasn't important to the

Athenian Socrates and his friends, because they regarded Athens as both a city and its surrounding area. A *polis* – a city-state, like Athens or Sparta – was not just a city, but also the lands around it. Athens needed its olive groves just as much as it needed its law courts. When the Spartans invaded Attica each year, at the start of the Peloponnesian War, the country-dwelling farmers withdrew behind the walls of Athens itself. They were just as entitled to be in the city as those who had houses and businesses there, even if the overcrowding caused by jamming everyone into a tight space probably led to the swift spread of the plague. Athens really was more than the sum of her parts: she had a city, farmland, a secure link to her port, Piraeus, and an almost unbeatable navy, which meant that the Athenians could import and export whatever they needed. One of the rules of warfare at this time, incidentally, was that no one could damage olive groves, even those of an enemy. The harm was too great, and took too long to put right: mature, fruit-bearing olive trees don't grow overnight, or even over a year. Like so many other good intentions, however, this unspoken agreement soon became a casualty of the war.

And quite aside from the costs of war, the countryside wasn't always a place of peace and tranquillity. Even in its literary form, the bucolic idyll has an ugly underbelly. Theocritus, a Sicilian-born poet who lived in Alexandria in the third century BCE, wrote plenty of pastorals describing the ideal, with scenes of serenading goatherds, a wistful, lovelorn Cyclops, and Eros pinching honey from the bees. But even Theocritus could embrace the dark side of the country. There might be country sing-alongs and love songs in abundance, but there were also tales of terrifying bacchic revels and murder. For the Greeks, Theocritus included, the countryside was the home of clear, cool water, shady trees and beautiful wood nymphs; but it was also the place where far less enticing inhuman creatures dwelt. Nymphs are often portrayed alongside satyrs, the priapic minor deities who pursue them with unceasing enthusiasm. Nymphs must turn into trees or leap into streams to avoid unwanted attentions. The countryside might be idyllic for those eyeing up a nymph, but it seems more stressful from her perspective.

Chastity is always difficult to preserve in the countryside: look at Deianeira, the wife of Heracles (or Hercules, to give him his Roman name). To get across the River Euenos, Deianeira needed a lift from a centaur, Nessus, another inhuman forest-dweller. She describes him, in Sophocles' *Trachiniae*, as 'archaiou thēros' – 'an ancient beast'. Nessus hired himself out as a semi-equine ferry service: a big fellow with four sturdy legs, he could carry people across the river. But he also had wandering hooves. 'In the middle of the crossing,' she explains, 'he touched me with groping hands.' This is euphemistic: Nessus wasn't just copping a feel, he was attempting rape. He had not, however, reckoned with Heracles, who promptly shot him with an arrow dipped in the poison of the Hydra, a serpent with several heads. The countryside may be pretty, but it is also full of lascivious and dangerous monsters.

Nowhere was more dangerous than Mount Cithaeron, a mountain in central Greece, with Boeotia on its northern side, and Attica (where Athens lies) on its southern side. This is where poets sent their heroes to meet a bitter end – or not, depending on their story. It's where Oedipus was exposed as a baby, left to die rather than fulfil his hideous destiny of killing his father and marrying his mother. We know, of course, that Oedipus is rescued from the mountainside by a shepherd. But Mount Cithaeron was the place chosen for his hoped-for infant death. And Actaeon, the hunter who offended Artemis, met a grisly end there. According to Callimachus, the third-century BCE poet and scholar at the great Library of Alexandria, Actaeon caught a glimpse of Artemis bathing. Even though he didn't mean to catch sight of her like this, there was no forgiveness: he was turned into a stag, then torn apart by his own hunting hounds. His mother was left to gather her son's bones from all over the mountain.

Mount Cithaeron was also the undoing of Pentheus, another ill-fated king of Thebes, whose story is told both by Euripides in *The Bacchae* and by Theocritus (perhaps, the authorship has been questioned) in his 26th Idyll. Pentheus refused to acknowledge the deity of Dionysus. This wasn't mere posturing: Dionysus was a late addition to the Greek gods, and not one of the twelve Olympians. More relevantly to Pentheus, Dionysus was the product of yet another of Zeus' excursions. This time, the dalliance was with Semele, Pentheus' aunt. Semele was tricked by Hera into demanding to see Zeus in his godly form, and promptly died when he turned into a thunderbolt. But if you are the king of anywhere, it makes perfect sense to refuse to believe that your cousin is a god; believing anything else could seriously undermine your position.

Dionysus, however, is a vengeful god. He converts Pentheus' mother, Agauë, and her sisters into Bacchae or Maenads: women possessed by Dionysus. Pentheus becomes increasingly obsessed with the behaviour of these Maenads, and begins to lose his grasp on reality. Although reality itself is becoming increasingly difficult to grasp: a herdsman comes to report that the Maenads are nursing gazelles and wolf-cubs, and that fountains of wine and streams of milk appear at their fingertips. The land of milk and honey cannot last, however. Soon the women notice the herdsman and his fellows, and become enraged. They wrench the cattle apart with their bare hands, and drive the men away with sticks. Pentheus is transfixed by these tales, and Dionysus soon humiliates him, persuading him to dress as a woman so he can spy on them. Dionysus lures him to the mountain, then reveals his presence to the Maenads. They, believing him to be a mountain lion, tear him limb from limb. Agauë, his own mother, carries his disembodied head back into Thebes, before she comes out of her trance and realises what she has done. For Sophocles and Euripides in Athens, and Callimachus and Theocritus in Alexandria, the mountain was a forbidding place. While the city and its environs were ordered in comprehensible ways, Mount Cithaeron represented the other, the alternative to order. It was a place where chaos could reign, where dogs turned on masters and mothers on sons.

And the Romans, too, had good reason to fear their countryside on occasion. The monsters that terrorised them between 73 and 71 BCE, for example, were considerably more real than satyrs and centaurs. To the Romans, the escape of Spartacus and his fellow gladiators, their magnetic lure for other slaves in the south of Italy and their victorious battles against Roman soldiers, must have seemed almost as unlikely as an attack by harpies or gorgons. The story of Spartacus' rebellion is incredibly familiar to us, thanks to Kirk Douglas's portrayal of the gladiator turned general. A Thracian by birth, according to the historian Appian, Spartacus had served as a soldier with the Romans. But something must have gone wrong somewhere, because he was imprisoned and enslaved, then trained as a gladiator in Capua. While there, he persuaded about seventy of his comrades to break out of the training school and do a runner. They headed to Mount Vesuvius (this was 150 years before the eruption that would wipe Pompeii off the map), and occupied the high ground. There, says Appian, many runaway slaves and 'tinas eleutherous ek tōn agrōn' – 'some free men from the fields' – joined them. Even after all the time that has passed, the best part of 200 years, between Spartacus' revolt and Appian's writing, his shock at this whole story is tangible in his writing. Free men from the fields – Italian farm-workers, in other words – joining slaves and gladiators to fight against the Roman army? And not just fight – win? Spartacus and his rag-tag army almost captured Varinius, a Roman praetor. And these near misses only added to his appeal: he soon had 70,000 men at his command, who kept beating Roman soldiers in battle, besieging cities, and terrorising the citizens of Rome. Spartacus remained at large for three years. His gladiators, whom the Romans had initially dismissed as laughable and contemptible, were formidable opponents. The wealthy Crassus, one of Cicero's contemporaries, eventually commanded a Roman force into battle against Spartacus and his men. The film has a much more dramatic ending, but Appian tells us that Spartacus died in the field, and that his body was never found. His 6,000 surviving comrades were crucified at intervals along the road between Capua and Rome.

The Romans must have found the whole Spartacus episode rather harrowing. They thought they knew their place in the scheme of things. A Roman citizen was at the pinnacle of the social strata. Games were put on for the entertainment of Roman citizens, and indeed to honour their dead. And gladiators fought and died in those games. There can be no greater signifier of power disparity than having the lives and deaths of other human beings at your disposal, for your pleasure. Similarly, slaves weren't people to the Romans, they were property. You owned a slave in precisely the same way you might own a piece of furniture. And suddenly there they were, these gladiators and slaves lurking in the countryside where you couldn't see them, and waiting to attack you. Their spirits should have been crushed, they should have known their role in the world was a mere cameo in the Roman story. When Spartacus raised an army of gladiators, slaves and poor field-workers, the Romans must have felt exactly as we would if our kitchen appliances suddenly declared war on us. They sent their soldiers to fight them, the finest-trained fighting force anyone had ever seen, but Spartacus kept on winning. And he wasn't winning battles far away, he was winning on the fields of Italy. He even besieged and took Thurii, a city on the Tarentine gulf. This is what happens when city-dwellers ignore the countryside: it comes up to the city and bites them. Horace published his third book of odes in 23 BCE, and in it he makes one mention of Spartacus: he wants a jar of Marsian wine, 'if roving Spartacus' left any intact. Fifty years after the rebellion, and the man who wandered the country wreaking havoc is still worth a mention.

But if Spartacus and his hordes were the story of the countryside Roman authors would prefer to forget, there were plenty of other stories they chose to remember and retell. Horace picks one of Aesop's fables, for example, to illustrate the superiority of country simplicity over urban complexity. He even addresses the countryside itself, declaiming, 'O rus' – 'O, countryside', and demanding to know when he'll be able to retire to the country, and spend his time reading books by ancient authors, sleeping and enjoying inactivity. He wants simple country food – beans and bacon: these would provide 'nights and suppers of the Gods'. It's a vision of retirement that has proven alluring for well over two millennia. And Horace is careful what he wishes for: he wants a comfortable, simple retirement, rather than untold riches at his disposal. Aesop's story of the town mouse and the country mouse is used as an example for precisely this reason. Since some people are praising another man's wealth, Horace's neighbour pipes up with the story. A town mouse (*urbanus mus*) and a country mouse (*rusticus mus*) are old friends. The country mouse has his friend to stay in his humble cave. He tries to share his simple fare, but the town mouse is too snooty to enjoy a meal of oats and a dry plum. He invites his friend to come and stay with him instead: like most city-dwellers, he finds it inconceivable that anyone could choose the country over the city. 'How does it help you, friend, to endure your life at the back of this steep grove? Wouldn't you prefer people and the city rather than these wild woods? Come with me.'

165

People love to quote Horace. For a start, he is responsible for the opening line of Wilfred Owen's poem 'Dulce Et Decorum Est', although he intends these words to mean something rather different from Owen (the whole line is 'dulce et decorum est pro patria mori' – 'it is sweet and proper to die for one's country'). But Horace's most renowned phrase, quoted extensively in the movie *Dead Poets Society*, appears in Ode 1.11. 'Carpe diem', says Horace in the last line: pluck the day, trusting as little as possible in the next. Life is short, in other words, and don't you forget it. His two-word phrase is almost invariably translated as 'seize the day'. This book of odes was published in 23 BCE, about seven years after his satires were produced. So it's great to find the precursor to the famous phrase here, in the mouth of the urbanite mouse. 'Come with me,' he tells his country cousin: 'carpe viam'. For the translator who can't resist the rare example of a pun which works in two languages, it might better be translated 'seize the way'.

The country mouse goes back to the city with his friend. The town mouse lives in palatial quarters, pretty carpets on the floor, ivory couches. And there are fancy leftovers to be eaten. But suddenly, the perils of city life bear down upon the mice in the form of the household dogs. The country mouse realises that luxury paired with insecurity is no luxury at all. He declares that this life is not for him, and returns to his solitary cave, and his humble food supply, where he won't be ambushed by mastiffs.

Like all fables, this sweet animal story contains a moral message. The town mouse may have all the glamour, the easily found sweetmeats and the warm, cosy home. But he might one day pay a hefty penalty for enjoying them. The country mouse, eating his oats in his pokey cave, might appear to have a boring life, but he is safe and untroubled there. Horace, we can assume, was with the country mouse all the way.

And who could blame him? Achieving a bit of peace and quiet was probably a common ambition for Romans at that time.

Cicero agreed on the advantages of rural life, too, at least for oratorical purposes. In his defence of Sextus Roscius in 80 BCE, he reminds the prosecutor that country living is the height of respectability: 'But I have known many men ... who think this rustic life is most honest and most pleasant.' He goes on to contrast his country-bumpkin client with the city-slickers who are trying to frame him, and draws an explicit contrast between the morality of the country and the lawlessness of the city: the kind of crime (patricide) that Roscius is accused of doesn't fit with a rural lifestyle. 'Every type of crime doesn't come from every type of life. Luxury is created in the city. Of necessity, luxury creates avarice. From avarice, recklessness bursts out. And from that comes every type of crime and wickedness. But the country life – which you call uncultured – teaches thrift, conscientiousness and justice.' Cicero, we should remember, loved Rome; the politics, the law courts, the power-brokers, the back-stabbers, he was born to rise through them all. But he knew perfectly well that a jury of Romans might well see the city/country divide rather differently, and he played to the crowd accordingly.

But the Roman countryside had a greater cheerleader than Horace or Cicero. It had Virgil, the man who would spend the last ten years of his life carving out *The Aeneid*, leaving it unfinished at his death (and had his wishes been followed, it would have been destroyed then). But before he embarked on his epic, he wrote *The Georgics*, a poem about farming and Italy. Virgil was born in Mantua, in the far north of the country. He lived for a while in Rome, where he and Horace shared a patron, Maecenas. But he was more comfortable away from the city, and so moved to Naples, in the south. He was pretty well qualified, therefore, to write about all of Italy.

The poem is divided into four books, on field crops, trees, animals and bees. Although ostensibly a didactic poem, this is no farmer's manual. Virgil writes extensively on vines, in the second book, but he has less interest in olives, for example, which he mentions only briefly. Poetry is more important to him than accuracy. He certainly took care writing it, according to Suetonius, who claimed that every day Virgil would dictate a large number of verses, which he had thought of that morning: 'Then he spent the whole day reducing them to a tiny number, wryly saying that he wrote his poem like a she-bear, finally licking it into shape.' If you've ever wondered where the phrase 'lick into shape' comes from, wonder no more. The Romans believed that a newborn bear wasn't yet bear-shaped, but a furry blob which needed some work. The mother bear licked her cub, not to clean it, but to turn it from protean bear-matter into the shape of a small bear. This may seem like a foolish thesis, but the Romans had the good sense not to get too near a mother bear with a new cub. And the phrase has stayed with us to this day.

Like Hesiod, Virgil saw the agricultural life as heroic, explicitly comparing, for example, the arrangement of a vineyard to a legion prepared for battle. They should both be neat, orderly and regularly spaced. And he, too, compares the life of the farmer favourably with its alternatives: 'O, how very lucky are farmers, if they know their good fortune!' Once again, the simplicity of rural life is viewed as superior to the city. In the countryside they may not have inlaid tortoiseshell doors, dyed clothes and endless hangers-on, but they have something far more important than status: 'peace and quiet, and a life that doesn't know deceit'. They aren't caught up in intrigue, they aren't corrupted by luxury, they aren't warmongers. Virgil is particularly caustic about those who wage war for personal gain: 'One man seeks to rain destruction down upon a city and its wretched homes, so that he can drink from a jewelled cup and sleep under a purple bedspread.'

The version of the countryside we see in *The Georgics* is idealised, of course. Quite aside from anything else, there are adorable anthropomorphic animals running through its pages. If you don't flatten out your threshing floor, warns Virgil, then a little mouse will move in, make her home and build her granary under it. Or an ant will pinch your corn, if you're not careful. He won't do it out of malice, but rather because he is 'metuens senectae' – 'fearful of old age'. Cute woodland bugs and creatures were around a long time before Walt Disney.

Was the Roman countryside really like a cartoon? Of course not. The ideal which Virgil, Horace and Cicero described was just that, an ideal. Although Athens had small farmers in abundance, in Rome the equivalent was dying out. In the later years of the Republic, especially, smallholdings had been bought up by wealthy men, paying the original owners a minor sum to take unprofitable land off their hands. It is hard to make a small farm produce enough food to sustain a family even now, and we have machinery and, crucially, fertilisers. Plenty of Romans preferred to sell up their plots for the best price they could get. This in turn resulted in the creation of *latifundia* – huge farms – owned by one man and worked by hundreds or even thousands of slaves. Pliny the Elder, the first-century CE author of *Natural History*, found this shocking: that Roman land which had once been tilled by free men, generals even, was now worked by shackled slaves. No wonder it was less fertile than it used to be.

And this brings us to the very crux of the countryside problem. The gap between ideal and reality is rarely more pronounced than when we consider the bucolic dream versus the actual fields. Roman authors managed to focus on the ideal, even if they lived in the real thing. But they were men who craved contrast: Horace, Cicero and Virgil all lived through the first century BCE, a time rocked by unprecedented political and social upheaval. No wonder they extolled the virtues of the simple life: the city had been a difficult home. And romanticising the countryside is perfectly understandable today, when most of us no longer live in it. For the first time in world history, more than half of us now live in cities – 50 per cent of the global population on just 3 per cent of the land. If the only experience of a rural lifestyle for most of us is a brief holiday, why wouldn't we idealise it?

The problem this creates is obvious. If we tend to live in cities, only think about food when it appears on a supermarket shelf, and have a mental picture of the countryside as a patchwork of rolling hills and gambolling lambs, we will struggle to understand or accept the reality. We'll lobby against genetically modified food because we don't like the thought of messing around with nature, never mind that messing around with nature is something we are all in favour of when it comes to finding cures for cancer and vaccines for flu. Those of us who rarely go hungry can rather lack imagination on the benefits of developing drought-resistant crops. But if we subconsciously believe the countryside myth, and think that it used to look like it does in costume dramas, or indeed in *The Georgics*, it's no wonder that we still want it to appear that way, even if that way never really existed. So we crave organic farms rather than industrialised ones, which is a luxury that only some countries, and indeed consumers, can afford. By focusing our attention on the boutique end of the farming spectrum – three free-roaming chickens and a couple of lowing cattle – we fail to notice that we're paying so little for milk in our supermarkets that dairy farmers can find it cheaper, if somewhat less humane, to slaughter cows rather than milk them.

We need to be realistic about what we take from the countryside, and what we need to give back to it. Food is very cheap for many of us, and the world's population is increasing. Countries like China are developing the same meat and dairy-intense diet that much of the west has enjoyed for decades. This is unfortunate, as we probably all need to be turning vegetarian, certainly according to Lord Stern, author of the 2006 Stern Review on the cost of global warming. Einstein once said that nothing will benefit human health and increase chances for survival of life on earth as much as the evolution to a vegetarian diet. And he didn't even know about vCJD, over-fishing or the Big Mac.

So why has the rural dream been so pervasive? Why do we want so much to believe in an idealised construct of non-urban life, from *The Waltons* on one side of the Atlantic to *The Darling Buds of May* on the other? And why do celebrated figures – from Virgil purporting to tell farmers how things are done to Marie Antoinette dressing as a shepherdess – get a kick out of playing at being simple country folk? It's not something that will soon go out of fashion, either. We're all dying to bring some pastoral idyll into the cities where most of us live. There are 100,000 people on waiting lists for allotments around the UK. In Camden, in north London, the waiting list is so long that if you added your name to it today, you'd get your allotment in about forty years. By which time, it's fair to suggest, you might have gone off the whole *rus in urbe* thing. And don't think this is just about growing vegetables, either. It has become increasingly chic to keep chickens in the gardens of British urban homes, and I once interviewed a teenager who kept honeybees on a Hackney rooftop. And the desire to bring the countryside into the city isn't just personal, it's political. Of the nine regions of the UK's Forestry Commission, which protects the Lake District, Sherwood Forest and many more world-famous green sites, one region covers just one place: London. The city may be home to more than 7 million people, but that doesn't mean it fails to take its trees seriously.

But are town-dwellers doing any more than flirting with a cute farmyard fantasy when they put bees in the back garden and chickens in the yard? Does it stem from a genuine unhappiness, because they wish they didn't live in cities and suburbs? And if it does, why not simply move to the place they idealise? The answer is obvious: most of us live in towns and cities because we work in them. However much progress has been made in broadband speed and access, many people still need to live near where they work, and most of the jobs are in areas with dense populations. And playing at being a chicken farmer with three or four hand-picked chickens to take care of is a very different proposition from making your living keeping livestock. The risk inherent in all this countryside fetishism is that we see it not just as a vague ambition – to retire and move to the country one day and keep alpacas, for example – but as the norm, which our lives fail to match. If we start to believe that everyone is keeping chickens but us, does that mean our ordinary urban life (which often won't include a chicken-friendly space) is wanting? What about those of us who like living in a city and the companionship of working in an office? Are those of us who love the city too eager to hide our enthusiasm beneath a patina of world-weary irritation? In other words, do we construct a countryside myth because we're dissatisfied with real, urban life, or do we simply dabble in a bit of beekeeping and vegetable-growing as a way of affirming that our sophisticated city really does include everything, countryside and all?

Perhaps ambivalence is simply an intrinsic part of city living. Proud Angelenos will still bemoan Los Angeles' traffic and smog. Neapolitans can love their city but hate their (occasional lack of) local services. And don't even ask Londoners about the Underground, unless you have been paid to do so, as your ears will start to bleed. But the thought of living anywhere other than London still seems impossible to most of its residents. Perhaps our natural state is to live in a city and complain about it; to get the criticisms in before anyone else can.

There is one man who precedes anyone who has ever moaned about their city while refusing to countenance living anywhere else. We are back to Rome's most articulate grouch, Juvenal. If there is one thing that the city can provide him with, it is a constant stream of material to incur his wrath. Everything he hates about Rome is his life-blood, his inspiration, his muse. No wonder comedians tend to die young: the bile gets them, even if the drugs don't.

Juvenal's Third Satire is all about the city. His friend Umbricius is moving out of Rome, and, like all true urbanites, Juvenal is appalled. Even allowing for the many failings of the place, how could anyone want to live anywhere that isn't Rome? It's the precise tone of bafflement you would expect to find from a Parisian or a New Yorker, on discovering that a neighbour is moving to Languedoc, or Vermont. Initially, Juvenal appears to sympathise with his friend's decision. Cumae, where Umbricius intends to move, is a lovely place, the gateway to Baiae, a fashionable tourist area. Not that the prettiness of the new place matters: Juvenal says he would rather live on a barren island than be anywhere near the Subura, a crime-riddled part of Rome that is most easily likened to a pre-gentrification Hell's Kitchen. However mean and lonely his barren island was, it wouldn't, couldn't, be as dangerous as Rome. Juvenal lists the perils: Rome is riddled with fires, and collapsing buildings, the many dangers of a savage city. But he saves the biggest peril to last: poets reciting their verses in the month of August. Anyone who has ever tried to walk the streets of Edinburgh in the month of August, which coincides with its world-beating Fringe Festival and a huge influx of street performers, mime artists, poets and musicians, can certainly feel Juvenal's pain. And Edinburgh is considerably cooler in August than Rome, for the most part.

Juvenal needs more than a few lines of verse to express his total horror at much of what is wrong with Rome. And dyspeptic, bigoted, racist and furious though he may be, his complaints echo through the ages. It is a rare city-dweller who hasn't voiced at least one or more of Juvenal's concerns, at some point or another.

Let's take them in order. Well, firstly, Umbricius is leaving Rome because 'There's no room in the city for honest work.' He has less money today than he had yesterday, and he believes he'll have even less tomorrow. This is precisely the problem faced by a younger generation of urbanites today, who feel comparatively poorer every day. House prices have shot stratospherically high, and even when salaries go up, house prices increase by far more. At the peak of the last boom, in 2007, average property prices for first-time buyers in London, for example, were seven times their average income. In spite of a contraction over the last couple of years, properties still cost almost six times average income. In the USA before the recession, median property prices reached almost five times median household income. If you live in a city, and do an averagely waged job – teaching, for example – you can't afford to do anything but rent. This might be fine in those cities where rents are controlled, but much harder if they aren't. A London-based teacher has little prospect of saving to invest in her own home, she is too busy paying the gougingly high rents of the buy-to-let landlords. And while it is tempting to dismiss this issue as an affectation – people rent property all over the world, without feeling cheated that they can't afford to buy – the fact remains that in the UK, the USA and plenty of other countries, home-ownership is seen as the norm. It's something for ordinary people to aspire to. And in the UK, our votes are tied to our electoral register, and that has traditionally been compiled according to where we live. Move house often enough (as renters routinely have to), and you can easily lose your political say in the city where you live, quite by accident. Although the Political Parties and Elections Act became law in 2009 (which changes the system from household registration to individual registration), it won't be implemented until 2011. A generation of younger voters are already criticised for not voting in elections, but very few commentators stop to ask if they ever received a polling card, sent out months after the electoral registration forms were filled in, often a house move or two behind the voters they needed to reach.

Juvenal, by the way, has plenty to say on the subject of landlords later on in this satire, and none of it is pretty. He considers the standard of properties in Rome compared with their country alternatives. No one, he says, fears that a house will collapse in Praeneste, Gabii or Tivoli, but in Rome, things are different: buildings are inadequately shored up. The landlord papers over the cracks – 'texit hiatum' – another great example of a phrase that works so perfectly it is still used in English today. Cheap buildings were on the verge of collapse at all times, in Juvenal's view. No wonder Umbricius wanted to move away to a place, 'where there are no fires or night-time panics'. Rome's poor lived in *insulae,* blocks of wooden apartments packed closely together in a grid formation. If you could go back in time and look down on imperial Rome from above, these sections of it would have resembled Manhattan: tight blocks in neat rows. But because the buildings were wooden, and because people used fire to keep warm or cook food, there were plenty of very serious fires. The Great Fire of Rome in CE 64 is remembered by us only because of its scale, but there had already been several major fires in Rome that century, in CE 6, 27 and 37. Others followed. Augustus had created a slave fire brigade in 23 BCE, but replaced it in CE 6 with the vigiles, Rome's hybrid fire brigade and police force. They fought a losing battle with the closely built *insulae*, however, which may have reached five storeys or even higher. Juvenal paints a grim picture of a first-floor neighbour calling for water, and moving his bits and pieces out of harm's way, while you're on the third floor, in complete ignorance of a fire downstairs. The smoke reaches you, but 'tu nescis' – 'you don't know it'. The alarm is raised at ground level, so 'the final one who'll burn is the tenant only protected from the rain by the roof-tiles.' As so often with Juvenal, the scene moves from cartoonish exaggeration to something genuinely horrible in a couple of words. Things improved a little for the poorest tenants who lived on the top floors after the Great Fire. Nero limited the height of new buildings, and ensured that the streets were wider, and that the building fronts were protected by colonnades. This didn't eliminate the risks of fire – the buildings were still largely wooden, after all – but it did make it slightly harder for a fire to jump from one building to another.

Back to Umbricius, getting poorer every day because there are no honest jobs in Rome. What does he really mean by that? What constitutes an 'honest job'? Well, Juvenal is a snob, so it's no surprise he doesn't hold with plenty of jobs that seem pretty honest to our ears: temple-building, river management, harbour construction, sewer-cleaning and carrying out the dead. Roman society, like so many before and since, saw landowning as the only really acceptable route to wealth. New money from trade was decidedly less the done thing. It's another example of what separates town from country: a city job is the sign of new money and vulgarity, whereas landownership conveys family wealth and no need to get your hands dirty with drains and dead bodies. But Juvenal is not a wealthy man, so his snobbery is particularly ruinous. If he or Umbricius had spent less time despising the men who did the jobs they considered beneath them, and taken on those kinds of jobs for themselves, they might have been richer and happier. However, it isn't just the work that Juvenal loathes, it's the men who do it, who (and this is, of course, another phrase that has passed straight into English) 'nigrum in candida vertunt' – 'turn black into white'. For someone who makes things up for a living, Juvenal has a great loathing for those who tell lies for professional gain. 'What can I do in Rome?' declares Umbricius, hopelessly. 'I never learned how to lie. If a book is bad, I can't praise it and ask for a copy.' Poor Juvenal: he and his friend even lack what it takes to be truly popular authors. He could at least have tried the technique Nancy Mitford employed, when asked what she thought of a terrible novel. She would invariably give the double-edged reply 'Good is *not* the word!'

So far, the score against Rome is that it is full of liars and charlatans, that there's no work for any other type of person, that property is expensive and dangerous, and that there are too many crummy writers jostling for some attention. But Juvenal is just warming up. The one thing he abhors about the city above all other failings is its immigrant population. He makes the odd snide comment about Jewish settlers, 'whose worldly goods are a basket and some straw'. But his heart isn't really in anti-Semitism this time. He saves his real ire for another group: 'Citizens of Rome! I cannot bear a city of Greeks.' Juvenal's dislike of Greeks in Rome matches that of any fervent Nationalist in any country you can name. All major cities, ancient and modern, are centres of immigration, whether their citizens embrace that or resist it. And Juvenal is very much in the latter category. It's not just the Greeks who bother him, either: 'How many of our dregs come from Greece? For a long time now the Syrian Orontes has flowed down into our Tiber.' The Greeks are bad enough, but now the Syrians are coming too. River metaphors are popular in highly charged rhetoric about migration; for Enoch Powell, immigration would result in the Tiber foaming with blood (a quotation from Book Six of *The Aeneid*, incidentally. These are the words of the Sibyl, who foresees a bloody future for Rome; Powell saw the same problem ahead for Birmingham). For Juvenal, though, ever one to enjoy bathos, it's wine dregs and sewage that he turns to for his metaphors.

The arrival of Greeks, Syrians and other foreigners in Rome might have bothered Juvenal less had they done what migrants traditionally do when they arrive in a new city: take on the jobs no one else wants to do, earn a pittance and be thankful for it. This is precisely what happens with migrants today all over the world: Hispanic women clean Miami houses, while Polish men fix the leaky taps of Manchester. And all over their respective cities, conservatives huff that there are plenty of native residents who could do these jobs if they weren't so damned idle, while liberals coo that migrants are so cheap and hardworking, it would be a disaster if they returned home. But the Greeks in Juvenal's Rome didn't play by those rules at all – they wanted more than menial labour. And in Juvenal's opinion, the Romans encouraged them far too much. They're soon using fancy Greek words instead of sensible Roman ones. And they don't seem to notice what Juvenal can see very clearly: that the Greeks are taking them for a ride, worming their way into powerful households, making themselves indispensable with their guile, audacity and ready wit. Plus, the Greeks are so damned clever, they can do anything. Juvenal demands that you guess the profession of a Greek. He can convince you he's simultaneously a schoolteacher, rhetorician, mathematician, painter, masseur, augur, tightrope-walker, doctor, magician. Tell him to fly, sneers Juvenal, and he's up in the air. And soon, of course, the Greeks are so valuable to their Roman employers that men like Umbricius and Juvenal are being squeezed out. The Greeks start getting the good seats at dinner parties, and all because they are so obsequious and deceitful. When Juvenal considers even harbour-building to be infra dig, it's easy to see why he might find the versatile Greeks a bit sickening, and for precisely the same reasons that we hear so often today on the subject of migration: no one is being racist, but they do take our jobs, houses, women, and so on.

Perhaps the cause of this bigotry, ancient and modern, is always quite simple: we resent those who do what we cannot. We are ashamed of our inability as a society to produce enough doctors, teachers or engineers, so we blame the incoming professionals for their capacity to make up for our shortcomings. And if we can find a way to blame them without admitting to those shortcomings in the first place, so much the better. So we focus on someone's poor English, religious enthusiasm or unusual dress, rather than the issues we are really bothered about. And certainly Juvenal, who needed a hefty dose of patronage to pay his way (given his antipathy to working for a living), must have found the rival claims of the Greeks – on the same wealthy Romans that he himself was trying to tap – absolutely horrifying. If you had a hundred sesterces going spare, would you give it to the flattering, helpful foreigner, or Juvenal, who can't even bring himself to tell you your crappy book is magnificent? No wonder he was furious. His real loathing of Greeks stems from what he sees as insincere over-empathy: 'si dixeris "aestuo," sudat' – 'if you say, "I'm hot," he sweats.' And that is hardly something anyone would accuse Juvenal of doing.

Rome's migration problem as Juvenal perceived it, therefore, was very similar to what we see in our time. The arguments haven't really changed: migrants are deemed to take more than their fair share of scant resources, to cheat their way to the best jobs and perks, to bow and scrape in the presence of a superior, but to stick the knife in the second you turn your back. Like many of the most vocal critics of migrants now, Juvenal isn't especially confident in his own Roman-ness: his father was a Spanish freedman, which made Juvenal a first-generation Roman citizen. Juvenal knows that it is only luck and timing that made him a citizen of the mighty Rome, rather than its slave. And so he fears and dreads the arrival of other slaves, freedmen and foreigners to the city, who might become more successful Roman citizens than he is. It doesn't take a psychologist to suggest Juvenal's aggression came from the fact that he felt threatened. He wrote the poetic equivalent of the first punch because he was sure the bigger kid would take him down if he waited. But, like most cities, Rome depended on the outside world: for its labour, its grain, its prosperity. Juvenal may have despised the immigrants that came with all that, but the city couldn't thrive without them.

What else was wrong with Rome, in Juvenal's eyes? The same things that town-dwellers complain about today: noise, overcrowding and crime. Noise may feel like a modern phenomenon, invented alongside the car and the aeroplane. But it certainly kept Juvenal awake at nights: 'Most invalids die from being kept awake ... what lodgings allow sleep? Only those with great wealth can sleep in this city.' The rich, then as now, could afford larger houses set back from the roads. They had rooms that didn't look out on to a busy street. The grimy poor had no such luck, with wagons racing past their homes at all hours of the night. Wheeled traffic was largely banned from the streets of Rome during the day: people needed to move around the streets on foot, and clogging up the roads with traffic would have made that impossible. Keeping Rome moving was crucial to its many residents and businesses; but carts and wagons had to arrive sometime. An undisturbed night's sleep was a luxury the city couldn't afford; the carts rattled past all night instead.

Juvenal may seem like an archetypal grumpy old man, even when he was still quite young, but he certainly sells his rage. All great observational comedians have the gift of making an audience think they share the same beliefs. They can convince us that they are putting all our frustrations, dislikes and fury into concise, funny phrases, building to a climax which will enable us to laugh at what previously left us annoyed. When comedy is cathartic, this is why: we stop feeling infuriated and start giggling instead. But comedy is so often transient. What was funny to Shakespeare or Chaucer rarely makes us laugh today, possibly because puns are now relegated to tabloid headlines and Christmas crackers. But Juvenal isn't lost to us at all when he moans about Rome, his humour jumps out of its time: we may have to tolerate unmuffled motorbikes, muzak and car alarms rather than wagons or carts, but our emotional response is exactly the same as his. Noise pollution, after all, is an incredibly distressing phenomenon: the World Health Organisation suggests that exposure to loud noise, especially at night, can produce physiological and psychological symptoms, from long-term sleep disorder to cardiovascular problems. They also believe that traffic noise alone is harming the health of every third European. Juvenal was a long way ahead of his time.

Walking through Rome's streets doesn't seem to have been much fun either. Juvenal is hemmed in by the crowds in front and harassed by those behind him. Elbows, poles and barrels attack him. Builders' wagons were exempt from the daytime ban, so cartloads of marble and other building materials were a common sight, and the risk of getting squashed by falling cargo was constant. Logs or marble could snap a cart's axles and crash down upon you at any time. And when that happens, Juvenal leaves us in no doubt of the consequences to the passer-by: 'Who could identify his limbs, his bones?' He sets up a small scene where the crushed man is on the bank of the River Styx, long before his household even know he's missing. The unpredictable perils of the city pre-date the hit-and-run.

But if Rome by day is a dangerous place, that is nothing compared with how scary it can be at night. All cities have this double character; a park full of children playing in the middle of the afternoon can soon be full of more alarming inhabitants at night. Streets that are deserted and shuttered all day suddenly come alive after the sun goes down.

The same places that give a city its vibrancy – its clubs, bars, entertainments – are only ever a breath away from causing panic. Cities are like drunks: all the fun in the world one moment, but with the ever-present risk that they may suddenly flip to violence and aggression.

Juvenal lists a selection of night-time perils. A falling roof-tile could land on you. People throw broken and leaky pots out of the windows – there were laws against this kind of thing, but who could see the guilty party in the dark? Look at the damage these missiles do to the pavement, warns Juvenal. Imagine how much they'd do to your poor head. Juvenal recommends that we take his concerns seriously: you'd be considered ignorant and reckless if you went out to dinner without having made a will first. If the worst thing that falls on you are the kitchen slops, he reckons, that's a good night.

But it isn't just the thoughtless behaviour of the tenement-dwellers that a night-wanderer should fear. Once darkness falls, the crooks come out to play. Specifically, the mugger (*grassator*, in Latin) might attack you. These men are drunk enough to start a fight, but never so drunk that they attack the rich, with their crowds of bodyguards. They wait instead for a man like Juvenal or Umbricius, invariably picking his way home alone by moonlight. The mugger adds insult to injury by mistaking his victim for a Jew (this is a financial slur rather than a racial or religious one, incidentally. Remember earlier that Juvenal had criticised the Jews in Rome for being little more than squatters with only a bit of straw to their names). Juvenal articulates perfectly the plight of the lone man who really doesn't want a fight: 'If you try to say something or you retreat in silence, it makes no difference. They'll beat you up either way, and then lay charges against you.' In other words, they'll start the fight, then claim you did. This is the double-peril of living in Rome: first you get beaten up and then you get sued. This, snarls Juvenal, is the poor man's liberty.

Perhaps we should bear Juvenal's satire in mind when our less temperate media commentators are castigating the young for the new offence of binge-drinking, something that never happened in their day, presumably because they were all too busy being high-minded and quaffing the occasional small glass of sherry. This kind of drinking only happens in Northern Europe, or on Spring Break in the USA, or whenever Brits go on holiday abroad, we are told. It certainly doesn't happen in Italy, or southern France, where everyone drinks in a measured way and no one picks fights in the streets. This distinction would have been news to Juvenal, who clearly had an axe to grind against the booze- and testosterone-fuelled culture of Rome back in the days when people usually drank wine heavily diluted with water. Antisocial behaviour, we should try to remember, didn't just begin when we became too old to drink vodka from a bottle in the street, and decided that anyone who was young enough to do so was a hooligan. It began when people moved into cities, became overcrowded and territorial. It began because there is a whole category of people who think that everyone else appears to be looking at them funny. The addition of the alcopop simply makes the whole scene happen a little earlier in the evening.

So after Umbricius' whistle-stop tour around the hellhole that is Rome, what conclusion are we supposed to draw? Juvenal can't persuade him to stay – his mind is made up, and he is off to Cumae. But has he convinced Juvenal to go with him? To leave the city for good, and avoid its endless dangers and injustice? A poor man in Rome is comparatively richer when he leaves, after all: everything is cheaper away from the big city. As Umbricius says, Juvenal could buy a house in the country for the amount he spends renting a dark grubby attic in Rome. And it is a safer, perhaps more equal society away from Rome, too. The sharp juxtaposition of unfathomable wealth and poverty is less pronounced elsewhere.

Juvenal has related Umbricius' complaints with such relish, how could he fail to be persuaded by these arguments against Rome? Because, of course, he would rather live in the centre of the world than anywhere else. Even when he is giving us Umbricius' sales pitch about the lovely house Juvenal could afford if he would only leave the horrible city, he can't resist mocking it. It's quite something, says Juvenal, to have enough ground to grow vegetables that would feed a hundred Pythagoreans (vegetarians). And his sarcasm only increases when he adds that it's a big deal to become master of the ground one lizard lives on. (Lizards in Italy, should you be wondering, are very small.)

It is, of course, in Juvenal's nature to mock everything. Ordinary people might hate the city and love the country, or they might feel the opposite way. It takes the spleen of Juvenal to loathe the city over several hundred lines of verse, and then mock the only alternative he offers. It is a very urban cynicism, and perhaps that is what the city really offers. A sense of having seen and done it all. Sophistication or jadedness, depending on one's perspective. If the construct of the countryside is a charming, small-scale, olde-worlde innocence that it doesn't really possess, then the city is also as much myth as it is reality. The construct of cities is that they are the only places where dangerous, important, society-changing things can happen. Governments sit, law courts judge, traders sell, thugs maraud, all of humanity eventually jostles each other in a city. We can fill our towns with parks and gardens, we can tend to our urban chickens, we can keep sheep and pigs in our back gardens. But what we can't do is change the essential nature of a place which convinces everyone who lives within its limits that it is the only place of any importance in the world. A city owes everything to the magnetic force it exerts over each new generation. Like Dick Whittington, who set off with his possessions in a handkerchief and a surprisingly well-trained cat at his side, young ambitious people flock to cities to live a different life from the one they grew up with. They want the construct, just as much as those who dream of a bucolic ideal want theirs. City-dwellers have museums, restaurants, cinemas, theatres: they get everything when it's new and they can decide whether they like it before anyone else does. They can see artists, hear musicians, buy groceries in the middle of the night and books on their way home from the pub. The city, for all its failings, so carefully enumerated by Juvenal, is still wonderful. So those of us who live in one should enjoy it for what is is, and always has been: a glorious, grubby, industrial, gastronomical, cultural, social mess.

7

No Business Like Show-business

It's time to play the music, it's time to light the lights. Whenever we need experiences that are most sensational, inspirational, celebrational – and, at a push, muppetational – culture is the answer. We all want some kind of art or entertainment: whether our tastes are high- or lowbrow, whether we prefer laughing or crying. And we want to share our cultural consciousness, too: to watch the water-cooler moment on TV so we can discuss it at work the next day, or make a playlist (once the long-defunct mix-tape) for someone we've just met and want to impress. Once, we held up our lighters at rock concerts during our favourite, saddest songs. Now we hold up iPhones, with the screens turned white. We may no longer be allowed to smoke at gigs, but we still want the band to know that this song is important to us. Our cultural tastes define us – which films we like, who's our favourite singer, why something is the worst show on TV, which team we support. These are the things that make or break friendships and relationships. And, by the way, if a shared sense of humour didn't matter to people, they wouldn't include it in their personal ads.

Culture also provides us with a profound emotional hit. We need the thrill of epic storytelling and the heartbreak of a sad love song. We want to look at beautiful paintings and race through page-turning books. In short, we want romance, excitement, danger, pain, fear and elation, ideally without having to undergo the experiences that produce those emotions ourselves, at least not all in the same day. From pop culture to fine art, we – the audience – derive a vicarious thrill from watching or hearing something we would certainly enjoy a lot less were it happening to us rather than to a character. The catharsis that Aristotle saw in great tragedy is no different from the catharsis we experience watching a great horror movie. We get an adrenalin rush, a sense of pity, a wincing desire to change the inevitable outcome. Whether we're watching Medea waver about killing her children, or Norman Bates oscillating between mild-mannered young man and homicidal mother, we're crying out for sanity to prevail. And we're crying out in vain. Drama allows us to face our darkest fears and walk away intact. Which is more than can be said for Medea's children, or Janet Leigh's Marion Crane.

The Greeks invented almost every literary form: tragedy, comedy, lyric poetry, history, philosophical dialogue, biography. It's no accident that the names of these genres are all Greek in origin. In contrast, the Romans invented only one literary form: satire. And all these literary genres affect what we watch and listen to now. The earliest poetry was epic in many cultures: tales of gods, heroes and monsters, composed orally and eventually written down. Traces of their oral beginnings can easily be found: Homer's epithets are still remembered today – the wine-dark sea, the rosy-fingered dawn. These stock phrases, repeated many times, would help a bard to sing long tracts of *The Iliad* or *The Odyssey* without needing to have it written down in front of him. And for the poet composing as he goes along, it buys time to think of the next phrase. If you want to see a variant of this kind of time-buying in action, watch any politician who's been asked a question he or she can't answer. They will inevitably begin their reply with the words, 'I think the question we should really be asking is ...', followed by a question they can answer. The stock phrase affords necessary thinking time, and enables the speaker to switch the subject from the initial question to one he or she actually wants to hear. It's rather less beautiful than the phrase 'rosy-fingered dawn', though.

These huge stories still entrance us today: *The Epic of Gilgamesh*, *The Iliad*, *The Odyssey*, *Beowulf*, *The Divine Comedy*, to name only a few. Epic stories have made their own direct contribution to popular culture, even if that popular culture has rather failed to return the favour: the films *Troy* (2004) and *Beowulf* (2007) lacked pretty much everything you might hope for from a decent epic, such as excitement and tension. They did have princesses with golden hair, but that's hardly enough. However, our love of epic has manifested elsewhere, in an undisputed triumph of late twentieth and early twenty-first-century culture: American television drama. The big series that have dominated broadcasting schedules and DVD sales for the past few years are often epic in scale: *The Sopranos*, *The West Wing*, *Deadwood*, *Buffy the Vampire Slayer*, *Angel*, *Battlestar Galactica*. The sheer number of episodes that constitute each series make them a fairly epic proposition. If you were to decide to catch up on *The Sopranos* now, you would need to set aside the time to watch eighty-six episodes, at fifty minutes each. And that's one of the shorter ones: *Buffy* notched up 144 episodes.

All these shows fulfil some criteria of epic beyond the simple issue of scale. Epic poems tend to begin in the midst of the action – *The Iliad*, for example, opens in the tenth year of the Trojan War. *The West Wing* begins one year into President Bartlet's term of office. We don't need to see the build-up in any of these shows – the moment when

Bartlet gets elected; the bit where Buffy finds out she's the Chosen One. We can find this out later: we see Bartlet first choosing his team of White House staffers in flashback at the beginning of the second series. Equally, Homer doesn't need to bore us with the background to the Trojan War at the beginning of *The Iliad*: we know why it began, we know how long it lasts, we know that the Greek forces are led by Agamemnon and their best warrior is Achilles. Instead, we jump straight into the fight between Agamemnon and Achilles that shapes the end of the war.

Buffy the Vampire Slayer and *Angel* adhere still more closely to the epic mould. They both feature supernatural creatures, super-strong heroes, magic, and gods intervening in the human realm. Buffy is an epic hero in every sense: she's stronger than her friends and enemies, like Achilles; she has a great sense of responsibility, like Hector or Aeneas; she is clever, using guile to overcome an enemy's superior force, like Odysseus; she has a connection to the divine, like all those heroes who are also demigods; she has a family to protect, like Hector; a stalwart gang of friends who help her, like Aeneas or Odysseus; she is angered by threats to her command, like Agamemnon. She especially reminds us of Aeneas, making impossible decisions when she is torn between what's right and what she wants. The disadvantage of being a hero is that you cannot always do what you would choose. Aeneas is always described by Virgil as 'pius Aeneas' – 'dutiful Aeneas'. His responsibilities to the Trojans, the gods and his descendants are far greater than his personal desire. He doesn't wish to leave Troy or lead a band of survivors across the seas to found a new city. When he tells the story of the Fall of Troy, in Book Two, he explains how his first wife, Creusa, lies dead somewhere in Troy, and he is desperate to find her. But her ghost suddenly appears, and urges him to leave, and he must. Again, when he stops in Carthage and falls in love with Dido, he tells her that he would prefer to stay with her, that he doesn't want to set sail for Italy. But duty calls: as usual, Aeneas must sacrifice what he wants for his divinely sanctioned responsibility. Buffy finds herself in the same predicament in the finale of Season 2, when she's obliged to kill the man she loves, rather than see havoc rain down upon the earth. It is more important that she saves the world than give in to her desires. For Buffy, as Aeneas also discovers, heroism can be a very lonely experience, one that means you sometimes have to betray those you love, in order to do the right thing. Being a hero may seem a very glamorous job description, but it's often not very much fun for the hero herself, who in Buffy's case sacrifices everything, even her own life – twice – to carry out her heroic duty.

What is the difference between an epic hero and a tragic hero? Is there a difference at all, when the same character – like Jason of Argonautic fame – might appear in both an epic (Apollonius' *Argonautica*), and a tragedy (Euripides' *Medea*)? Epic heroes often die tragic deaths, like Hector does in *The Iliad*, so one might be tempted to see them as essentially the same. But they are not. A tragic hero, like Sophocles' Oedipus, has particular characteristics, and follows a particular path. The great tragic heroes are extremists – Oedipus is much cleverer than his compatriots, and more quick to anger. He is a great dramatic figure, but would be a terrible dinner guest. His cleverness leads to intolerance and impatience; his anger swiftly advances to aggression. Medea grieves a disproportionate amount when Jason leaves her: he is undeniably a crummy husband, and common sense alone should tell her that she will be better off without him. But she cannot see things that way at all – her judgement is clouded by a furious jealousy which harms everyone around her, herself included. Even characteristics we might see as positive, such as loyalty, become deviant when possessed by a hero. So Antigone, who loves her brothers to distraction, irrespective of their characters, should be a praiseworthy figure in Thebes. But her loyalty becomes obsessive: she buries her brother in breach of the law and her own safety. A initially positive character trait is distorted through the tragic prism into a destructive one.

Tragic heroes have these deviant, excessive emotional responses, and they inevitably cause their own downfall. Oedipus cannot let mysteries lie: he must pick at the truth until everything unravels, no matter what it costs him. And it costs him everything – Jocasta dies, he is blinded, exiled, driven from his children and his home. Similarly, Medea doesn't hesitate to destroy everything she holds dear, if she can cause Jason only a fraction of the pain she causes herself. Disproportionate response is hard-wired into heroes: Medea isn't delusional when she kills her boys, or confused. She makes a conscious, intelligent decision that causing her enemy pain is worth it. Extraordinary though her behaviour seems to her audience, to her it is the best, and only, course of action.

Tragic heroes have never gone out of fashion; they are a staple of most drama, on stage or on screen. Tragedy is cathartic, after all. We never tire of seeing someone else go through the wringer. Perhaps the detective genre has come closest to replicating the tragic flaw. It's hard to imagine a great detective who doesn't remind us of the Greek tragic hero. Sherlock Holmes is brilliant but self-destructive. His drug use calms his excessive intelligence, but with only limited success. His depression is usually provoked by boredom, by not having anything sufficiently taxing to exercise his enormous intellect. It leaves him isolated: even Watson eventually marries and moves away. And Holmes's total commitment to his job leads him to extraordinary lengths: spending weeks at a time in disguise, faking his own death, and detatching himself from Watson, Mrs Hudson and Lestrade, the very people who care about him the most.

Raymond Chandler and Dashiell Hammett gave us differently flawed heroes. Sam Spade may not have been a big fan of Miles, his partner, but he still stakes everything on solving the guy's murder. 'When a man's partner is killed,' he explains, 'he's supposed to do something about it. It doesn't make any difference what you thought of him. He was your partner and you're supposed to do something about it.' Sam Spade and Philip Marlowe both drink too much, get in too deep with women of dubious virtue, and risk their lives too often and without hesitation. It's hard not to have a crush on them, but equally hard to imagine any involvement with them could possibly end well. Like the heroes of Greek tragedy, their character flaws are what make them heroic – in their case, able to solve the seemingly impossible crime – but they are also what keep them sad, broken, isolated men.

The cliché of the modern police detective is that he or she is a loner, with a broken marriage or two in the background: Jane Tennison, John Rebus and Kurt Wallander, for example. Tormented by their demons, these super-sleuths are married to the job, and living proof that Nietzsche wasn't kidding when he said that if you gaze long into the abyss, the abyss gazes also into you. They truly are the tragic heroes of our time: their excessive commitment to their cases impedes any hope of a social life. Their rule-breaking need to catch the murderer drives away most of their colleagues. Their superior officers hate them (even though the crime clear-up rate would be roughly zero without them), because they don't follow orders or understand office politics. Even when the murder is solved, these detectives aren't happy: there are always more criminals, more crimes. The ultimate tragic hero is Inspector Morse, who drinks because he can't relax any other way, and dies from the diabetes that his beer-drinking can only have exacerbated. It is, perhaps, a sign of our times that self-destruction should have become rather more internalised and rather less about poking out eyes with pins.

Our appetite for catharsis hasn't changed at all – crime novels and TV series have filled our minds with horrible, violent murder, torture and rape. We, just as much as the Greeks, need to see our fears acted out, if we are to fear them a little less. And the more taboo a subject is, the more cathartic the dramatised version seems to be. Most ancient societies saw incest as something truly terrible (although their idea of incest was rather more limited than ours), so it's no wonder that Oedipus is such an emblem of suffering: killing your father and marrying your mother are horrific crimes, and in no way reduced merely because he did so unknowingly. In contemporary crime fiction, paedophilia is often the recurrent theme, perhaps fulfilling the same role as the ultimate taboo.

And if we want to find an even closer parallel to Greek tragedy than crime drama, we couldn't do better than to watch HBO's *The Wire*, a critical hit on both sides of the Atlantic, and deservedly so. It is a huge, complex story with a hefty cast of characters, any of whom can suddenly step up to take centre stage for a while. It makes no effort to slow down and introduce the audience to the characters, but drops us in the middle of Baltimore's badlands and lets us work out for ourselves what's going on. So far, so epic. But the story arc of one particular character, the compelling Stringer Bell, is purest Sophoclean tragedy. At the start of the first season, Stringer Bell is a highly successful drugdealer, and not just because he is in his thirties and still alive. He was brought up in Baltimore's Projects, and has made himself a fortune in the only way he knows how. He is the brains behind the Barksdale gang, and doesn't hesitate to have people murdered or tortured to keep their position secure. The police spend years trying to obtain evidence on the gang, and although their doggedness puts some of his crew behind bars, Stringer remains elusive. He is too clever and too careful to be caught.

Stringer, in other words, is doing an excellent job of living the destiny he's been given, just like Oedipus did in his early life in Corinth, living with the king and queen he believes to be his parents. When Oedipus discovers the prediction made about him, he leaves Corinth immediately, desperate to avoid hurting the parents he knows and loves. He has no idea, of course, that the parents he is desperate to avoid are only adoptive ones; that staying where he is would be his best course of action; that by running away from his destiny, he is actually running straight into it. Oedipus' fate is pitiless, as is Stringer Bell's. He too decides to shun the destiny he was given. He distances himself from the day-to-day ugliness and dangers of drug-dealing. When other members of the gang end up in jail, Stringer seizes the opportunity to reorganize the business. He becomes an unrivalled financial and managerial figure in the gang's hierarchy. He even attends college courses to learn about effective business management, and implements what he learns in the running of the Barksdale organisation. In other words, he does exactly what exasperated teachers must have told him to do when he was a boy: get an education, apply yourself, use the brains God gave you. He has already begun investing in property, but begins to focus his attention on developing a fully respectable business portfolio, without dirty money moving around his empire. Drugs may have provided his start-up capital, but he is determined to move into the non-criminal world. This desire to change himself and his livelihood drives a wedge between him and his friend and colleague Avon Barksdale. Barksdale doesn't want to be removed at all from the casual, consummate violence of drug-dealing. He sees something Stringer does not: that men cannot run away from their destiny, however hard they try. Stringer is soon ripped off in the property market, and by a seemingly respectable US senator, who turns out to be as much of a crook as any of the drug lords. Just like Oedipus, it is precisely when Stringer tries to live a better life than the one he was born to that he ends up fatally weakened.

The conflict between Avon and Stringer causes both their downfalls: Stringer betrays Avon to the police; Avon betrays Stringer to two men who want him dead. It's only here that Stringer Bell's story moves away from Sophoclean tragedy – he isn't killed or maimed off stage, only to have his miserable fate told in a messenger's speech to a shocked chorus and audience. Stringer goes down in a hail of bullets in an empty building. His tragic arc is complete. By fleeing a destiny that made him a criminal thug, he not only fails to improve his life, he loses it. You can watch *The Wire* without reading Sophocles, and it's still brilliant. But it's even better with Oedipus lurking in the back of your mind: no less contemporary, no less extraordinary, just even smarter than it looked first time round.

Greek tragedies were performed in competition in ancient Athens: sets of trilogies were staged, with a satyr play at the end. A satyr play was a less traumatic way to end the day than a tragedy. After a trilogy of murders, suicides and self-mutilations, a tragi-comedy with a chorus of satyrs and plenty of phalluses presumably sent the audience away in a jollier frame of mind. The Dionysia, at which the plays were performed, was a dramatic festival held around April: every performance was an offering to the god Dionysus, as well as an entertainment for the masses. It's important for us to remember this, living as we do in a time when Greek tragedy has attained the status of high art. It is, of course, high art. The poetry is exquisite, the characterisation is simple and clear, the stories are compelling. But Greek tragedies weren't originally performed for the middle-class, theatre-going few. Rather, they were part of a big, public, drunken celebration: Dionysus was not just the god of theatre, but of booze as well. The Athenian audience would be in a celebratory mood when they watched Aeschylus' *Oresteia*, something it would do us no harm to remember, whenever we find ourselves sitting through a serious, respectable production of Aeschylus today. If we were really committed to reliving an authentic Athenian experience, and mindful of the lack of an interval in Greek tragedy, we would surely remember to have a hefty gin and tonic, at the very least, before taking our seats.

The prize-giving was a very serious business, too: it was a source of great pride to a playwright to win, although the prize was ornamental – an ivy-wreath – rather than financial. The same might be said of the Oscar trophies, which cannot be resold unless they are first offered to the Academy (another Greek name, after Plato's school) for the bargain price of $1. And the Oscars have traditionally rewarded tragedy, too: the winning and nominated films alike are overwhelmingly tragic rather than comic. One could argue that this is because tragedy is intrinsically the finest art-form, or one could be more pragmatic. Acting Oscars are awarded to men and women equally, and tragedy is a genre that features women in numbers one doesn't see in, say, action films, buddy movies, war films and so on. Even if you do happen to get two women in a road movie, it will surely end in tragedy, like *Thelma and Louise*.

Tragedy – ancient and modern alike – often focuses on the family. And that family is invariably less than wholesome, whether it is the disastrous, destructive House of Atreus (where a father kills his daughter, his wife kills her husband, and her children kill their mother) or the empty life of Lester Burnham, played by Kevin Spacey in the film *American Beauty* (husband falls out of love with his unfaithful wife, and develops lust for his teenage daughter's friend, inadvertently convinces his deeply repressed neighbour that he is gay, and is shot dead). The family under pressure is a tremendous source of dramatic tension, whether it's in Greek tragedy, Oscar-winning films or lowly soap operas. Either way, we get suffering matriarchs, deviant relationships between sexual partners, and an insupportable strain on the parent–child bond. Professor Edith Hall has suggested that Greek tragedy has been performed more in the last forty years than at any other point since fifth-century BCE Athens. Productions of *Oedipus*, *Medea* and *Hippolytus* happen all over the world, every year, in numbers that simply aren't matched by performances of Greek comedies or Roman tragedies. If there is a *Medea* showing at a theatre near you, you can be almost certain it will be Euripides' version, rather than Seneca's. It's worth thinking about why it might be that the tragic motifs of broken vows, barbarity in war and damaged families are so enthusiastically rediscovered by each new generation of theatre-goers. Perhaps it is because the plays are so simple that we can insert our own subtext with ease: Euripides' *Bacchae* has featured a homosexual relationship between Pentheus and Dionysus; Sophocles' *Philoctetes* has been afflicted by AIDS; Antigone has fought against apartheid in South Africa and stood up to civil war in the former Yugoslavia; and Euripides' *Trojan Women* have represented the victims of brutality from Hiroshima to Ceaușescu. And the rise of feminism perhaps means we are more eager to see strong female characters on stage. The murderous Medea, scheming Electra and vengeful Clytemnestra are roles that most actresses would kill for. Certainly they ask far more from a performer than any Shakespearean heroine. Lady Macbeth has nothing on Hecabe, the old woman who sees almost every one of her sons and daughters killed or enslaved during the Trojan War, before she discovers that her one surviving son, sent away for safety, has been killed by his guardian, Polymestor, for money. She is so ravaged by grief that she kills his children, and then puts out his eyes with brooch pins. The last thing he will ever see is his own children paying the ultimate price for his greed and perfidy. In a world where women over a certain age never appear on the big screen unless they are either Meryl Streep or Judi Dench, perhaps it's not surprising that audiences might want to see the occasional vengeful old broad on the stage.

And tragedy isn't just beautiful, it's also useful. In Plutarch's life of Nicias, we read the sorry saga of the Sicilian Expedition, one of the Athenians' great military blunders. In 415 BCE, after sixteen years of war with Sparta and running low on cash, Athens decided to launch a money-grabbing raid on Syracuse, in Sicily, as they had been told that vast sums of money were stored in temples there. However, the Athenians had overreached themselves, and although they had some early successes in battle, they were annihilated in 413 BCE. A huge number of Athenian men and their allies were killed, and many more enslaved. Thucydides puts the figure at 'no less than 7,000'. Those who had been captured were kept in quarries – as so often in history, the distinction between prisoner-of-war camp and death camp was non-existent. Thucydides tells us they were overcrowded, and had no roof, so the men burned in the sun before being frozen in the cool autumn nights. Dead bodies weren't removed, disease soon spread and their rations were horrifyingly small: one cup of water a day, and two cups of corn (a cup was about half a pint). They were kept in these conditions for seventy days, before most were enslaved. The Athenians who had not gone on the expedition, but were waiting eagerly back in Athens for the news of their compatriots' huge military success and financial reward, knew nothing of this. According to Plutarch, the first they heard about their loss was when a foreigner arrived at the Piraeus (Athens' harbour) and went for a haircut. He chatted with the barber about the Sicilian disaster as though everyone knew what had happened there. The barber raced into town and told everyone what he had just heard. Declining to believe such an awful thing, the Athenians decided he was a liar and tortured him on the wheel (blaming the messenger barely covers it). There is one bright spot in this miserable story, however. The Sicilians were enormous fans of Euripides, and prized his poetry above all. Some Athenians were freed if they could recite his works, or given food and drink for knowing small excerpts. Plutarch tells of Athenians arriving home and thanking Euripides for their safe return. Tragedy, in this instance, was a life-saver.

Tragedy isn't the only way to experience catharsis, however. At the other end of the emotional spectrum is comedy, which also provokes a feeling of relief in its audience, whether that is because it mocks the world they know and recognise (observational comedy), takes them into a different world and lets them forget about their mundane worries (surrealist comedy), or provides them with a pseudo-tragic experience of gratitude that they are better off than the poor sap they're watching (comedy of embarrassment). These categories aren't at all exclusive: a great observational stand-up like Bill Hicks or Billy Connolly can easily jump into surrealism, taking a joke about the real world into a fantastical one. *The Office* is pure comedy of embarrassment, but its setting and characters remind plenty of office-workers of their own workplaces: acute observation is what makes the embarrassment so very toe-curling. *The Simpsons*, which isn't far off its 500th episode, cheerfully flips between every type of comedy: it satirises the American family and way of life, it creates huge, surreal flights of fancy and it invites us to cringe at Homer's stupidity, even while we hail him as the ultimate comic everyman.

The Simpsons is the most obvious descendant of Aristophanes' comedies – anarchic, satirical, parodic and political. Aristophanes was fifth-century Athens' king of comedy. He wrote plays that were spectacular and surreal – featuring a cast of politically disenchanted birds, for example, or a chorus of old men wasps. Comic playwrights like Aristophanes would have had a *choregos* – a wealthy citizen benefactor – to equip their choruses with costumes, instruments and training. Perhaps it was seen as a status-symbol: if you were rich enough to pay one of these Athenian super-taxes – equipping a theatrical chorus or fitting out a warship – you really were in the money. It might have been the equivalent of having a wing of the National Gallery named after you, following a handsome donation. Although Aristophanes cheerfully suggests in one play that these donors actually are paying the penalty for being unpopular with the politically influential, rather than doing their civic duty. 'I'll make you a trierarch,' declares Cleon, in *The Knights*, 'and you'll get an old boat.' A trierarch had to fit out a trireme – the Athenians' prized warships. Presumably it was just good luck if you were responsible for a boat that had been well maintained (at some cost to the previous trierarch) in the past year. But an old boat was a terrific threat: a leaky hull and broken oars would doubtless be ruinously expensive to make shipshape.

Aristophanes spent literally years bating Cleon, his political nemesis, calling him names, and putting these kind of sentiments in his mouth. If Bill Clinton once suggested that you should never pick a fight with people who buy ink by the barrel, then Aristophanes' career is testimony to the fact that you also shouldn't pick a fight with a comedian, because you will inevitably lose. Aristophanes can make all the scandalous, slanderous accusations he wishes about Cleon, and Cleon can do nothing about it. The bad blood between them dated back to Aristophanes' second play, *The Babylonians*, which was performed at the Dionysia in 426 BCE, but which sadly doesn't survive. In it, Aristophanes attacked every important Athenian official, and Cleon, who failed to see the funny side. He prosecuted Aristophanes before the Council for speaking ill of the Athenian people. We don't know exactly what happened at the trial. Aristophanes was then only twenty years old and new to the comedy business. In *The Wasps*, produced in 422 BCE, the chorus leader (borrowing Aristophanes' voice for a moment, as theatrical convention allowed) says that he was flayed alive and remembers the audience laughing as he squawked. Allowing for comic exaggeration, we can perhaps assume this means Aristophanes was fined. Suffice it to say, the message Aristophanes took from the whole experience was that he should live within the letter of the law from then on, if not its spirit. He wasn't prosecuted again, but his vengeance against Cleon was long-lived. Even now, 2,500 years later, whenever his plays are read or performed, Cleon is once more a figure of fun. He must be the longest-standing butt of any joke in history. It's made all the worse by the fact that there's every reason for us to keep reading Aristophanes: he's still extremely funny and smutty now. There's a masturbation joke before we're even thirty lines into *The Knights*; modern comedians seem positively restrained in comparison. Luckily Aristophanes is good, and on top of that, he knows it. The chorus of *The Knights* addresses the audience at one point, reminding them how rare is Aristophanes' talent: 'The art of writing comedy is the most difficult task of all. For many attempt it, but few do it well.' One only has to peruse the television listings to see how true that remains.

Aristophanes never lost his desire to mock the shortcomings of his fellow Athenians, in spite of the early prosecution. But he had loftier ambitions, too. *The Frogs* was produced in 405 BCE, just as Athens was suffering her final months in the Peloponnesian War. It tells the story of the god Dionysus making a trip to the underworld to find a poet who will save the city. Aeschylus had arrived in Hades some fifty years earlier, but Euripides and Sophocles had both died only recently. And Athens had made some terrible decisions in the latter part of the war

– she had struggled to fight on after the losses of the Sicilian Expedition eight years earlier. The democracy had been overthrown, albeit temporarily, in 411 BCE, in an oligarchic coup. Athens' allies, who hadn't always been treated well when Athens was at the height of her powers, were keen to revolt now she was struggling. And then in the summer of 406 BCE the Athenians had seized defeat from the jaws of victory: they won a huge naval battle at Arginusae, near the island of Lesbos, sinking seventy-five enemy ships. However, a storm blew up and the Athenians fell apart. Fifty more enemy ships got away in the chaos. Many damaged Athenian ships were abandoned, with the loss of all their men. The Athenians were devastated, and summoned their generals home to stand trial. Six Athenian generals returned home and were promptly executed after an Assembly vote. The Athenians instantly regretted their mistake: quite aside from the unpleasantness of executing your fellow countrymen when they make a mistake or are overwhelmed by bad weather, Athens now had six fewer men with military leadership experience to help them in their war. Actually, they had eight fewer – two of the generals made a run for it before they could be tried and executed.

After Arginusae, since both sides had suffered severe losses, the Spartans offered to make peace, keeping the former Athenian allies that they had gained, over the years, but leaving Athens the ones she had retained. This was pretty clearly a good deal for Athens. Of course, she would have preferred to keep all of her cash-cow allies, funding her building works and her fleet. But the very fact that she had lost so many men and so many tax-paying allies meant her war effort couldn't be sustained much longer. Nonetheless, the Assembly was persuaded by a man named Cleophon to reject the peace offer. According to Aristotle, he turned up drunk at the Assembly, wearing his armour, and saying he wouldn't allow peace to be made unless the Spartans gave back the allies they had pinched during the war. Rather than give him the ancient equivalent of a strong black coffee, the Athenians voted along with him, and missed the chance to make peace. No one needed to consult an oracle to foresee that they had blown a perfect opportunity to keep themselves a free city, and that they had little war left in them now.

Aristophanes responded to this catalogue of woes with *The Frogs*, a play about the Athenians' god of theatre, Dionysus, going to Hades. He has one aim in sight. 'I've come down here to find a poet,' he declares. 'What for? To save the city, so she can keep staging plays.' It wouldn't be Aristophanes without a touch of self-interest, after all. But while this may seem like a simple comic fantasy to us now – how could a poet save a city? They can barely pay rent – Aristophanes isn't completely joking. We've already seen above how the words of Euripides made the difference between life and death in Syracuse. But there was more to poetry than just beautiful verse. Poets were special, extraordinary people. They had a clearer vision than the rest of us, a more powerful intellect, a connection with the divine through their muses that gave them an insight the rest of us can only dream of. In short, poets would not vote to execute perfectly able generals in a moment of anger. They would offer wise counsel, and help ordinary people to make better decisions and be better human beings. The public performances at the Dionysia meant that tragedians had an extraordinary capacity to reach the masses, and educate them. As Aeschylus intones in the play, 'A teacher explains things to school-children, poets explain things to adults.'

Aristophanes might be making a serious point with his play, but that doesn't mean he does so in a serious way. The first half of the play follows Dionysus as he makes the treacherous trip down to Hades, in a haze of cowardice, confusion and mistaken identity. The second half takes place in Hades, as Euripides and Aeschylus battle it out to be named the Chair of Poetry in the underworld, and win a pass back to the land of the living. This plot allows Aristophanes to indulge in some tremendous parody: Aeschylus speaks in flowery pompous verse; Euripides is a sophist and a smart alec. Aeschylus is affronted by the very idea that Euripides might be the better poet, and the two of them tear strips from one another: Aeschylus' plays are boring because the main character never says anything; Euripides' poetry is so predictable that you can insert a banal phrase at the end of every line and it scans just as well. Aeschylus' verse is full of made-up words, so no one watching has a clue what's going on; Euripides' plays are full of grimy characters – even the kings are in rags, and the women are a disgrace. Aeschylus is repetitive; Euripides encourages the lower classes to ask questions instead of doing as they're told. Dionysus is at a loss over which poet he should choose to take back to Athens with him. As he eventually says, 'The one I consider clever, but the other one is pleasing to me.' Hades tells him to make his mind up, and Dionysus picks Aeschylus. Euripides is appalled: Dionysus promised he would favour Euripides. How could he be so dishonest? Dionysus replies, 'My tongue swore that, but I choose Aeschylus.' It's a partial quote from one of Euripides' most famous lines, when Hippolytus, in the eponymous play, breaks an oath of secrecy he has pledged to the Nurse. 'My tongue swore,' he says. 'But my mind was unsworn.' It's a classic piece of sophistry, exactly the kind of thing Euripides is always saying and should be thoroughly ashamed of, according to the other characters in *The Frogs*. After all, in a world without much writing, a man's word really was his bond. If someone could swear an oath before all the gods, and still break it, then no one could trust anything at all. Aristophanes obviously loves the line as a perfect representation of what he likes to mock in Euripides: he quotes it more than once in his plays. And so Euripides pays the ultimate price for being clever, rather than pleasing – he stays behind in Hades, while Aeschylus trots back to Athens with Dionysus.

The one thing no one questions is that he has his work cut out for him. 'Go,' says Pluto, as he sends them on their way. 'Save our city with your good advice, and educate the fools. You'll find plenty of them.' Even after his prosecution some twenty years earlier, Aristophanes is still mocking his fellow Athenians and calling them names. We must assume they took it as teasing rather than slander. At one point, Xanthias, Dionysus' servant, looks out into the audience and calls them a bunch of villains. It doesn't seem malicious, but rather the kind of tart comment that might provoke a few good-natured boos amid the laughter. Stand-up comedians will perform the exact same trick when they are on tour. There's virtually no audience in the world that doesn't laugh if a comic implies either they or their nearest neighbours are crooks and idiots. Perhaps collective self-deprecation is one of the things that unites us with our fellow spectators.

And mocking an audience is not the only technique Aristophanes uses that remains unchanged in modern comedy. 'We sank twelve or thirteen enemy ships,' declares Dionysus at the start of the play, boasting to Heracles. 'Just the two of you?' asks Heracles. 'Yes, by Apollo,' Dionysus replies. 'And then I woke up,' mutters Xanthias. This is a classic pull-back-and-reveal, a technique comedians still use for a laugh today. The scene suddenly switches, and what seemed perfectly normal in one context is now inappropriate and therefore funny. In the words of the underrated stand-up Michael Redmond, 'People often say to me ... get out of my garden.' A banal phrase which the audience expects simply to be introducing a joke suddenly turns out to be the joke, because the setting flips into one we didn't expect.

Aristophanes' comedy is full of slapstick, too – a performing style that transcends language and culture. The highbrow among us may be sniffy about, say, the enormous international success of the slapstick Mr Bean when we all prefer the verbal gymnastics of *Blackadder*. But there is a good reason why Charlie Chaplin, the Marx Brothers and Laurel and Hardy are still popular today. People falling over is funny. People getting knocked over with a ladder is funny. It's not even species-specific – children wouldn't laugh at *Tom and Jerry* if a cat getting slammed in the face with an iron didn't fulfil a basic love of violence and Schadenfreude. Aristophanes grasps this completely, and his plays are full of cowards and bullies getting a smack in the kisser. In *The Frogs*, Dionysus and Xanthias get flogged by Aeacus, the doorkeeper of Hades. He is trying to discover which one of them is a god. They both claim to be immortal, and it is quickly resolved that the best way to test who is telling the truth is to flog them both and see who winces first – a god would feel no pain from such a trifling injury. The audience is then treated to the sight of two men howling in agony while pretending they don't feel a thing but have simply noticed a passing horse or suddenly remembered a religious festival. It's precisely this kind of knockabout fun that Aristophanes does so well, because he doesn't do too much of it. His successors – Menander, Terence, Plautus – are pretty much all slapstick, puns, long-lost children and cuckolded husbands. The sophistication, the political critique, the real intellect behind the jokes that Aristophanes brought to fifth-century comedy, these don't reappear for a very long time.

Aristophanes is also not afraid to make jokes that might well put him into the territory ear-marked for tragedians. In the middle of *The Frogs*, the chorus leader breaks out of the story to address the audience directly, not as the author (examples of which we saw above), but as the chorus. 'It is right and fair,' he says, 'for the sacred chorus to join together and advise the city, and to educate it.' The idea of the comedian as educator is one that might not seem familiar to us. Comedians are fools, after all. They're jesters, who might chime in and say what no one else dares to say, but they're not serious educators of the masses. And certainly there is plenty of brilliant, silly comedy around that makes no effort to change hearts and minds: the quick-fire jokes of Phil Silvers, Eric Morecambe or Harry Hill were never intended to change the way we think. They're merely intended to make us laugh, and they work perfectly. But there is another category of humorists who embrace their role as teacher as well as comedian – the late, preacher-like Bill Hicks, the deceptively languorous Stewart Lee, the politically charged Mark Thomas or Mark Steel. These performers offer something more to their audiences than pure laughter: they want you to laugh, but they also want you to think. Aristophanes' chorus leader lectures the crowd on their perceived inconsistency – they have granted citizenship to some slaves who helped them in battle, but deprived Athenian-born men of their citizenship for backing the wrong side in the oligarchic coup of 411 BCE. Aristophanes is pretty conservative in his outlook (rare, in political comedians today) – he would like to see the oligarchic sympathisers forgiven. He worries that Athens is depriving herself of men she needs. 'Come now, dimwits, and change your ways. Use the useful people again. If it all works out, you'll be considered sensible, and if you stumble, at least you'll hang yourselves from a worthy tree.' That may not have seemed like much consolation to the beleaguered Athenians, but their decision to vote with Cleophon and refuse peace had effectively signed the death warrant of their democracy. Perhaps that is the real weakness of comedy as a medium for changing the world: by the time a phe-nomenon is sufficiently widespread for an audience to get the joke about it, it's already too late to change anything. After all, comedians made jokes throughout the premierships of both Margaret Thatcher and George W. Bush, and it changed precisely nothing about their re-election prospects. Maybe it even hardened the resolve of their supporters – no one likes to be mocked.

But perhaps the most interesting weapon in Aristophanes' arsenal is his fondness for a joke that his audience might well consider to be in extremely poor taste. In their battle for poetic supremacy, Aeschylus and Euripides are arguing about the character of Oedipus: Euripides says he was happy at first, before he suffered his terrible fortune. Aeschylus argues that in fact Oedipus was always the most wretched of men: even as a baby he was fated to live a horrible life. He enumerates why, building to a gruesome climax: 'He married an old woman, even though he was young, and on top of everything else, she turned out to be his own mother. Then he put his eyes right out.' Euripides is not convinced. 'Well, he was happy, then. Compared with how he'd be if he'd fought alongside Erasinides.' Erasinides was one of the generals from the Battle of Arginusae who had been executed for their conduct. Given how many Athenians had lost loved ones in that battle, and given how controversial the executions of the generals had turned out to be, this was a pretty risky joke to make. Certainly, if a parallel joke about a general in Afghanistan were broadcast today on the BBC, we would see the complaints flood in. We don't like jokes about soldiers dying, for the excellent reason that they are widely perceived to be in poor taste. And many of them may well be just that – poorly conceived, and delivered with little or no thought for the consequences or the hurt feelings they might provoke. But not all jokes on bad-taste subjects are in bad taste. There is an assumption among the holders of the moral high ground that making a joke of something is the same thing as making light of it, that laughing at something proves you consider it trivial. Actually, the reverse is often true. When a comedian approaches a difficult subject – death or illness, for example – the very last thing they are doing is trivialising it. They are giving it their full professional attention. If you make your living by making jokes, then making a joke about something is proof that you consider that subject to be genuinely important. That is why so many comedians will make jokes about the death of a loved one, a broken relationship, a time they were genuinely afraid, angry or hurt. It isn't because they are pathologically unable to feel emotion and use humour to disguise it, it's because jokes on negative subjects need to be made. No one needs jokes when their day is all flowers and kittens. They need jokes when things are difficult. This gallows humour is part of how we cope with horrible events and circumstances. Someone should make jokes about senseless loss of life, because otherwise we would all simply weep at the futility of existence, and that doesn't get anything done. Aristophanes knew perfectly well that a risky joke on a painful subject was an important thing to include in his huge, ridiculous play. Jokes shouldn't always be simple and painless, precisely because the world isn't simple or painless either. If art imitates life, even low art like cheap jokes, it can't just pick the nice bits. And the Athenians could obviously take it on the chin: they awarded Aristophanes first prize for *The Frogs*.

For the ancients, just as for us, entertainment wasn't limited to the stage, however. They loved chariot-racing, mock sea-battles and gladiatorial fights. Our vision of ancient Rome is coloured by several epic films that revolve around the games and races: Stanley Kubrick's *Spartacus*, about the rebellious gladiator, and William Wyler's *Ben Hur*, which depicts a chariot race between our hero, Ben Hur, and his friend-turned-nemesis, Messala. More recently, Ridley Scott's *Gladiator* pitched Russell Crowe's Maximus into the arena, and a literal and metaphorical fight to the death with the emperor Commodus. It's tempting for us to see these lethal entertainments as proof that the Romans really were a bloodthirsty bunch. In all three films, after all, we're asked to sympathise with the non-Romans: Maximus may have fought in the Roman army, but he is actually a Spaniard. When he and his fellow gladiators fight as the characters of Hannibal and the Carthaginians, in a staged re-enactment of the Battle of Zama, they are supposed to lose, like the Carthaginians did in real life. But they cannot resist the chance to thwart history and beat the gladiators who represent Scipio and his Roman army. Spartacus, meanwhile, is foreign-born, probably Thracian, and rises up against the Roman oppressors. When he and his band of gladiators escape, we don't want the Roman army to crush them, we root for the underdog. We don't see the gladiators as criminals on the run, we see them as heroes, freedom fighters trying to make a stand against an impossible foe. Similarly, in *Ben Hur*, we want Charlton Heston to avenge himself and his family against the Roman occupiers, represented by Messala. The films are cast to play to our prejudices: beautiful Kirk Douglas as plucky Spartacus, and mean Charles Laughton (whose career had already included the killjoy Javert in *Les Misérables*, the vile Captain Bligh in *Mutiny on the Bounty*, and the never popular King Herod in *Salome*) as the Roman, Crassus.

And it is true that the Romans placed a very low value on a large proportion of human life. Slaves and criminals were fair game to be slaughtered in the arena, on a regular basis and in huge numbers. And the Roman writers whose work survives were almost entirely uncritical of this. Livy mentions a dictum doing the rounds that a man who could organise a banquet and put on games knew how to win a war. These were all skills the Romans valued: their huge success in brutal warfare paid for the games and the banquets and it provided a vast supply of prisoners of war to fight in the arena. The very existence of the games reasserted the natural, Roman order of things: those who had committed criminal acts, or fought against the might of Rome, could then appear as gladiators, dying for the ephemeral pleasure of the very Romans they had injured.

Incidentally, one of the most widely known things about gladiators is their salute to the emperor when they entered the arena to fight. 'Ave Imperator,' they shouted. 'Morituri te salutant' – 'Hail, Emperor. Those about to die salute you.' It's a phrase that cries out to be quoted, and it has been, extensively. But it appears only once in Latin literature, and even then it isn't said by gladiators. Suetonius tells the story of a *naumachia* – a staged sea-battle fought for the entertainment of an audience. In CE 52 the emperor Claudius was giving a *naumachia* at Lake Fucinus, in central Italy. The *naumacharii*, or sea-battlers, suddenly shouted out the well-known phrase. Claudius replied, 'Aut non' – 'Or not'. Whereupon the sea-battlers refused to fight, saying he'd pardoned them. They'd said they were about to die, he'd said they might not, that was surely a pardon. Claudius saw things rather differently, and had to issue a series of threats and promises to induce them to fight. So, if '*morituri te salutant*' is a phrase that fighters usually said, why does Suetonius report it here? And why does Claudius reply at all to a stock phrase? And why, when his reply is so vague – if one really is about to die, 'Or not' doesn't really resolve one's concerns for certain – do they refuse to fight altogether? It seems much more likely that Suetonius tells the story precisely because it was so remarkable, not because it was commonplace. Those condemned to die didn't usually indulge in speechifying, they simply went out and died. But somehow the phrase has become entwined over time with stories about gladiators, and has morphed into our version of their opening gambit.

Perhaps it's not surprising that we should be so fascinated by the idea of men (and sometimes women, although this was rarer, and seen as the lower end of the gladiator market) who knew perfectly well that they were about to die. Violent death is often compelling – hence the popularity of crime and horror genres, which explore it – no more so when it seems that the victims were ordinary people like us. So no wonder we want to believe that those facing such a terrifying, brutal ritual would express their emotions in language. But gladiators weren't the only Roman entertainers who faced death whenever they went out on to the sand (the Latin *harena*, meaning 'sand', gives us the word 'arena'). The Circus Maximus saw plenty of deaths, too. Chariot-racing was an extremely dangerous profession. Roman charioteers, unlike their Greek predecessors, didn't hold the horses' reins in their hands. Rather, they had them wrapped around their bodies. This meant that if the chariot did tip, and the rider did lose his footing – hardly a rare occurrence, given that ramming another chariot with your own was fair game during a race – he would be dragged along the ground. Being trampled by horses or crushed by chariot wheels were very real possibilities. The charioteers did carry a small knife with which they could try to cut themselves free. But reaching for the knife and chopping through leather reins while being dragged along the racetrack at high speed cannot have been very easy. Nonetheless, there was no shortage of riders – the slaves among them had no choice whether they raced or not, and freedmen-charioteers could become rich. There was also the intoxicating prospect of fame: the Circus Maximus could hold around 250,000 spectators, perhaps a quarter or more of the entire population of Rome. You don't need to live in celebrity-obsessed times to see that it might be exciting to appear in front of a crowd like that.

And excitement wasn't limited to the racetrack itself, either. Ovid saw the races as the perfect place to seduce women. In *The Art of Love* he has plenty of advice for those seeking illicit city affairs. The races were a terrific cover: you could sit by your mistress and press up against her, you could chat about the horses, find out her favourites, flick imaginary dust from her clothes, provide her with a footstool, ensure no one else was rubbing up against her. The Circus Maximus might appear to be more an opportunity for frottage than chariot-racing, but at least Ovid appears to be enjoying himself.

This isn't always true with other Roman authors, who often see the games as a corrupting influence on the Roman audience, in almost exactly the manner of a disapproving broadsheet journalist decrying the mob mentality of an audience of *X Factor* viewers. Juvenal, for example, thinks gladiators are far too much admired by people who really ought to know better. His contempt is turned on a senator's wife, Eppia, who had embarked on an affair with a gladiator called Sergius. What was it about him, asks Juvenal, that made her put up with being called the Gladiatrix? He had a scarred face, a warty nose, an injured arm and a gammy eye. But it made no difference: 'sed gladiator erat' – 'he was a gladiator'. The job description makes him a pin-up even if he is physically unappealing. Some jobs just come with the kind of glamour that bewitches sense and reason. Anyone who has ever dated a person of considerably inferior talent and beauty, merely because he was in a band, must surely hang her head in shame at Juvenal's words.

Tacitus has a salutary tale about a gladiatorial show held in Pompeii in CE 59. Some trivial slight at the games provoked a day of terrible rioting between the Pompeians and the visitors from nearby Nuceria. It began with insults, developed into stone-throwing, then all-out fighting with weapons. The Pompeians came off rather better, since they had numbers on their side. The Nucerians took the corpses of their children and parents to Rome to show what had happened to them. The Senate exiled Livineius Regulus, who had paid for the show, and various other agitators. Pompeii, meanwhile, was banned from holding gladiatorial games for ten years. Sport-induced hooli-ganism and street violence certainly didn't begin with football.

The mob mentality that thrived at the games and could cause such a tragedy was also disliked by the philosopher Seneca. Writing to his friend Lucilius, he shows a real squeamishness about the goriness of gladiatorial combat which is hard to find elsewhere in surviving literature. 'In the morning,' he says, 'men are thrown to lions and bears. At lunchtime, they're thrown to the spectators.' Although he elsewhere writes admiringly of the stoic acceptance that gladiators show when they offer their neck to the sword, this particular trip to the games seems to have left him badly shocked. He describes the mob baying for blood: 'Kill him, whip him, burn him! Why does he fall upon the sword so fearfully? Why does he fall so meekly? Why does he die so unwillingly?'

Was it Seneca's philosophy that made him less enthusiastic than his contemporaries on the whole subject of death for entertainment? It is one of the oddest things for the modern reader of ancient literature to accept: that people who wrote such extraordinary works – touching, sensitive, funny and clever – were so often unconcerned by the brutality that surrounded them. How could love poets like Horace or Ovid not care about the death of innocents? How could any Roman who had done military service, like Juvenal, not be shocked by the Roman war machine into pacifism? And how could they care so little that people died in the name of entertainment? The simple answer is that our notion of humanity is very different from those who lived in ancient Greece and Rome. While we have many things in common with our ancestors, we also diverge dramatically on this point (and plenty of others). It's tempting to believe that we are the pinnacle of moral evolution – our views on women, slavery and gladiators are clearly superior to the Romans' views in every way. But perhaps future generations will judge us just as harshly for beliefs that now seem entirely uncontroversial. Either way, we can't simply assume that people in a totally different culture would respond to the same stimuli in the way that we would. Most of us, surely, would blanch at the notion of killing as entertainment. But that isn't true everywhere, even now. Public executions have taken place in football stadiums in Afghanistan and Iraq in the past decade. The link between violent death and the sporting arena is not yet consigned to history.

We live in a culture defined by celebrity obsession. If we aren't buying endless magazines with pictures of celebs looking fabulous (or terrible), we're reading about their burgeoning romances (or incipient divorces). We can love or hate this model, that singer, this actress, but we have to struggle to ignore them. Reality television makes stars of ordinary people, and the paparazzi's long lenses make ordinary people out of stars. Even the most respectable broadsheets occasionally assume they should have an opinion on, say, the names of children of two semi-famous people we've never met. Those who dislike this cult of celebrity can find an early sympathiser in Tertullian. He was a Christian who wrote in the early years of the third century CE, and he produced a work called *De Spectaculis*, 'On the Shows'. His disapproval of the Roman way of life wasn't limited to a dislike of their low entertainment, but his absolute bemusement at their love/hate relationship with their stars is striking. What really baffles him is that the gladiators and charioteers are often slaves – men with no rights whatsoever. Tertullian complains that the Roman people clearly despise slaves. They give them no voting rights, no civic office, no office of any kind, in fact. Yet they adore them, or in Tertullian's words: 'Charioteers, actors, athletes, gladiators – those men to whom men surrender their souls and women even their bodies too'. The Romans glorify and degrade them for the exact same quality – being a gladiator, an actor, a chariot-racer. 'What perversity!' he exclaims. 'They love those they punish, they despise those they consider good, they celebrate the art, they stigmatise the artist.'

Tertullian's words cannot help but resonate today, when celebrities fall in and out of favour with a fickle public in an almost entirely arbitrary way. We too praise and loathe the same people for the same behaviour: one person's good-time girl is another's problem drinker. A lovable rogue is only millimetres away from the lowest type of love rat. We love music, and we love musicians. But wear the wrong outfit, give the wrong performance or say the wrong thing at an awards ceremony, and we turn like the weather. We consume these celebrities, judge them, and find them wanting. And yet there is no shortage of candidates to replace them. And why should there be, when a humble Mr Universe can end up as the Governor of California? Not that the path from performer to political power is one way: even those who hold high office are happy to play at being celebrities. Tony Blair gave his voice to *The Simpsons*, and Bill Clinton played saxophone on *The Arsenio Hall Show*. At the time these performances were received with some criticism – Clinton was called the 'MTV President' – but they still stick in our minds as examples of political leaders using pop culture to appeal to a mass audience. Besides, Clinton and Blair were following in a long tradition. The emperor Nero drove a chariot at the Circus Maximus and especially loved the stage. He would embark on a performance whenever possible: he wasn't fiddling about (i.e. doing nothing) when Rome burned, he was fiddling (i.e. playing a musical instrument – not exactly a fiddle, but near enough). He sang in operas and acted in tragedies. But the great difficulty with supreme leaders believing they have supreme artistic talent is that nobody has the courage to cut their act short. Suetonius tells us that no one was allowed to leave the theatre when Nero was mid-recital. Pregnant women had to give birth in the aisles, and men pretended to be dead so they could be carried out. So perhaps the real question isn't whether our leaders' dignity is damaged by their passion for the arts, but whether the arts are damaged by our leaders' infatuation with them. If nothing else it proves an incontrovertible truth – that no matter how powerful and successful people become, they still want to entertain.

8

The Price of Everything, the Value of Nothing

Money, as Kander and Ebb once wrote, makes the world go around. However much we may try to console ourselves that the best things in life are free, the sorry truth is that the best things in life may well be an absolute bargain, but many of the necessary things – food, shelter, heat, light – cost hard cash. Money is a driving force in virtually every life – ancient or modern. Even hermits have to eat, after all. But without the Romans, money would certainly have another name: the Roman mint was on the Capitoline Hill, near the temple of Juno Moneta (Juno who Warns, or Reminds). It is from Moneta that we derive the word 'money'.

The economy has, over the past few years, encapsulated everything that anti-capitalists most loathe about money. The very rich became so ridiculously wealthy that their incomes dwarfed those of large companies and small countries. The very poor may have been objectively less impoverished in relation to the cost of a pint of milk, but they became infinitely poorer in relation to the wealth of some of their compatriots. Then, just as we began to choke on conspicuous consumption

– a hundred-million-pound flat was put up for sale in London just before the recession began – suddenly we all lost our collective shirts as the markets wobbled and the currencies wavered. The bankers had already incensed us when they drove prices up everywhere they went – where Wall Street employees lived and worked, property cost more to rent and half-fat lattes cost more to buy. Now they incensed us all over again, as it became clear that it was their fault we couldn't get a mortgage to buy a flat at a price still overinflated by the last influx of bonus-wielding bankers with a mind on buy-to-let. Manhattan and London both heard mutterings of rebellion. We watched people queuing hopelessly on the streets, trying to dig their money from the tottering institutions they'd considered a safe bet. The UK threatened Iceland with terrorism laws to freeze assets. The USA saw several high-profile Ponzi schemes collapse. And as tax-payers' money bailed out the banks, effigies of bankers were burned in the streets. Even those who'd considered banking, hedge funds and private equity to be the pinnacle of boring vulgarity had to acknowledge that, whether we liked it or not, we were now all connected. As so often, when bubbles burst and prices crash, those who lose the most tend to be the least responsible for either bubble or collapse. And those whose careless, foolish, hubristic or criminal behaviour precipitated the crisis seem to have dusted themselves off with remarkable speed. As Dorothy Parker once observed: if you want to know what God thinks about money, just look at the people he gives it to.

Whether we have money or not, whether we long for a big pay cheque or despise it, we live in a world that is ruled by money. How much you have, how much you earn, what you spend it on, how much things cost, how much tax you pay – these are questions that define our times. Money might appear to be a mere tool of society, but it has its own morality: cautious savers bemoan the fecklessness of those with credit-card debt and overdrafts. They don't just view them as financially broke but as morally bankrupt too. 'Neither a borrower nor a lender be,' they intone, as though Polonius were a wise role model, instead of an interfering old fusspot. On the other side of the balance sheet, canny borrowers protest that cheap credit has kept the economy moving – if we all stash our cash away in the bank instead of spending it in the shops, the consequences for everyone else would be disastrous. Corporations offer rewards to high-spenders – discount vouchers, free products, Airmiles – as though purchasing goods or services were an act that somehow deserves to be rewarded. Meanwhile, the Archbishop of Canterbury feels perfectly comfortable attacking bankers for a failure to repent their wrongdoing. It seems that receiving enormous bonuses is no longer merely obnoxious, but against Christian morality. And he may have a point: if it was easier for a camel to pass through the eye of a needle than a rich man to enter heaven in the first century CE, imagine what size animal you'd need to shunt through the needle nowadays, when the richest are so very many more times richer than the poorest. Even Croesus, the axiomatically rich king – and Midas, with his golden touch – would struggle to compete with Russian oligarchs, Saudi oil magnates and American software gurus.

The conspicuously rich have always excited envy. In fifth-century Athens it was Nicias whose great wealth provoked correspondingly great irritation. Pericles, said Plutarch, led the city using his natural virtue and power with words. 'But since Nicias lacked these qualities, but had considerable wealth, he used this to rule the people.' The sniffy tone of disapproval is unmistakable. Money is the route to power and influence for people who don't have talent. And not only is Nicias rich rather than able, but his wealth is a little suspect, because he made his money from the silver mines at Laurium. No one pretended that mining was a pleasant job – large numbers of slaves died in mines every day, from the hard work and the terrible conditions – and Plutarch leaves us in no doubt that he considers mining-money less pure than other kinds: 'He kept a soothsayer in his house, and pretended he was always asking about the people's affairs, but most of the time he was asking about his own affairs, especially about his silver mines. He had major interests at Laurium, which produced huge profits for him, although the work was not without danger.' The Greeks had perhaps a less utilitarian attitude to their slaves than the Romans. This isn't to suggest that all Greeks saw their slaves as human beings and all Romans saw them as glorified farm animals. But the Greek model of a decent way of life is very much along the lines that we have seen from Ischomachus, in Xenophon's *Oeconomicus*: a household would comprise a man, a woman, children, a few slaves and a few animals. Most Athenians weren't trying to create huge revenues each year; the ideal was to produce food and goods that would feed and clothe your family, with a little left over to sell on or trade. Everyone in the household, at least according to Ischomachus, should know their role and do their bit, whether it is hard physical labour in the fields, or storing and organising goods in the home. And so the slaves working on a Greek farm would be known personally to their master, and he might well work with them, on days when he didn't have voting, council business or jury-duty to do. There was not, in other words, a huge distinction between the average Greek man and his slaves, who were very probably also Greek, but had been on the losing side in a war, resulting in their enslavement. The Athenians would share a language, even if dialects differed somewhat, with the slaves they used.

Nicias, on the other hand, had mining slaves, probably several thousand of them. The personal connection between slave and master was non-existent. Mine slaves were simply there to work until their early death, they were never going to be part of someone's family. This model is far closer to our idea of what slavery in the ancient world was like. It's also far closer to the Roman model, where citizens had moved away from the small-farm ideal. The Roman Empire was enormous, and their slaves were correspondingly far flung. A Roman might well have highly educated Greek slaves as his secretaries, then Gauls, Germans, Britons, Egyptians and Syrians, to name just a few, as cooks, bodyguards, litter-bearers and so on. If the slaves all spoke different languages from one another, of course they couldn't follow in the footsteps of Spartacus and rebel. How does a Briton negotiate with a Parthian to achieve anything? Even if they could find a way to understand each other, they'd still have to explain things to the German down the hall before they could get their co-conspirators up to three. So once we start looking at the huge households of wealthy Romans, we find more distance between slave and master, just as Nicias had in Athens with his silver-miners.

What would Nicias have spent his money on? Why did people need a lot of cash in Athens? The market for luxury goods that the Romans loved was still hundreds of years away. Well, as Plutarch suggests, Nicias could use his money to buy influence. Although the democracy meant, in principle, that everyone had equal power over the direction of the state, the reality was rather less even-handed. The major political figures of the fifth century BCE were usually from the wealthier end of the social spectrum. Pericles may not have been as rich as Nicias, but he was certainly upper class. Alcibiades – the playboy with whom Athens enjoyed a love/hate relationship in the latter part of the fifth century – was the son of Pericles' cousin, another member of an old Athenian clan with an unimpeachable family tree. So money could put Nicias into the same realm as those who, at least in Plutarch's view, outstripped him in terms of ability.

Money could also buy him popularity: the wealthiest Athenians would pay huge sums for projects that mattered to their fellow citizens, such as fitting out a trireme or kitting out a chorus for the dramatic festivals. When the prizes were handed out at the drama festivals, they were jointly awarded to the author of the play and the *choregos*, who paid for the chorus. It might have been an expensive task, but it came with huge public recognition of wealth and generosity. Similarly, equipping a trireme was a huge public statement. These ships weren't rowed by galley-slaves, as we might expect, but by ordinary Athenian working-class men, *thētai*. Think how incensed we (rightly) become today when we believe that the Ministry of Defence has skimped on its spending and sent soldiers into battle without the proper equipment. The Athenians were no different: those who stayed behind in the city – the old, the young, the women – knew that their menfolk were sailing into danger. Athens was a huge sea-power: her navy was a source of immense national pride. So if your husband or son returned home from a sea-battle, you might well have thought the man who paid for his ship was the one you had to thank. Conversely, if you lost someone in a shipwreck, you often started looking for someone to blame. Nicias' wealth could make him a hero or a villain in the eyes of thousands of his fellow Athenians.

Lower down the social scale, money could still mean the difference between life and death. While Athenian rowers could expect a rich compatriot to kit out their boat, Athenian cavalrymen simply received some money to help buy equipment. But they needed a certain amount of property to qualify for the cavalry in the first place. If you could afford to be considered for the cavalry, rather than the infantry, your chances of surviving a day's fighting were greatly enhanced. The regular foot-soldiers – or grunts, to give them their *Jarhead* name – were the ones most likely to fall in combat. Those on horseback had much better chances – higher up, better armoured and swifter. So cash really could mean the difference between life and death to many ordinary Athenians.

And not just in battle, either. Doctors weren't free in the ancient world, so if you became ill, or injured, money could be a life-saver. Aulus Cornelius Celsus may have been a doctor, or perhaps just an educated layman, but either way he wrote an eight-book encyclopaedia on medicine and the human body, *De Medicina*. Celsus' life remains opaque to us nowadays, although he was probably born in the later part of the first century BCE, and he may have lived in Rome, Gaul or elsewhere. He wrote extensively on literature, agriculture and military affairs. Quintilian, the rhetorician, practically defines the notion of damning with faint praise when he refers to Celsus as 'vir mediocri ingenio' – 'a man of mediocre genius'. But while Celsus may have been unimpressive to his contemporaries, he gives us a terrific idea of what medical understanding and treatment was available in the ancient world. The opening to his book is a précis of earlier medical knowledge, almost all gleaned from the Greeks. Hippocrates of Cos is the one most remembered today: when doctors take their Hippocratic oath – 'first do no harm' – it's Hippocrates whom they commemorate. And Alexandria became a real hub of medical activity in the Hellenistic period. It was a home to many Greek doctors: Herophilus and Eristratus, for a start. These men lived in the late fourth and third centuries BCE, and they were medical pioneers – they performed experiments, theorised about blood vessels and nerves. When Celsus explains to us the treatments for neuralgia, the perils of gangrene or the remedies for fever, he is sharing the wisdom of dozens of earlier thinkers like them. Celsus also tells us how to treat wounds, how to remove weapons from wounds and what kind of injuries are the most worrisome. He knows how to remove cataracts and repair fractures. If you had money, the ancient world could be a far less painful place (at least in the long term. One imagines that treatments of bone fractures in a time before anaesthetic made the short term pretty horrendous either way). Doctors thrived in the Roman world, where people had enough money to keep them in business. Ancient medical science probably reached its pinnacle in the second century CE, with the physician Galen, from Pergamon in Asia Minor – modern Turkey. Galen began to produce a more sophisticated analysis of human anatomy, dissecting monkeys since dissecting people was not allowed. His anatomical discoveries contributed hugely to medical science for an incredibly long time: they didn't begin to be overturned until the 1500s.

And, incidentally, we may have medicine to thank for most of our knowledge of Socrates. Socrates' final words, in Plato's *Phaedo*, were to his friend Crito: 'Crito, we owe a cockerel to Asclepius. Give him his due, and don't forget.' Asclepius was the Greek god of healing, and normally one owed him a sacrifice when he had healed someone. Given that Socrates had drunk hemlock at this point in the dialogue, and was in his final moments, his remark puzzled scholars for a very long time. What could he possibly mean? Asclepius couldn't save Socrates now. And Socrates didn't want to be saved – he chose to drink the hemlock, after all, rather than escape prison and live in exile. So could Socrates be suggesting that his death was somehow a cure for his life? Could he have been employing the rather anachronistic Christian notion that the afterlife was better than the present one? Plenty of tortuous explanations have been proposed. But by far the most ingenious – and convincing – is one that requires no foisting of later moral or religious belief on to a fifth-century BCE Athenian like Socrates. Something that people did believe at this time was that in a person's final moments they could develop second sight. A final gift for a dying man might be a vision of what's to come when he's gone.

At the beginning of the dialogue, Phaedo lists who was present in Socrates' last hours. Plato was (unusually) absent because, says Phaedo, he was ill. So the most satisfying interpretation of Socrates' last words is to suggest that he had been given the gift of second sight. And that his second sight had revealed to him that Plato's illness had passed, that he would recover and go on to write his dialogues, sharing his mentor's wisdom with the rest of the world and setting up the whole future of Western thought. So Crito needed to discharge a debt to Asclepius, not for curing Socrates, who was beyond repair, but for curing Plato, who was not. We should remember that whether or not we believe in second sight – and it's probably fair to assume most of us don't – isn't relevant here. Plato most probably did believe in it, and it's his version of Socrates' last moments that we're reading. So let's choose to believe that Socrates' friends, who were often so generous with their money to help their friend, spent at least a few drachmae on a sacrifice to Asclepius, god of medicine, and saviour of Plato. If nothing else, there is something immensely gratifying about this detective-story solution to a long-standing mystery.

If money could buy you health in the ancient world, it didn't necessarily buy you a long life. We tend to assume everyone died young in ancient times, for the seemingly good reason that their life expectancy was much shorter than ours. This just goes to prove that many of us should have paid more attention in maths lessons at school. Because clearly, plenty of people did reach a considerable age: Socrates was seventy when he died of hemlock poisoning. Several hundred years later, another philosopher-suicide, Seneca, was about the same age when he died. These men, and plenty more people like them, weren't freaks of nature, either: Aristophanes loves nothing more than a chorus of grumpy old men (*The Wasps*) or grumpy old men and women (*Lysistrata*). Plenty of people, in other words, lived past their apparent sell-by date. The reason life expectancy was so short wasn't because no one was old, but because so very many people died young. The first year of life was extremely perilous. If you survived being born, you still had an uphill battle ahead of you. Roughly a third of children would die before they reached the age of six: childhood diseases were a grim business in a time before vaccination. By the age of sixteen, perhaps 60 per cent of live births had died. Make it through childhood alive and you still had perils ahead of you: soldiering for men, childbirth for women. No wonder life expectancy was so low. But the rich must have had better chances of surviving illness or childbirth, for example – their living conditions were less cramped, they had better hygiene and access to doctors.

It makes it all the more dispiriting that the correlation between riches and life expectancy today remains so strong – a baby born in Kensington, in wealthy west London, will live for probably thirteen years longer than one born in Glasgow. In the Western world, at least, very few children succumb to lethal childhood diseases; youth is no longer synonymous with fatal risk. But poverty still means a much shorter life. Particularly worrying is the fact that it is personal, relative poverty that seems to be the key, rather than the objective wealth of the society in which we live: in 2008 the World Health Organization found that children born in the most deprived areas of Glasgow had a lower life expectancy than their contemporaries born in India, where 80 per cent of the population lives on less than £1 a day. Considering Glasgow has universal health care, that's a damning statistic. Perhaps we haven't moved away from the inequity of the ancient world as much we might have hoped.

Ancient Athenians might also have spent their money educating their children. Here, they differed from their Peloponnesian counterparts: Spartans scooped up their offspring at the age of seven and put them into a state-run educational system that was a cross between a boarding school and a military academy. Children were taught to fight, to steal food and to obey orders. It was a type of education, but not one that left the populace literate or cultured. The Athenians, on the other hand, educated their children privately. It's hard to say exactly what that education entailed, but it certainly included poetry and music, wrestling and athletics, and some degree of literacy. There was far more widespread literacy in Athens than in Sparta, and it's tempting for us, in our literate societies, to view this as a measure of educational worth. If a child left school today without being able to read and write (as many do), we would consider that the educational system had failed them. We require literacy for the most basic aspects of our lives – signing our names, filling in forms, reading instructions. To lack literacy is to lack the ability to communicate: go to a country that uses a different alphabet from your own, and you can quickly imagine how isolating illiteracy is: you can't read maps or menus, and unless there are pictures, you can't tell what's inside a carton of drink or a can of food. But we have to remember that the ancient world wasn't like ours. If there isn't a blanket assumption of mass literacy, then being illiterate isn't such a big deal.

We can also see, from the process of ostracism, how a literacy issue could easily be resolved, even in a practice that involved writing. The Athenians could ostracise someone for ten years, either as a punishment for perceived wrongdoing, or as a pre-emptive strike to prevent it. There was no rule about what someone had to have done to be proposed for ostracism – if you disliked your cousin, say, and decided to write his name down, there was nothing preventing you from doing so. You might struggle to get sufficient votes from your fellow citizens for it to have any effect, however – by the 480s BCE, a candidate for ostracism needed to receive 6,000 votes before they were booted out of Athens. That's a lot of peeved acquaintances. The votes were cast by scratching the name of your nemesis on a shard of pottery, called an *ostrakon*. For a long time, the practice was seen as conclusive proof of mass literacy in fifth-century Athens. Then an archaeologist noticed that on 191 *ostraka* naming Themistocles as the man who should pack his bags and leave, only 14 different handwritings could be seen. Something fishy was going on. Perhaps it was fraud, and someone was mass-voting for their personal enemy. It should be remembered that these kinds of scandals routinely hit reality TV programmes, newspaper polls and so forth, so perhaps a fondness for rigging a ballot is deep-seated in human nature. But there is a more innocent explanation: perhaps the Athenians who couldn't write but wished to vote could simply approach one of a few scribes, and dictate the name they wanted. Either way, the opportunity to commit electoral fraud was considerable – how would the illiterate voter know that the name scratched on the shard was the one he wanted? But today we still allow postal voting, in which a ballot paper can be cheerily sent through the mail with no one actually checking that the voter and the form-filler are the same person, or that the voter has not been coerced into voting for a candidate they don't want. Once again, we seem to have learned virtually nothing in two and half millennia.

If most Athenian children got at least some education, only the rich got what we might call a higher education, usually at the hands of the sophists we met in Chapter 3. Sophists could teach grammar, geometry, astronomy, rhetoric, virtue and plenty more. There's good reason to believe that the mass of ordinary Athenians found them rather suspect: Socrates (who was often viewed as a sophist, even though he didn't call himself a teacher) was put to death, and Protagoras may have seen his books burned. As so often in history, a cluster of intellectuals was seen as dangerous, especially if young men were drawn to them. It was easy to blame their teachers when the young men turned out badly – like Alcibiades, who fought both for and against the Athenians in the Peloponnesian War, or Critias, one of the Thirty Tyrants, who helped to overthrow democracy and ruled Athens briefly in 404 BCE. Both men were known associates of Socrates and his fellow intellectuals, and their choices undoubtedly reflected badly on their teachers. Although, as teachers might well argue today, there's a limit to how much influence they can really have over their students. In ancient Athens, money could buy you an education in virtue, but it couldn't make you virtuous.

So money could buy you what we would see as essentials in ancient Athens – not just food, but medical treatment, and education. And it also allowed you to buy slaves, which enabled you to participate in the democracy – by going and voting – without your livelihood suffering: whether you were a farmer or a tanner, you couldn't afford to take much time away from your work unless you had other people who would take up the slack. But while the Athenians no doubt looked profligate to the Spartans, their spending paled compared with later generations. After Alexander's death the Hellenistic period developed a hefty bureaucracy, both political and personal: in 248 BCE a papyrus receipt for several pigs was given by a man called Heracleides to an Egyptian pig-farmer called Petosiris. Although Petosiris lived in Fayum, in Egypt, the receipt was written in Greek. We have, of course, no way of knowing if an Egyptian pig-farmer could read Greek, or even if he could read at all. What we do know is that the world was changing – when people have the time and resources for bureaucracy, they must have access to papyrus, ink, literacy education, sufficient goods to be worth selling and documenting, and so on. A time when men owned small farms and made just enough for their households to thrive was morphing into a culture of buyers and sellers. And if you were buying, Rome soon had a lot for sale.

The Romans waged war against Jugurtha, the king of Numidia, in North Africa, at the end of the second century BCE. Jugurtha was an unscrupulous man, and not one to hesitate before ordering illegal executions and the like. Nonetheless, during a temporary cessation of hostilities, even he was shocked by the levels of corruption and venality he found in Rome (at least according to the historian Sallust, who spent much of his career despairing of others' shoddy morals, never seeming to notice that his own morals weren't exactly pristine either). Jugurtha looked back on Rome as he left to resume the war, and exclaimed, 'That is a city for sale, and she will soon perish, if she finds a buyer.' Had he only known what was to come in Rome – the imperial system, and with it the unimaginable luxury and waste – he might have been lost for words.

Roman authors were invariably critical of the state Rome was in today. Luxury and vice were their preoccupations – Rome was on the slide from its moral high point, and nothing could be done to stop it. The strange thing about this mentality is that it still pervades everywhere today. Turn on any news station, open any newspaper, and the prevailing mood is one of despair. If only we hadn't become the slaves of capitalism, if only women had stayed at home, if only the welfare state hadn't destroyed people's will to work. There's always a nebulous time at some point in the past when things were, in some formless way, better: when young people didn't roam the streets, when old people were looked after by their families, when no one ate ready meals and there was never any swearing on TV. This type of Norman Rockwell fantasy is enormously seductive. Remember, the author seems to be asking, when people lived in better, more innocent times? Only we never do remember, because we weren't there. The better time is like the end of a rainbow, always a little out of our reach, no matter where we are. When we're presented with an apparently perfect world in film or on TV, we know there's an ugly underbelly – that the wives of Stepford are robots, that *The Truman Show* is a reality programme, that the Desperate Housewives have dark secrets and drinking problems behind their perfect picket fences. We realise that perfection means artifice when we're in the fictional world, yet when it's the real, historical world, we often forget to be quite so critical. Luckily the Roman writers give us a perfect sense of the perspective we desperately need. Sallust, living in the first century BCE, looked back at the second century and thought the Roman world then was terribly corrupt. But Cicero, Sallust's contemporary, raged against the collapse of the Republic that they were living through in the first century, because he wanted things to be like they were before power grabs and civil war. In other words, he wanted things to be like they were in what he considered to be more innocent times. But the time before Cicero was also the time of Jugurtha, and as Sallust tells us, Rome was rife with corruption and bribery even then. And by the time of second-century CE authors like Juvenal, or Tacitus, the whole period of the Republic had become a yardstick to which their time could not possibly compare: Sallust and Cicero would have been horrified. But the imperial writers were quite sure they live in a worse time than previous generations. If a paragon of virtue from the Republican past, like Scipio, popped up in Rome today, says Juvenal, 'The first question would be about his wealth, the last one would be about his morals.'

What we are so quick to forget, just as our Roman predecessors were, is that it isn't a time or a political system that makes people venal. It's people that make a time or a political system venal, and they are the same whenever and wherever they live. Ordinary people looked on in astonishment when the banks brought capitalism to its knees in 2008. But we'd been here before, less than a hundred years earlier. Franklin D. Roosevelt, in his first inaugural address, in March 1933, said this:

Practices of the unscrupulous money changers stand indicted in the court of public opinion, rejected by the hearts and minds of men ... Faced by failure of credit they have proposed only the lending of more money. Stripped of the lure of profit by which to induce our people to follow their false leadership, they have resorted to exhortations, pleading tearfully for restored confidence. They know only the rules of a generation of self-seekers.

It's hard to imagine that anyone speaking in 2008 could have put things any better; somehow we'd found ourselves in precisely the same mess all over again. If we learn nothing else from the ancient world, we should at least try to break this Roman habit of living in a state of low-level hysteria because we believe that our contemporary moral and financial problems stem from the fact that we're sliding away from a mythical time of moral and financial rectitude. We aren't: there is no once upon a time.

Rome was an easy place for people to be bitter about luxury and money, however. It was a city where a few people had incredible wealth, and everybody knew people far richer than they themselves were. Rome's social structure was basically pyramidal. At the bottom of the pyramid were the plebs. Above them, a far smaller number of equites – what we would call the middle class. Above them was a still smaller number of patricians, those of senatorial class – the aristocracy. And from Augustus onwards the pyramid narrowed again, down to one man at the very top: the emperor. The emperor was the ultimate patron in a world that thrived on patron–client relationships. Augustus, for example, had unrivalled wealth and influence once he was emperor. If you wanted a job in the higher echelons of government, like running a province (and making wads of cash from it), Augustus was the man you needed to know and impress. If you were a little lower down the social ladder, and you wanted a job working for the governor of a province, then you needed to impress the man who'd impressed Augustus. And so on. As the client of a wealthy patron, you could expect some cash or food handouts, and in exchange you had to give them a public display of gravitas. When someone walked past the house of an influential man, they might see a queue of his clients waiting to talk to their patron and maybe get that day's handout. If that influential man wanted to stand for office, his clients could easily be marshalled into a rent-a-mob, making him look like he had plenty of keen voters in the bag. And, of course, if you were hoping for high office – to be made governor of Macedonia, for example – you might want to look really popular. So popular that the emperor would prefer you to be a long way from Rome. Your clients, meanwhile, might be thinking of all the contracts you'd award them to run building projects or tax collections in Macedonia once you got there. Everybody was a winner in the patron–client relationship, so long as they didn't mind constantly being reminded that they were less well off than the man one rung above them on the social ladder.

And it wasn't just those who worked in the bureaucracy of the state who needed patrons – artists did, too. The most celebrated patron of Imperial Rome was Maecenas (himself a friend and client of Augustus). Maecenas had terrific taste – he was patron of Horace, Virgil and the love-poet Propertius. Without his financial backing, some of the most extraordinary poetry of the age might never have been written. But if we want to see an alternative vision of what the client–patron relationship looked like, we need to turn our attention back to Juvenal, who despises his fellow Romans for their acquisitiveness, their need to keep up with the latest fashion, even on borrowed money. 'Omnia Romae cum pretio,' he snaps. 'Everything in Rome comes with a price.'

Juvenal, as you might expect, doesn't see the client–patron

relationship in a positive light at all. He devotes a whole satire to the story of what a dinner party is like for the poor. A wealthy patron invites plenty of guests to dinner, including, very infrequently, his clients. They resent being invited so rarely to share in his largesse. But then when they actually do go to a dinner, they are humiliated at every stage – so much so that Juvenal asks his friend Trebius if he really thinks that the highest good he can expect from his life is to live off another man's crusts. And this from Juvenal, who despises anyone's idea of an honest day's work. But Juvenal thinks his friend's role as a client is even worse than working for living. How bad can your hunger be? he asks. Aren't there bridges you could beg under instead? Anything, in other words, to avoid '*inuria cenae*', 'the insult of dinner'. It is for phrases like this, by the way, that you should forgive Juvenal his mean-spiritedness. Who else would have slammed the idea of a dinner being an insult into two words that read like a slap in the face? This is the fruit of your great friendship, he adds: food. Juvenal is simply too grumpy to look at patronage any more generously than he looks at, say, marriage. Perhaps we can assume that since there are some happy marriages (something Juvenal can't countenance), there might have been a few happy patrons and clients, whose mutually beneficial friendship was an inspiration to all who saw it. That isn't the story we're ever going to get from Juvenal, though: Trebius' patron, Virro, is a parsimonious snob who invites his clients over once every couple of months for one lousy dinner. And then he offers them horrible, rough wine, while drinking a prized vintage himself. He has a jewel-encrusted goblet, they get an ordinary cup. And even that's got cracks in it. His slaves are too superior to bring you anything you ask for, even if it's just some water. You are given bread that will break your teeth; his is finely milled and fluffy. In other words, Virro expects constant bowing and scraping from Trebius, and when he offers him a favour in return, he uses every opportunity to ram home the difference in their respective statuses. 'Perhaps you think Virro is just cutting back on his expenses. No, he's doing it to upset you.' But if Trebius suddenly struck it rich, Virro would change his tune and they'd be instant best friends.

The anger that Juvenal expresses is so pungent it seems impossible to believe it's manufactured simply for the poem. His fury at a social order that emphasises relative poverty and wealth, and allows the rich to treat the poor like scum, is surely heartfelt. Isn't it really Juvenal who has been passed over at dinner, ignored by uppity slaves and made to feel every bit the hanger-on? And if we lack sympathy with him because he himself is a snob, then we should at least feel his pain in Satire Seven, when he points out that a hundred lawyers have barely the same amount of cash as one charioteer on the red team. Even if Juvenal were prepared to take on what we might consider a proper job (writing comedy is never that), he'd still be miles behind the earnings of a horse-racer. This is surely the subtext behind every furious editorial about Premier League footballers' wages: they aren't even clever, but they're getting paid thousands of times more than most of the hard-working children in school will ever earn. What's the point in sucking it all up and working in an office if you're still going to be poor, compared with them?

And if Juvenal felt that he'd been mistreated by the rich, at least he was a free man who could walk away and beg under nearby arches if he really wanted to. It's more than slaves could do. For all Juvenal's dislike of what he viewed as the self-satisfied slaves of the very wealthy, they were still slaves. And although they could sometimes earn enough to buy their own freedom, their choices were completely curtailed by another person. Perhaps Virro's slaves did enjoy belittling his hangers-on, and saving scraps of the nicest food and wine for themselves, while feeding dross to the likes of Trebius. Scholars have often suggested that the slaves of the well-to-do were actually better off than the free-but-poor. Slave women would do household chores rather than turning to prostitution (so long as they weren't surplus to household requirements, whereupon they might well be sold into prostitution). And slaves might not be free, but they would at least be fed and sheltered. Slaves in a household might well form attachments and be allowed to marry and have children. It's easy for us, with no idea what slavery would feel like, to compare them to the servants on a large estate in the time of, say, Jane Austen. And perhaps it was just like that. But instinct surely tells us that it was much worse. Take the story of Vedius Pollio, which Seneca tells in his work *On Anger*. Pollio was a rich man, and he had the crystal goblets to prove it. One of his slaves broke a goblet, which anyone knows is always a risk with expensive glassware. Vedius was considerably less sanguine about the breakage, however, than his slave might have hoped. Rather than shrug it off and buy another, or simply accept that he would have less than a full set, Vedius ordered the slave to be seized and put to death. But not in any obvious way. Rather, he ordered that the hapless slave be thrown into a pond filled with giant lampreys, which would eat him. If you're trying to work out who this reminds you of, it's Blofeld, in *You Only Live Twice*, when he has Helga Brandt thrown to his piranhas. It really takes a Bond villain – or Vedius Pollio – to keep such ugly fish purely for the purposes of feeding your unwanted underlings to them. It was, says Seneca, showing a commendable gift for understatement, an act of cruelty. Luckily for the slave, he slipped from his captor's grip and begged the emperor Augustus for mercy. Interestingly, he didn't beg not to be killed, only not to be eaten alive by fish. Perhaps he couldn't imagine that he didn't deserve to die for breaking a cup. Augustus was so moved by the novelty of Vedius' cruelty, he ordered that the slave boy be released. Then he had every one of Vedius' crystal goblets smashed before his eyes. And his fish pond filled in. History doesn't record what happened to the lampreys.

Dinner parties – with or without blood-sucking eels – were a feature of wealthy Roman life. The minute a society has money going spare, it appears, its citizens can think of little they would like to do more than invite the neighbours round for a meal. The Romans, like many of us, were house-proud hedonists. They liked to fill their homes with statues, mosaics and art. They liked to buy fancy plates and dishes. They liked to spend their money on exotic foods and chefs who could prepare those foods in unlikely ways. And then they liked to invite their friends over and show all of it off. Even the emperors weren't immune to the hospitality bug: Augustus, according to Suetonius, gave plenty of dinner parties. And he seems to have been a thoughtful host, too, encouraging his shyer guests to talk, and hiring actors or circus performers to entertain the company. He wasn't, by Roman standards, especially free with the food, which he usually limited to three courses. On his most generous days he might stretch to six. This may sound like a lot to a modern, Western reader, since we no longer conflate wealth and the sating of appetites. Quite the reverse, in fact. We see that obesity is intimately linked with poverty – the fatter you are, brutally, the poorer you look. And the converse is true: the very rich are far more likely to be thin than the very poor, in parts of the world where food is, for the most part, incredibly cheap and available. When we see a Hollywood actor with a perfectly honed physique, we know very well that it has taken literally hours of work every day: exercising; eating carefully prepared, low-fat, low-sugar food; perhaps having a little surgery to help things along. A city worker with an enviable figure doesn't get that way because she grabs a doughnut on the way in to work each morning. She gets that way by refusing to take the cheap, easy route, by getting up early to go to the gym before work, and by eating a sensible bowl of porridge before she sits down at her desk, so she doesn't snack on energy-dense junk at eleven o'clock. No woman, the Duchess of Windsor once proclaimed, could be too rich or too thin. It's an opinion that shows little sign of going out of fashion.

When cheap, calorific food is both plentiful and easily accessible, it takes a certain commitment to avoid it. Eating fresh vegetables and organic meat costs more than scarfing a burger and fries. So the burger and fries diet, with its contingent waistline, becomes a sign of poverty, both financial and spiritual. The ire people will cheerfully vent about the obese on long-haul flights, for example, is often more than mere territorial irritation that a fatty is taking up a bit more of your arm-rest than you would like. Rather, it comes with real, moral disapproval, often masked by an ersatz concern for safety issues. It's not that the fat person is fat, it's that they might not be able to do up their seatbelt, or lock their seat upright, and that would be dangerous. Plus they might block the route of virtuous, thin people to the emergency exit. Fatness is a signifier of changed times. It used to mean you were rich enough to eat more than you needed to survive; now, it means you're poor enough or lazy enough to prize junk food over a media ideal of the perfect body.

But the Roman love of excess was so pronounced than even Romans would mock it. Petronius was a courtier of Nero, with the job title, according to Tacitus, of 'arbiter elegentiae' – 'the arbiter of elegance'. This was the man who decided what was hot and what was not. He was also most probably the same Petronius who was the author of *Satyricon*, a comic novel that has survived in fragmentary form. It's not a novel as we would understand it – even in the bits we do have, the plot is decidedly peculiar – but it contains an extended piece about a dinner party of lunatic extravagance, given by a freedman, Trimalchio. Trimalchio is the model of vulgar greed and stupidity. He is incredibly rich, but his impoverished background means that he has no taste, no restraint and no idea how proper Romans do things. When he does realise that he is more expansive than is customary, he assumes his deviation (since it is always on the side of finer wine, more courses, heavier spoons and so on) is something to be admired. Our narrator, Encolpius, meets Trimalchio in a town in Campania, perhaps Puteoli – modern Pozzuoli, near Naples. He and his friends are invited to dinner at Trimalchio's house, and this experience forms the largest single chunk of the book that survives, often given its own title, *Cena Trimalchionis* – 'Trimalchio's Dinner'.

Dinner and drinking parties were a favourite literary theme in the ancient world. Plato's *Symposium* is at the more high-minded end of the spectrum, and even that has a drunk comic playwright, a bevy of flute girls and a hefty dose of flirtation going on. But Petronius, with his ruthless eye for the weakness and vulgarity of his fellow Romans, had no pretensions to philosophical dialogue. He simply couldn't pass up a chance to laugh at the stupid, uneducated nouveaux riches. And Trimalchio is a huge comic creation.

His character was inspired at least in part, we can assume, by the enormously wealthy freedmen who came to prominence under Nero's predecessor, Claudius. Narcissus and Pallas, both ex-slaves, became prodigiously wealthy and extremely influential, right down to helping Claudius choose his fourth wife. Authors like Tacitus were always likely to disapprove of freedmen (instead of honest Romans) reaching positions of power. It was bad enough that Rome had ended up with emperors of any kind, but worse when their weaknesses or tastes made those emperors seem like oriental kings. A supreme ruler surrounded by lackeys who did his bidding was not the Roman ideal at all. And the fact that those lackeys attained untold riches while they did it just added insult to injury. It is worth mentioning, however, that Trimalchio estimates his wealth at about 30 million sesterces. It is notoriously impossible to convert money through time – inflation is extremely hard to measure, and our spending habits have changed. We consider the price of a pint of milk to be a good objective value, but obviously the Romans didn't drink many lattes, so milk wasn't so important to them. However, you could probably buy two decent loaves of bread for one sesterce. Two loaves of bread in a British supermarket today would set you back about £1.50. So let's presume, with all due caveats, that those values are roughly equivalent, and that 1 sesterce = £1.50. In that case, Trimalchio is worth £45 million in today's money. But Narcissus, the imperial freedman, was said to be worth some 400 million sesterces, or £600 million. The financial crisis of recent years has perhaps left some of us with an inability to consider any number truly large if it doesn't come in billions. Even after the banks had wobbled and begun to recuperate, *Forbes* magazine still listed 1,011 known billionaires in 2010. And compared with Bill Gates, Warren Buffett or Ingvar Kamprad, Narcissus certainly looks pretty poor. But in a pre-industrialised society he was an impossibly rich man. No wonder so many Romans hated him.

So Trimalchio is super-rich by virtually any standard, and especially given that he lives away from Rome: the richest people tend to congregate in large cities, after all, either because they offer unrivalled opportunities to spend money, or because they offer the best opportunities to make more money. But Trimalchio's money has come from the import business – wine, perfumes, slaves. Like all self-made men, he has tales of near-disaster: his first five ships, filled with wine, sank, and he lost a fortune. 'That one day, Neptune swallowed up 30 million sesterces.' But his wife sold all her jewels and finery, and funded a second attempt. The loss, he explains, meant nothing to him. He built more and bigger boats, and tried again, and what the gods want soon happens. Trimalchio believes he was destined to be rich.

However, he wasn't destined to be tasteful, and Petronius has huge fun at his expense. He's routinely described by the narrator as being extremely elegant, usually at the precise point where he is being indefensibly common. He has too many entertainers, for a start. Anyone who serves anything does so while singing. Acrobats and other performers leap into sight at every possible moment. Trimalchio serves too much of everything, too extravagantly, and doesn't hesitate to mention that he's giving today's guests better wine than yesterday's guests received, even though yesterday's guests were much more impressive. And as for the food, you'd be wise to read this book on an empty stomach. The Romans liked food that pretended to be other food – one animal made to look like another, or hidden inside another – but Trimalchio's chef goes too far. He makes pastry eggs with little figpecker birds inside. Encolpius is about to throw his away, before he realises that it isn't an inedible, embryonic hen's egg, but a treat. A huge pig is brought to the table, and Trimalchio pretends the chef has failed to gut it, and prepare it correctly. When they cut it open – surprise – it's been prepared and then filled with sausages and black pudding. There's a hare given wings to look like Pegasus, had Pegasus been a rabbit. One course appears in which every dish has been made to resemble a different sign of the zodiac. Our narrator and his friends are no better than Trimalchio, really – for all that they sneer and giggle at his lowbrow friends and these ludicrous displays, they still eat everything and drink as much as they can, long after they're full. They don't hesitate to look down on him while taking advantage of his hospitality.

Trimalchio's staff are almost as bad as he is. When the guests arrive, they're greeted by a boy who begs them to help him: he's about to be flogged for having lost the steward's clothes while they were at the baths. He was supposed to be guarding them, but failed. Encolpius and his friends ask the steward to let the boy off, and receive a decidedly haughty response: "'It's not the loss of them that annoys me,' he said, "so much as the carelessness of this awful slave. He lost my dining clothes, which a client once gave me as a birthday present. They were real Tyrian purple. But they had been washed once. So what good were they? You can have him.'" The steward, suddenly remembering that his expensively dyed clothes have been to the laundry a single time, no longer cares about them. And Trimalchio has a slave sweep up a piece of silverware along with the rubbish, just because it had fallen on the floor. Ostentation is the theme of the story, and Petronius plays the urban sophisticate, poking fun at these awful, provincial rubes. One might wonder if the Roman Empire would have been a little more stable if more men had been like Trimalchio, running a business, and fewer had been like Petronius and Juvenal, scorning their efforts. But the last laugh goes to Trimalchio, who has planned his funeral to the last detail, and has it acted out during dinner, safe in the knowledge that his loved ones will give him the memorial he desires. Petronius, meanwhile, was accused of treason in CE 66 – a trumped-up charge made by a jealous rival – and had to slit his wrists. Life in the big city had its risks.

So, after you'd paid for a good life – whatever that entailed for you – could money buy you a good death? Or did it merely invite jealousy and resentment, and an earlier death than one might hope? Think of poor Valerius Asiaticus, who was a wealthy ex-consul during Claudius' reign. He had purchased the beautiful gardens of Lucullus, and was making them especially magnificent, according to Tacitus. But Claudius' third wife, Messalina, coveted the gardens, so she trumped up charges against Asiaticus, finding an informer to say that he was a threat to the throne. Asiaticus, realising that there was no escape from Messalina's fury, slit his wrists. But only after he'd had his funeral pyre moved, so the smoke wouldn't damage his trees' foliage. A gardener, even in death.

Money, for Trimalchio, means a huge funeral, with dozens of mourners, including all his slaves, whom he will free in his will. It also means a huge monument to mark his life – with a statue of him wearing golden rings, and of his wife, Fortunata. He wants a picture of his dog on it, and paintings of wreaths, vines and fruits. In other words, he doesn't just want a beautiful house when he's alive, but one when he's dead, too. And a guard to keep it in good condition. Finally, he wants a big inscription that concludes with the following: 'He left 30 million sesterces, and he never heard a philosopher.' It's hard to decide exactly what the joke is here. Is it another jibe at Trimalchio's total lack of culture and education? All that money and he never spent a bean on his intellectual betterment? Or is it a different joke: that philosophers were still not to be trusted by anyone with sense, and so Trimalchio is rightly proud that in spite of his considerable fortune, he will have lived and died without giving cash to any of those intellectual charlatans that so many others have been taken in by? As so often with a good joke, you can take your pick.

Trimalchio's funeral and monument are, like his life, a gaudy exaggeration of what normal people might have wanted. But the principle is the same: like everyone else in the ancient and modern worlds alike, he wants to be remembered. When Achilles and Agamemnon clash in the first book of *The Iliad*, it is over their respective honour – kudos. What looks to the casual reader like a stupid tiff over girls and treasure is something far more profound. The more slaves, the more treasure you pile up in a conflict, the more you have objectively achieved. And the more extraordinary your feats of bravery and strength, the more poets are likely to sing of your exploits. In a world before photographs, printing presses and film, what other way could you become immortal?

Being the subject of song for poets tens and hundreds of years after your death is a way of living for ever. Achilles died young, but his story survives even now. For those less heroic, a handsome monument that might remind passers-by of your name and achievements – financial, political or professional – was the next best thing. And money could certainly buy you that.

But could it buy you a good death, before the memorial was built? The ancients were obsessed with the idea of a good death: it's no accident that we have so many stories of people dying in pleasingly telegenic ways. Socrates issues his final words in seeming comfort, with none of the agonies one might expect from someone poisoned with a neurotoxin. When Arria Paeta stabs herself in the heart, she has time to encourage her wavering husband before slumping to a neat death. There's no mention of her resembling Carrie on prom night. And if you couldn't die in a philosophically serene state, there were other good deaths – in battle, saving your country, for example. Tough Spartan women used to tell their boys to come back either carrying their shields or on them: death was far preferable to the disgrace of cowardly chucking your shield down so you could run away. But a good soldier's death is no prettier than any other kind: that's another fantasy from the ancient world that we sustain today. The Romans, for example, looked back on the Second Punic War – which culminated in Scipio finally vanquishing Hannibal, and earning himself the name Africanus – as a major victory. It was a vital war for them to have won: the soldiers who fought and died saved Rome from being conquered by the Carthaginians. They had archetypal good deaths: in battle, keeping their loved ones safe from a horde of foreigners. But their deaths don't sound so good in Livy's history. In 216 BCE, Hannibal massacred the Roman army in a terrible battle at Cannae. According to Livy, Hannibal is so astonished by his success, and his proximity to Rome, that he needs a day's rest to consider everything that has happened. It is generally believed, says Livy, that the day's delay was enough to save Rome and her empire. So the sacrifice of the soldiers at Cannae certainly wasn't in vain. Their deaths held Hannibal off for a precious twenty-four hours. But then Livy takes us back to the battlefield the next day, in the aftermath of the Roman defeat, to survey the wounded and dead. 'They even found soldiers with their heads buried in earth they'd dug up. The soldiers had made these small pits for themselves, and heaping on the earth which lay over their faces, it appeared that they had managed to suffocate themselves.' These brave men were so badly hurt, and so utterly without hope, that they choked themselves to death where they lay. Soldiers only die a good death if no one sees them actually die.

So perhaps there is no such thing as a good death. Does it really make any difference if you are forced to slit your wrists or if you die on the battlefield? Is Vespasian's death – managing a final joke on becoming a god – somehow better than Nero's? Nero had to commit suicide when it became clear that rebellion had forced him from the throne. He eventually drove a dagger through his throat – with the help of his secretary, Epaphroditus – after wailing repeatedly, 'qualis artifex pereo' – 'Such an artist! But still I die!' Surely none of us wants to die by being stabbed through the neck by someone who usually does our filing. Yet Vespasian is just as dead as Nero, in the end. The only difference is that he gets a better write-up, which is all any of us can really hope for.

The only other thing we might wish to spend our money on, as we hurtle towards the great unknown, is a book or two to assuage our fear of dying, and perhaps our fear of living. Lucretius wrote a poem called *De Rerum Natura* – 'On the Nature of Things'. An Epicurean philosopher and physicist, Lucretius wrote his poem for a friend,

Gaius Memmius, and urges him not to be afraid of death. 'Death is nothing to us,' he proclaims. If Mother Nature suddenly found a voice, she would wonder why we make such a fuss about dying. If we've had a good life, she would ask, why aren't we happy to leave it, like a guest who's had a lovely time at a party? And if we've had a rotten time, why prolong it? We don't remember what it was like before we were born, and that is Nature's mirror of how things will be after we die. 'Surely nothing about dying seems sad. Doesn't it seem more untroubled than any sleep?'

Lucretius believes that our fear of death makes us live in ways that don't make us happy – amassing wealth and power at any cost, for example. 'These wounds of life,' he says, 'are in no small way nourished by a fear of death.' In this, Lucretius the calm, cool thinker finds an unlikely ally: the markedly less calm, less cool Juvenal. After all the splenetic fury he has enjoyed in earlier poems, in Satire Ten, Juvenal offers us something unexpected: a realisation that looking at what other people have (if it's more than we have) is a recipe for unhappiness. He finally accepts that wishing for money, luxuries, power and influence (all things he bemoans his lack of in the earlier satires) is actually a terrible waste of time: the rich are targets of jealousy; the powerful rarely die of old age. In this satire, Juvenal tries to work out what we should pray for, instead of these obvious choices. He dismisses plenty of options, with historical examples. Don't wish for power, he warns, or you might end up like Sejanus – the one-time friend of Tiberius – who only yesterday was the second most-powerful man in the world. Now he's fallen from grace and died for it. All his statues are crackling as people melt them down and turn them into pots and pans. And don't wish for good looks, he adds, or a woman with no scruples but huge power, like Messalina, will want you. If you refuse her, she'll have you killed. If you go along with her plans, you'll also be killed, but by the emperor instead when he finds out what you've been up to with his wife. So what should we wish for, then? The gods know best, says Juvenal – don't pray for specifics, because they know better than we do what is best for us. It's an inspirational idea that has carried through the ages: this very passage is inscribed, in Latin, in the courtyard of Rubens's house in Antwerp. But if we really can't leave it to the gods to decide and we have to wish for something – spend our money, perhaps, on an offering or two – what should we wish for? Juvenal is in no doubt: 'mens sana in corpore sano' – 'a healthy mind in a healthy body'. He goes on: 'Ask for a brave mind, with no fear of death, which puts a long life last among Nature's gifts, which can bear any hardship, which doesn't know anger, and which lusts after nothing.' Rich or poor, it isn't bad advice.

Epilogue

In the words of Lieutenant Columbo, just one more thing. The classical world is, as I hope you agree, an extraordinary, fascinating place for us to spend our time. Studying the Romans, Carthaginians, Athenians, Alexandrians and Spartans gives us a unique opportunity to understand the way we live today, partly because of the incredible similarities between ancient and modern worlds, and partly because of the huge differences. Thucydides was absolutely right when he said that his *History* was a work designed to last for ever: human nature changes very little over time, and we can learn a considerable amount about ourselves if we look hard at our predecessors. But we also need to set our world in relief against ancient societies; to look at how much we've changed and how far we have come in all kinds of fields since then. By acknowledging the skill and ingenuity of the ancients, we give ourselves a context. Sure, the Romans had central heating, and that is amazing. But we have central heating and computers as well, and that's even more amazing. It doesn't hurt to look back to the past and realise how much we've achieved. If nothing else, it enables us to look to the future with optimism and courage, instead of a creeping fear that things inevitably get worse as time goes on.

The Greeks gave the world towering philosophical and artistic figures. The Romans gave it limitless ambition and technical mastery. And here we stand, a couple of thousand years later, with so many of their achievements to inspire us, and all of our own triumphs as well. No one seriously believes that we would be making the best of ourselves if we simply ignored everything that came before us and trotted about our daily lives in blissful ignorance of everything that isn't immediately in front of us at any one time. History is a passport to understanding ourselves as well as the societies and people we're studying.

Edmund Burke, the Irish statesman, once said that those who don't know history are condemned to repeat it. Well, he was half right: the periodic banking crises and stock-market crashes prove pretty conclusively to my mind that some aspects of our history are repeated, regardless of whether we know it or not. But knowing history means more than simply knowing the facts of what went before; it means interpreting those facts, deciding which causes had certain effects. If the Athenians overreached themselves in war – by carrying out too many conflicts for which they had insufficient money and manpower to succeed – don't we want to know about that for several reasons? Firstly, because the history of the Athenians is interesting in its own right. And secondly, because we can judge our own behaviour, and its likely consequences, in the light of their mistakes.

But history isn't prescriptive: the lessons we draw from the past are obviously up to us. Don't get involved in too many wars; don't get involved in wars at all; intellectual golden ages are accompanied by aggressive foreign policy; democratic government is unsustainable; direct democracy leads to poor decision-making; philosophical thought is not compatible with free societies: we could draw any of these conclusions from the golden age of Athens. And in reading and thinking about Athens, we formulate the questions we need to think about ourselves. History in general – and Ancient History in particular, because I am clearly biased – is a learning process that enlightens us on multiple levels. We know more history than we did when we began, and we know more about the human condition too.

And given the general usefulness of historical learning, you would think it would be a priority for every education system all over the globe. Teach us our past, teach us other people's pasts, and we will become more rounded, more tolerant and more engaged human beings (there are obviously exceptions to this rule, Holocaust deniers being only the most glaring ones that leap to mind). Socrates really wasn't kidding when he said that an unexamined life is not worth living. So what on earth is the point of living when we do – in an era of mass access to untold information – if we don't use our time to learn about the world we live in and our predecessors lived in? Wiki-pedia may contain mistakes and inaccuracies, but at what other point in history did ordinary people all over the world have instant and free access to a vast encyclopaedia? Cyberspace is fiercely democratic, in spite of the attempts of governments and corporations to curtail it. And the Internet is an extraordinary resource for classicists especially: masses of texts – in Latin, in Greek and in translation into English, French, German and more – are online, free to access and read. No one needs to be rich enough to buy piles of Greek plays, or live near a library that is unusually well stocked. All over the world, geeks are making sure you can sit in your living room, tap into your laptop – or even your phone – and find all of Euripides, right there waiting for you. If there is a heaven for scholars, these people will have a free pass.

But for too many of us, history is or was an afterthought at school.

I was beyond lucky with my Latin, Greek and Ancient History teachers: the school was committed to running courses in these subjects, the staff were incredibly good at teaching them. But that isn't true in very many schools now. Parents often need to buy a classical education for their offspring – if they choose to spend their money that way – because Classics has fallen off the curriculum for too many children, making way for subjects that seem more relevant. They are not. If we don't learn languages – ancient or modern – how can we hope to understand our own? Find me a kid who studied Greek who can't then spell words perfectly in English. And find me a managing director who wouldn't pick a perfectly spelled CV over one riddled with mistakes.

And if we don't learn any languages, the door to all the books written in something other than English is closed to us. I will probably never know enough Spanish to read Borges, which is a miserable truth to acknowledge. My French isn't good enough to read Racine. But if I can't read Molière – and I definitely can't – I can read Plato, and that's a start. And reading anything in another language is mind-altering: you can't help but look at the world differently once you've done it. Other languages have words we can't translate at all, because the concept they describe doesn't exist in our culture. If nothing else, this realisation – aged about twenty, because I was a slow learner – made me understand that all the stuff I couldn't read as a student, still haven't read now and will never have time to read is worth someone's time, even if it isn't getting mine. I stuck with being an Arts student, but I did finally understand that the physicists with their dense textbooks and impenetrable equations were just a different tribe, and not – as I had previously assumed – dull.

Learning something for its own sake – because it is worthwhile to learn it and to know it, rather than because it is useful for another purpose, even if it is also that – is a wonderful thing to do. For too long we have allowed a public discourse that equates 'difficult' with 'boring'. Maths is hard, so it must be dull, so why bother? Well, here is why: because everything that is worth knowing is hard to learn at first. We should be suspicious of any information or understanding that we didn't have to sweat to gain. And learning to do something difficult is infinitely more satisfying than learning something easy. Learn to ride a bike, and you feel pretty smug: you can ride a bike. It's an end in itself, and it's also one that enables you to do other things. You can ride a bike to school, or work, or to see friends. But learning to ride a unicycle: now that's hard. And it doesn't enable you to do much but ride a unicycle. Not that many people commute on one wheel. But still, you can do something no one else you know can do. You're halfway to joining a circus. And if the circus doesn't work out, who's to stop you wheeling into your office on it one day?

Classics is, to me, the unicycle of education. It isn't especially practical or useful to learn Ancient History. It isn't necessary to learn Latin, or to read Virgil, however much it helps your spelling. It won't get you a well-paid job in a fancy office, and it won't necessarily make you attractive to the opposite sex (maybe just to the really good people). But none of that is important compared with the simple fact that studying Classics is brilliant. It's terrific to know an alphabet you didn't learn as a five-year-old. It's amazing to learn about a world far away from your own. It's wonderful to find a whole new world of literature, history, art, architecture, religion, philosophy, politics and society. Classics is just waiting for us to get our priorities straight and find it. It's been very patient as generations of politicians have turned on it, dismissing anything they were bad at at school as 'elitist'. It has even restrained itself from pointing out that if you boot a subject off the timetable in every school but the fee-paying ones, it is a bit rich to then accuse the subject of being elitist, since you're the one limiting it to an elite. Classics is making a comeback – in cinema, in fiction, in children's books, on TV. And like I said in the introduction for this book: it repays whatever time you give it. If you don't fancy a month with *Kennedy's Latin Primer*, then read a historical novel instead. Classics is everything we used to be, and much of what we are now.

And that is quite enough.

Acknowledgements

There are so many people I should thank that I have had to edit the list ruthlessly, just to make it look like I did any of it myself. So to those of you who aren't here, but without whom there would be no book: I'm sorry. But really, you were stealing my limelight.

This book wouldn't exist at all if it weren't for the cohorts at Conville and Walsh, who are uniformly splendid. Especially my irrepressible agent, Patrick Walsh, a literary matchmaker whose ability to pair author with publisher is verging on psychic. Lucky he lives now, because a few hundred years earlier he would have been burned as a witch. Everyone at Profile Books also deserves my thanks for being magnificent, especially Valentina Zanca, Diana Broccardo, Penny Daniel and Andrew Franklin. There are all too few maple-syrup loving, vulcanologist copy-editors in the world. So thanks to Caroline Pretty for being mine. And Peter Carson is the best editor a person could hope for – the kind that authors should never mention in public, so they don't lose them to other writers. Actually, scratch what I said above.

I was lucky enough to have extraordinary teachers at every stage of my Classics career: without them, I would have been a different writer, and a different person. So my heartfelt thanks to Tim Cooper, who started me off as a Classicist. David Sedley, at Christ's College, Cambridge, is not only the cleverest person I've ever met, but one of the kindest. He gave me a place at college because I could change the oil on a Morris Minor, and he taught me everything I know about Plato, Aristotle and much else. He also took time out from inspiring another generation of classicists to read Chapter 3 of this book, for which I am immensely grateful. Stephen Anderson taught me more Latin and Greek than I should have needed to know, and has been my friend far longer than he was my employer. The perfect boss, in other words.

The op-ed team at *The Times* gave me space to write the column that began all this: comparing modern political leaders to Roman emperors. So many thanks go to Anne Spackman, Tim Rice, Robbie Millen and Paul Dunn.

Michelle Flower came up with two of the chapter headings, and proofread at least one chapter when she was locked out and needed somewhere to sit. That'll teach her to come to me in an emergency.

Phil Tinline produced the Radio 4 documentary *OedipusEnders* which I was working on when I should have been finishing the final chapter. He asked me difficult questions about ancient and modern, and never failed to make me try harder and be smarter. All writers need someone like that.

Christian Hill has run my website for ten years, even though he is busy being a physicist. He also fends off the crazies when they swarm, a veritable knight in geek armour. I'm very lucky to know him.

When I'd forgotten entirely what my job was, Joss Whedon reminded me that it is to make more stuff for him to read. I didn't then, and I don't now, have the words to say how much that means to me.

My family have always been incredibly supportive of my writing career, which you sort of assume everyone's families are. But they aren't, so a million thanks to mine for being the good kind. My brother, Chris, offered advice that every writer sometimes needs to hear ('Man up'). My father, Andre, answered questions about modern history whenever I lobbed them at him (often). My mother, Sandra, read each chapter as I went along – even when she was busy – and said she loved them all. It takes a rare reader to see that everyone else will offer constructive criticism, and that unconditional enthusiasm is often a greater spur.

This book, like so much else in my life, wouldn't exist without Dan Mersh. Thank you, most of all.

Some Modern Guides to Ancient Life

Unless you are a particularly sturdy type of reader – which you may well be – bibliographies can easily be an off-puttingly dense list of titles and publishers in a tiny font, which only the keenest of eyes can discern unaided. There will be none of that here. But I hope very much that this book will persuade you to read other Classics books, so here are some that I recommend.

If you are interested in reading classical texts in the original Greek or Latin, then you probably already know the editions to look out for. The Oxford, Cambridge and Bristol university presses' editions are fantastic, and sometimes come with notes and vocab at the back. This should never be underestimated. Loeb editions set a page of Latin or Greek with the corresponding translation on the facing page. The translation often dates back many decades, leading one to the occasional delight of discovering that the olde English makes no more sense than the Greek. As a schoolchild, I rolled my eyes at the stupidity of this. Now I think it's kind of heroic. I also know what more of the English words mean these days, which is a relief to my editor.

If you would rather go for translations, then the Penguin Classics are usually pretty good. In some cases – Peter Green's *Juvenal*, Michael Grant's *Tacitus*, Rex Warner's *Thucydides*, Philip Vellacott's *Euripides*, to pick just a few – they are terrific. I shamelessly used Rex Warner's translation in this book, knowing I couldn't come close to doing anything half as good myself.

As for books about the Classics, here are some I found especially good:

An Introduction to Plato's Republic by Julia Annas
Ancient Literacy by William V. Harris
Juvenal and the Satiric Genre by Frederick Jones
The Heroic Temper by Bernard Knox
Socrates and the State by Richard Kraut
The Hellenistic Philosophers by Anthony Long and David Sedley
Tacitus by Ronald Mellor
Goddesses, Whores, Wives and Slaves by Sarah Pomeroy
Everything by Paul Cartledge, Robin Lane Fox and Mary Beard

If you fancy some classically influenced historical fiction, you can't go far wrong with Robert Graves's *I, Claudius* and *Claudius the God*. Similarly, Mary Renault will send you on campaign with Alexander the Great (*Fire from Heaven*, *Persian Boy*, *Funeral Games*), and into the bull pit with Theseus (*The King Must Die*, *The Bull from the Sea*). Lindsey Davis and Stephen Saylor both write gumshoe mysteries set in Rome, and Caroline Lawrence's *Roman Mysteries* series for children ensures that no one has to wait till they're older. Robert Harris has brought Cicero back to life in *Imperium* and *Lustrum*. And Zachary Mason has reimagined Odysseus in the extraordinary *The Lost Books of the Odyssey*.

This is only a very small list of the books that helped, informed and inspired me with this book; my heartfelt thanks to the authors, particularly the ones still alive to appreciate them.

Index